"As colorful on the page as he is in person, Cianci is a natural story-teller with a lot to say." —*Kirkus Reviews*

"A relentless charmer. . . . A shrewd intelligence shines through; it's easy to understand why he kept getting reelected. Cianci readily admits to the role luck and money played in his success, and even admits to some major mistakes. More subtly, the former mayor reveals the intricacies of the horse-trading that makes politics go." —*Publishers Weekly*

"Cianci is a character, a one-of-a-kind, bigger-than-life politician the likes of which I have never met before. I find it difficult to even think of anyone I could come close to comparing him to—he's that unique." —*Norwich Bulletin*

*To Scungilli Harvo
all the Best!
Enjoy!*

Buddy Cianci

Politics and Pasta

A Memoir

VINCENT "BUDDY" CIANCI, JR.

with David Fisher

Thomas Dunne Books
St. Martin's Griffin
New York

THOMAS DUNNE BOOKS.

An imprint of St. Martin's Press.

POLITICS AND PASTA. Copyright © 2011 by Vincent Cianci, Jr., and David Fisher.
All rights reserved. Printed in the United States of America..For information,
address St. Martin's Press, 175 Fifth Avenue, New York, N.Y. 10010.

www.thomasdunnebooks.com

www.stmartins.com

The Library of Congress has cataloged the hardcover edition as follows:

Cianci, Vincent Albert, 1941–
    Politics and pasta : how I prosecuted mobsters, rebuilt a dying city, dined
with Sinatra, spent five years in a federally funded gated community, and lived
to tell the tale / Vincent "Buddy" Cianci, Jr., with David Fisher.—1st ed.
        p. cm.
    Includes bibliographical references and index.
    ISBN 978-0-312-59280-6
    1. Cianci, Vincent Albert, 1941–   2. Mayors—Rhode Island—Providence—
Biography.   3. Providence (R.I.)—Politics and government.   4. Political
corruption—Rhode Island—Providence.   5. Providence (R.I.)—Biography.
I. Fisher, David.   II. Title.
    F89.P953C533 2011
    974.5'043092—dc22
    [B]   2010040345

ISBN 978-1-250-00652-3 (trade paperback)

First St. Martin's Griffin Edition: July 2012

10   9   8   7   6   5   4   3   2   1

To my father, who taught me

To my mother, who loved me

To my sister Carol, who has always loved
and supported me far and beyond

To my daughter Nicole and her children,
who give me a special joy of life every day

To my family, friends, and supporters,
who never gave up on me

And to the people of the great city of Providence,
who elected me six times to be their mayor.

Thank you.

Acknowledgments

The wonderful life and the long careers I have enjoyed would not have been possible without the friendship and assistance of so many people I love and admire. There aren't enough pages in this book to name them all. Suffice it to say, you have my gratitude forever.

But I would like to acknowledge those people who gave their time and effort to assist me in the preparation of this book, in no particular order of appreciation. So to each of you, thank you: Joe Vileno, who served in my administrations and remembers them well; retired Congressman Ed Beard; President of the Providence Central Labor Council, Paul MacDonald; President of the Providence Teachers Union and State Representative, Steven Smith; the Honorable Judge Frank Caprio of the Providence Municipal Court; Paul Campbell, the former Deputy Director of Policy and the author of several extraordinary books on the history of Providence; Steven Patriarca, the former Director of the Mayor's Council on Drug and Alcohol Abuse; Charles Mansolillo, my former chief of staff and my City Solicitor; attorney and former Deputy City Solicitor, Ray Dettore; Linda Verhulst, my former executive secretary; Beryl Kenyon, our former press secretary; Joseph Paolino, the Mayor of Providence from April 1984 to January 1991 and the Ambassador to Malta, 1994–1996; Scott Millard, my executive assistant and the former Aide in the Advance & Constituent Affairs Office; Municipal Judge Joseph Abbate, the former Deputy Director of the Planning and Development Office, city of Providence; my invaluable aide Fred Passarelli; Stephen Day, former Batallion Chief of Maintenance of the Providence Fire Department and former President of Local 799 of the International Association of Firefighters; the Honorable Superior Court Judge Stephen Fortunato (Ret); the Honorable former Councilman Philip Almagno; my friend Frank DiBiase; my friend, Norman Gauss, for all his visits; Lynn Singleton, Director of the Providence Performing Arts Center; former Director of Communications, Providence Public Safety/Police and Fire Departments, Manny Vieira; Albert Notta; Providence Police Chief (Ret) Bernard Gannon; Artin Coloian; the Honorable Ronald DelSesto; Ron St. Pierre, cohost and producer WPRO; Nick Blair, Assistant Program Director and Producer WPRO; Joseph Phillips, WPRO Assistant to Programming Department; former city photographer, Isabelle Taft; Paul Giammarco and Barbara Haynes of Citadel Broadcasting.

I would also like to acknowledge and express my appreciation to those stalwarts at St. Martin's Press who have supported this effort from the beginning: Sally Richardson, Tom Dunne, Peter Joseph, Joe Rinaldi, and Margaret Smith; as well as my agent who made it possible, Jay Acton; and my collaborator, David Fisher.

David Fisher would also like to acknowledge and express his appreciation to all the people at St. Martin's for their support not only for this effort, but for all those projects on which we have worked, as well as Scott Millard for his efforts night and day and night to make this book a reality. I also would love to thank my beautiful wife, Laura Stevens Fisher, and our boys, Taylor and Beau, and our small but loud dog, Belle, for their support while working on this book. Finally, I want to thank Buddy Cianci for taking me along on his astonishing ride through history. I have enjoyed every minute of it.

Politics and Pasta

One

No city in the United States is at the present time making greater preparations for the future than the city of Providence. Her citizens believe that she is destined to occupy an important place in the development of the nation during the coming years, and they have shown their faith by inaugurating a comprehensive series of both private and public improvements, which will put the city in the very front rank of municipalities.

The New England Magazine, February 1896

There are many people who think they know my whole story, the Buddy Cianci story. But they don't, not even close. Here it is, the successes and failures, the politics, the fireplace logs and all:

I became the thirty-second mayor of the great city of Providence, Rhode Island, on January 6, 1975. I was thirty-three years old, a former special assistant attorney general and prosecutor for the state's anticorruption strike force and, let me be candid here, on the day I took office I knew as much about being mayor as I did about brain surgery. If I had known then what the job actually required, I wouldn't have voted for myself. I walked into that office completely inexperienced and unprepared—but confident. Believe me, I was confident. Maybe I didn't know precisely what I was doing, but I was confident I could save the city.

Like most aging Northeastern cities that had lost their manufacturing base, Providence was suffering terribly. We were pretty much out of business. The great city of Providence is one of America's oldest cities, founded in 1636 by Roger Williams as a religious haven, a place, as he called it, to find "God's merciful Providence." It had grown to become an important industrial center, producing textiles, jewelry, and precious metals, silverware, machinery, and tools. That was our history; our present was pretty depressing. The textile mills were shut, the factories were gone, the shipping industry was barely hanging on. Our downtown was practically deserted; the once grand hotel, the Biltmore, was closing; and, perhaps symbolically, the week I was inaugurated a crane was pulling out the grand piano from the second floor. The situation was so awful that even the American Bible Society, one of the last successful businesses we had, had packed its Bibles and moved out of town. Let me illustrate it this way: On the night of my inauguration the police got an emergency phone call that several monkeys were escaping from our zoo. You know you're in trouble when your monkeys are trying to get out of town. A *New Yorker* writer reported that after spending a night in Providence he was buying a train ticket back to New York and was asked, "One way or round trip?" When he replied, "One way," the ticket seller complimented his choice: "Smart bastard."

But I had tremendous confidence I could lead the renaissance that would restore Providence to its former grandeur and prosperity. While I had no specific plans, I had great dreams. I was going to rebuild the crumbling infrastructure, convince industry and people to return, and create one of the most livable cities in America. And I was also going to get rid of the one business that was still booming in Rhode Island: political corruption. I had vowed during my campaign that I was going to clean up the corruption, run the most ethical administration in the city's history, and deliver the services the good people of Providence were paying their tax dollars for and deserved. As mayor, it was no longer going to be political business as usual.

I meant every word of it. However, that vow lasted about two hours into my administration. As I very quickly learned, experience and preparation, good intentions, and even intelligence have never been prerequisites for political success.

So my first day as mayor of Providence, Rhode Island—by the way, if you've never been to Providence you are missing a wonderful experience; come for WaterFire—I was sitting in my beautiful office, admiring the chandeliers, the oriental rugs, the beautiful artwork on the walls, and the antique fireplace, trying to determine what the hell I was supposed to do first. How do you start being mayor? I had run for office as a Republican, not because I had any deep political commitment to the philosophy of that Grand Old Party, the party of Abraham Lincoln, but rather because Democrat was already taken. I wanted to run for mayor and I knew I could get the Republican nomination. Actually, almost anybody could have had the Republican nomination, since for more than four decades Providence had been run by the Democratic political machine without any real opposition; nothing happened without the permission—and participation—of the city council. But with my election that had all changed! Or so I believed.

On that first morning of my first day in office when my secretary, Margaret McLacken, announced my very first appointment, I buttoned my jacket, centered the knot on my tie, and prepared to begin doing the business of the great city of Providence, Rhode Island. It was the dawn of a New Era. As it turned out, my first meeting was with the politically powerful Democratic boss of the Seventh Ward who had risked his political career by supporting my candidacy. "Bring in Mr. Rossi," I said.

A veteran Ward healer named Arthur Rossi walked in. Rossi was a big, heavyset guy, and walking a few steps behind him was a midget. The midget was a man named Bobby whom I'd met during my campaign. I didn't think Rossi was there simply to offer his congratulations; I may have been inexperienced, but I wasn't naive. What I couldn't figure out was what he was doing with a midget.

Rossi sat down and Bobby kind of climbed up onto the chair right next to him and folded his legs under him. After we exchanged pleasantries Rossi got down to political business. "Mayor, I told you I was going to deliver the Seventh Ward for you, right?"

"You definitely did."

"And did I do it?"

"Absolutely."

My intention to run the most ethical administration in the history of Providence was suddenly confronting reality. "Well," he said, "there's a certain few things I gotta get here."

"Oh? Really?"

Rossi pointed a finger at Bobby. "See him?"

This was long before anybody ever heard of political correctness. In fact, in those days political correctness meant taking care of the people who supported you. So I looked at Bobby and said, "Barely." In 1975 that was a joke you could make.

"Bobby's gonna need to make a buck and a quarter, buck and a half a week."

A hundred fifty a week? That was a pretty good salary in 1975. I didn't know what Rossi had in mind or his reasons, but this was my first lesson in municipal politics. "To do what?" I asked.

"I don't give a shit," he said. "Make him an inkwell on your desk. Long as he gets paid."

"Okay." The election was over, I had won, it was time for me to begin my education. "What else?" Rossi smiled, reached into his pocket, and took out his list.

I hired Bobby to work in our Recreation Department, paying his salary out of a federal CETA (Comprehensive Employee Training Act) program that supported employment for minorities and the disabled. It turned out that Bobby was a hard worker with a terrific personality and he endeared himself to everyone. Eventually he became the deputy director of the department, a position he definitely had earned. But slightly more than twenty-five years later, I was serving my sixth term— there had been that unfortunate interruption in my career when I was accused of assaulting my estranged wife's lover with a fireplace log, which wasn't true, I never hit him with it—anyway, Bobby came into my office again, and climbed up onto the chair again. I could see he was furious. By this time Bobby was no longer a midget; he had politically correctly become a "little person." And I was no longer a naive kid learning how to be mayor; I was the longest-serving mayor of a city with a population over one hundred thousand people in America. I was appearing frequently on national radio shows and television programs; I even was selling my own marinara sauce. "What's the matter, Bobby?"

He said, "They're fucking me, Mayor, I'm telling you they're fucking me."

"What do you mean? Who's fucking you."

"The retirement board. I put in for my pension and they don't want to give me my disability."

Adding a disability to a city pension raised it to about two-thirds of the final year's salary—tax free. But I couldn't believe what he was saying. "Your what?"

"My disability pension."

I leaned across the desk. "Bobby," I said evenly, "what are you talking about? Your disability is why we hired you in the first place."

I was elected mayor of Providence six times and served a total of almost twenty-two years before leaving unexpectedly—and unfairly— for a five-year all-expenses-paid vacation in a gated community at Fort Dix, New Jersey, where my neighbor was a Mafia killer. Let me admit this right here: I wasn't an angel; I played a tough game of politics and I played to win. Certainly I made mistakes and I have some regrets, but I never took a bribe, never put one dime in my own pocket. I was acquitted of eleven charges of public corruption brought against me and convicted of one charge, a RICO (Racketeer Influenced and Corrupt Organizations) violation, a felony that had been created to attack organized crime. According to this charge, I was running the city government as a criminal enterprise. In other words, I was responsible for crimes committed by other people about which I had no knowledge. In fact, as a respected union leader and Rhode Island state representative, Steven Smith, explained so accurately, "They found him guilty of nothing but responsible for everything."

One of the prosecution's main witnesses against me was a real genius. He had been caught laundering money by the FBI and faced going to prison. Instead, he claimed that he had given me several bribes. In one case, he eventually testified, he had arranged for a young urban planner to pay me a five-thousand-dollar bribe in exchange for a nine-dollar-an-hour part-time job. With no benefits. Maybe I can move rivers, but convincing someone to pay five thousand dollars for a nine dollar-an-hour part-time job in the exciting field of city planning? Even I'm not that good a salesman. But this witness claimed that at my direction he had given the cash to one of my aides. Of course, when he was asked during cross-examination the denomination of the bills, he revealed with great confidence they were fives, tens, and fifteens.

But the city I left behind when I went to prison was better in every possible way than the city I had taken over in 1975. In 1994 *The Livable Cities Almanac* cited Providence as the "safest city" in the continental United States. In 1997 *USA Today* named Providence one of the nation's five "Renaissance cities." CNN cited Providence as "Perhaps the most dramatic downtown renovation in history." The *New York Times* wrote in 2000 that "Providence has become more like those vibrant European cities with rivers running through them." *Money* magazine selected Providence as one of the nation's best places to retire. I won my share of awards, too; in 1996 the American Association of Government Officials selected me "America's most innovative mayor."

While Cleveland's polluted Cuyahoga River had actually caught on fire, we had rerouted our three rivers and created a popular art project in which we intentionally set as many as one hundred bonfires in the river— and we even offered gondola rides. We had moved the railroad tracks, revitalized the arts community, and rebuilt our downtown—which included an ice skating rink two and a half times the size of the one at New York's Rockefeller Center, and the completely refurbished Biltmore Hotel. We'd built the 1.4-million-square-foot Providence Place Mall, which attracted many of the nation's most desirable merchandisers; repaved four hundred miles of streets; and improved and maintained seventy-five parks. We'd successfully preserved and renovated historic buildings and nurtured a restaurant industry that eventually included several of the finest restaurants in the country. We substantially reduced the crime rate, rehabilitated our neighborhoods, and attracted national conventions and the top touring Broadway shows to the city. By 1999 *Travel and Leisure* named our zoo one of the top ten in the country, which I'm assuming made our monkeys happy. But in my opinion, by far the most important thing I accomplished was that I raised the self-esteem, hope, and pride of the citizens in our city to a level no one had ever believed was possible. Rather than claiming they were from New England or Rhode Island, as they had been doing, our residents were proud to admit that they lived in the great City of Providence, Rhode Island.

And they gave me credit for the transformation. According to a Brown University poll, on the day I was indicted my approval rating actually went up four points.

The city of Providence has been the center of my life. It has been my passion. There hasn't been a day of my life when I haven't loved this place. I've had a remarkable life because of this city; I mean, how many people can say they've been to the White House for dinner, slept in Windsor Castle, and spent five years in a prison cell? As I said during the press conference when I announced I would be resigning, "It is a city of awesome beauty and splendor."

It never occurred to me growing up that I could become the mayor of Providence. I'm Italian, and Italians were not elected mayor; the Irish controlled the Democratic machine that picked the mayor. My family came from the village of Roccamonfina, which was just outside Naples. My grandfather Pietro Cianci immigrated to America in 1896 and settled in the Italian neighborhood of Federal Hill. Eventually he and my grandmother had thirteen kids, then they finally realized how that was happening, so they stopped. My father, Vincent, was born in Providence in 1900. The Cianci family embraced all the traditional immigrant values: family first, hard work second, education when you had time for it. The Ciancis were in every kind of business imaginable; they were contractors and cement workers, architects, and construction workers; they were in the car business, and during Prohibition my uncle Jimmy ran a famous speakeasy, the Coconut Grove. But my father was the only member of the family to go to college.

He wanted to be a doctor—who knows where that dream came from? After graduating from Cranston High School he spent two years in premed at Providence College, transferred to Harvard Dental School, and finally got his medical degree from Saint Louis University. With a little help from his family but mostly through his own hard work he paid his way through college and medical school, sorting freight for the railroad on the Mississippi River and driving cement trucks in the summers. At first he was a family doctor, a general practitioner, but eventually he specialized in proctology—believe me, I've heard all the jokes and I've actually been the butt of many of them—at Tufts. Dr. Vincent

Albert Cianci was the immigrant success story. I can remember lying in bed at night listening as patients came to our house for help. I don't think my father ever turned away a patient, and I know he accepted poultry or eggs or fresh vegetables as payment.

My love of politics comes from my mother's family. Esther Capobianco's great-grandfather was the mayor of Benevento, Italy. His grandson Nicolo immigrated to America, to Federal Hill, just after the turn of the century. Eventually, he became an active member of the Democratic Committee in the Fourth Ward. My mother and father were a natural match; the young doctor and the beautiful business school graduate, both of them from highly respected families in the Italian community. They were married in 1937. I was born in 1941, and named after my father, Vincent A. Cianci, Jr.

But I was always Buddy. I don't know where that came from, either, although at the time it was a popular nickname. For much of my political career every time I walked into an event the band would play that old classic, "My Buddy." It was only years later that I found out it had been written about a dog.

My parents taught me their values, which basically came down to respect everybody until they give you a reason not to. If you start something, you finish it. And whatever happens in life, first take care of your family.

The work ethic was very strong in the Italian community. Ironically, I think that's one of the reasons there are so few Italians in the hierarchy of the American Catholic Church. Italian fathers needed their sons to work: I'm a shoemaker, I'm teaching him to be a shoemaker. I'm a bricklayer, my son works with me. The Irish sent their kids to the religious schools; the Italians sent them to church on Sunday morning but wanted them home ready to work in the afternoon.

I was born with confidence. I would venture to say that no one has ever used the words "Buddy" and "shy" in the same sentence. By the time I was seven years old I was performing regularly on WJAR's *Kiddie Revue,* which was broadcast every Sunday morning from the Outlet department store in downtown Providence. I suspect it would surprise none of my critics to learn that even at that age I was a comedian—and a singer. Our producer, Celia Moreau, would dress me up in Italian immigrant work clothes and have me sing songs like "Where D'Ya Worka, John?" One of my favorite songs was called "Sunbonnet Sue." A great lyric, "Sunbonnet Sue, Sunbonnet Sue, Sunshine and roses are second to you. I kissed you once, I kissed you twice, under your sunbonnet Sue."

While my mother made sure I had singing lessons and wanted me to pursue the arts, my father would have liked me to become a doctor. In fifth grade my parents took me out of the public school and enrolled me in the extremely toney Moses Brown School. The school, founded in 1784, was a Quaker school whose teachings were based on the philosophy of tolerance preached by Moses Brown, a man who had freed his slaves—and instead ended up with a school populated mostly by upperclass white Anglo-Saxon Protestant young men training to become their parents. I remember driving up to the beautiful Moses Brown campus, across the street from Brown University, with my father and thinking, Oh my God, what is this place? I knew instantly it would be a tough fit for me.

I was thrown into an entirely alien atmosphere. In the 1950s there were not a lot of Italian Americans there. Until that time my whole world had been ethnically diverse, I'd been shielded from bias, discrimination, and prejudice. Suddenly I was the minority. Moses Brown was the best experience I could have had because it taught me how to deal with discrimination. I developed a very thick skin there.

Let me describe what it was like: Several years ago I was invited to a lovely dinner in Newport, Rhode Island, at the magnificent estate of Eileen Gillespie Slocum, who was considered the grande dame of Newport society. She was a lovely woman who became a close friend and she would often invite me to her small dinner parties. Usually the other guests included people like Count this and Countess that; Jackie Kennedy's mother, Janet Auchincloss; the von Bülows. This particular dinner party was being held in honor of General William Westmoreland, who'd commanded our military in Vietnam. At one point Mrs. Westmoreland stood up to make a toast. "Westie and I never miss our summer in Newport," she said. "Even when Westie was in Vietnam I was here.

And this is what I love most about Newport. This is so representative of America."

I looked around the mansion at the Louis XVI furniture, the Carrera marble fireplace, the life-size oil portraits, the magnificent grand piano, and the marble bust of our hostess; I leaned back as the waitstaff served us gourmet food prepared by a personal chef on bone china, and I thought, this woman is completely out of touch. I was the closest thing to an actual ethnic in the room. It was pretty obvious to me that some of these people didn't have the slightest concept of what the world outside the high granite wall that surrounded the Slocum mansion was really like.

That's what life at Moses Brown felt like to me when I first got there: isolated and protected from reality. And I was the outsider who didn't belong. Because of my heritage, there were on occasion events in which I was not included. In didn't happen often, but those times it did made a strong impression. There was little overt prejudice and eventually I made good friends there, but I lived with the feeling that there was a great party going on to which I hadn't been invited. At first I felt tolerated rather than accepted. It was a feeling I never forgot and, maybe more than anything else, it is that feeling that drove me to succeed.

I played football and I was a heavyweight wrestler, making up for my lack of natural ability with perseverance and intensity. Among my football coaches were Jerry Zeoli and Al DeRobbio, who taught us that football was a tough, physical game and that the way to win was to be tougher than your opponents. They taught me how to be tough when I needed to be. The highlight of my wrestling career was reaching the Rhode Island state championship. My opponent in the semifinals was favored to win. He was bigger than me, but I was quicker. We tied on points but I won on riding time, meaning I maintained control longer than he did. I never forgot the feeling; this was a real upset, something in which I took great pride. In fact, as the years passed, my opponent in the story continued to get bigger and tougher. By the time I got finished building up the story, the kid was practically a legend. But my ego was deflated—well, somewhat deflated—years later when I ran into him while campaigning, and discovered that he had become a very successful hairdresser.

I boarded at Moses Brown my last two years. My roommate was the first black kid ever to attend that school, Adrian Hendricks. What a coincidence that they put the Italian kid and the black kid in a room together. Adrian became my best friend; he was captain of the basketball team and the football team. I was his biggest advocate. When I ran for mayor in 1974, the fact that I carried the black neighborhoods may have made the difference in the election. An Italian Republican was not supposed to get black votes, especially after Watergate and Nixon's resignation, but somehow I did. During my campaign I never talked about the fact that I'd roomed with a black student for two years, at just about the same time Southern states were using the National Guard to keep black kids out of public schools—not that I didn't want to—but somehow that fact did appear in an article somewhere that might have been seen by the black community.

Moses Brown shaped me in many ways. A wonderful teacher there named Eleanore Monahon taught me to appreciate the hidden beauty of Providence. She sent me on field trips to visit the historic buildings and houses of the city, "historic" being basically a nice way of saying old and falling apart. Most of those structures were decrepit and covered with grime; you really had to look with more than your eyes to see their value. Across the country other cities were tearing down these buildings to put up glass towers, but Providence couldn't afford to do that and didn't need the office space. Business was moving out, not in. But it was because of Mrs. Monahon that I realized that for Providence, our history was our future.

It was never my ambition to become the first Italian American mayor of Providence. Of course, it also was never my ambition to serve almost five years in a federal prison. But both things happened. When I began college, my dream was to get a master's degree in international relations and join the foreign service. Like so many other young people in the early 1960s, I had been inspired by President John Fitzgerald Kennedy. I was going to bring American values to the world. As it turned out, the one place young Americans were bringing our values to was Vietnam. So after graduating from Fairfield University, I enrolled at Villanova to get my master's in political science. I completed one year and was four credits shy of that degree. Truthfully, it wasn't as exciting as I'd anticipated; the most interesting research paper I wrote that year was an investigation of the relationships between Portugal and its colonies. Ask me about Mozambique. But it was at about that time my father wondered loudly, "Do you have any idea what you're going to do as a foreign service officer?" And, probably more to his actual point, "Did you ever check the pay scale?"

My father was always a very practical man. He said things that made sense. So when he suggested, "I think you should go to law school because you'll always have that degree to fall back on," I paid attention to him. I got my law degree from Marquette University, and during the summers I returned to Villanova to complete my master's. I found that I didn't have a great passion for the law, more an intellectual curiosity about why decisions were made and how they affected people. The first year of law school they scare the hell out of you, the second year they work the hell out of you, and the third year they bore the hell out of you. I remember being in the library one afternoon with a close friend named Bob Ott, who needed to use the phone. When the librarian told him that that was not permitted, he shook his head and replied, "I don't know why I can't use the phone. I don't use the books!"

I graduated in 1966—and was immediately drafted. I took a train down to Georgia for basic training. I was twenty-five years old, considerably older than most of the kids traveling with me; I had my law degree and my master's. It really did set me apart and I assumed the army would recognize my capabilities. And that's what happened: The train stopped inside Fort Jackson. The drill sergeants were there to welcome us. They lined us up and one of them asked, "How many of you boys went to college?"

This was my opportunity. I raised my hand. "Right here, Sergeant."

"Good," he said. "You go ahead and grab that broom over there and start sweeping. I want the rest of you to watch him, you might learn something." When I finished basic I applied for a direct commission and ended up as a second lieutenant in a civil affairs unit assigned to Military Police. I was assigned to a holding company for officers waiting to be deployed to Vietnam, and I was there only a brief time before my father died suddenly of a heart attack on the Fourth of July, 1967. For some unknown and never-to-be-explained reason, while I was home for his funeral, a colonel who liked me called and asked if rather than going to Vietnam, I would prefer to be transferred to Fort Devens, Massachusetts, where I would be closer to my mother.

Let me repeat that: The army of the United States of America called and asked if I would rather serve in a war zone or be stationed not far from my home. Sure, you're probably thinking, next thing he'll claim is that he's innocent of all those charges against him.

I became the supply officer of a military police unit at Fort Devens. Mostly, it was a nice place to hide. Nobody bothered me. I would sit around an old potbellied stove with a sergeant who'd put his feet up on a chair and explain his philosophy of life: "I keeps my feets warm." Among my responsibilities was counting the blankets. I did a fine job; every barracks always had precisely the number of blankets they were supposed to have. But one day I noticed that after we had counted the blankets in one company this sergeant would pack up all the blankets and deliver them to the next barracks, where we would count the same blankets again. It turned out that's how he was keeping his feets warm, selling army blankets.

Who knows how many times I would have counted those blankets, but another sergeant who was fighting an Article 32, an AWOL charge, knew I had a law degree and asked me to defend him. This was the first law case of my career, and at that time I still believed in Perry Mason. It was a simple case that I won by proving that his commander had failed to provide him with proper notification that he wasn't there.

My problem was that this case attracted considerable attention on the post. I learned an important lesson here: The absolute worst thing you can do in the army is attract attention to yourself. The colonel got very upset that the army lost the case. The provost marshal, who until that moment had not known I existed, got upset because the colonel was upset. Not only did I lose my job counting blankets, I was promoted to assistant operations officer for the provost marshal. No more would I be sitting around the potbellied stove keeping my feets warm. This job actually required work.

It was an all-night job and my responsibilities included filing numerous reports, inspecting barracks and being in charge of the night shift. After numerous escapes from the stockade, I was put in command. Supermax this stockade was not. Supposedly it was a secure military prison, but we probably were averaging an escape a day when I took over. Just before I was assigned there, one prisoner had folded soap wrappers into lieutenant's bars and put them on his shoulders, then ordered the guards to call a cab for him and went to Boston. The next day I replaced the confinement officer.

We had about two hundred prisoners in there and I told them, "Let's be realistic about this. None of us want to be here. I want to get you out of here as quickly as possible. But every time there's an escape I have to stop what I'm doing and report to the provost marshal and the general. Then I have to file reports and meet with the provost marshal. All of that takes away the time I need to process your paperwork so you can get out of here. Every time somebody escapes, they're keeping the rest of you in here. So the quickest way out of here for most of you is to stop the escapes."

That marked the end of the escapes. Eventually, I got the place organized. I issued a strict order that no one, absolutely no one, got in or out of my stockade without showing proper identification. Unfortunately, one morning I had a sentry at the gate who did not understand that in the army "nobody" does not include the commanding general. This kid refused to open the gate for the post commander until he showed his ID. As a result, the general was furious with me. Until that time I had had a good deal; I lived off the base in a small rented house on a lake and I was able to eat my meals pretty much anywhere I wanted to, so I ate well. When I was assigned to the stockade, the meals had been awful, but only two days earlier I'd traded a jeep to Personnel for a new cook. He wasn't a good cook, and he definitely wasn't a candidate for Mensa. The general decided to stay for lunch and asked him, "Cook, what's for lunch?"

"I don't know what it is, sir," the cook answered enthusiastically. "But I'll find out." That was the last time I ate outside the stockade, for a long time.

My worst moments in the military took place after Dr. Martin Luther King, Jr. was assassinated in April 1968. About a year earlier I had volunteered to attend a three-day training program in riot control being conducted in Quantico, Virginia. I stayed at Quantico about three hours, signed the papers, and went to Washington. My purpose in life was not to learn riot control. But in response to Dr. King's assassination, riots were breaking out in various cities. Fort Devens was ordered to assemble a brigade and prepare to go down south to Memphis, Tennessee, to maintain order. When my name popped out of the computer as an expert in riot control, I was made provost marshal of this brigade. Oh, how well I remember that beautiful first morning when I met the troops I was going to lead. I stood up on a training platform and looked out on several hundred well-armed and very angry African American soldiers preparing to travel to Memphis, where Martin Luther King, Jr. had just been murdered, and I remember thinking, Boy, this is a seriously bad idea.

Fortunately for all concerned, our deployment was canceled.

I had begun working in politics in Herbert DeSimone's 1966 campaign for state attorney general while waiting to being inducted after graduating law school. It often has been said that Rhode Island has a rich political history, which in fact is a nicer way of saying that in Rhode Island politicians got rich. Our tradition of political corruption was already well established by the time President George Washington complained just after the Revolution, "Rhode Island still perseveres in that impolitic, unjust—and one might add without much impropriety— scandalous conduct, which seems to have marked all her public counsels of late." But like many immigrants I had been brought up to respect politicians. Every Sunday morning we would go to Saint Bartholomew's, which at that time catered to the immigrant community. My father was the parish doctor so we sat up front. When politicians like Senator John O. Pastore walked in just as the service was ready to begin, everybody turned and looked up with great respect—especially for Pastore, who was the first Italian-American in Rhode Island history to serve as governor and later senator. Now this was long before the lies of Vietnam and Watergate, long before the media began exposing politicians.

My parents knew DeSimone casually. Though my father was an Independent, DeSimone was Italian, which was all that mattered. DeSimone ran against the Mafia, promising to fight organized crime, and his campaign was helped immensely when his four-term Democratic opponent claimed there was no organized-crime problem in Rhode Island. Who was he kidding? Raymond Patriarca, the founder of the Patriarca crime family, the man who ran New England and at that time one of the most powerful Mafia bosses in the world, must have been surprised to find out that he didn't exist.

When DeSimone began his campaign, few people thought he had any chance to win. For some reason, though, when someone suggested I work on his campaign, it made sense to me. I volunteered and ended up driving DeSimone around and attending events with him. This was my very first lesson in campaigning. Eventually, we became close friends. DeSimone won that election, and when I was discharged he offered me a part-time position in his office as a special assistant attorney general. I accepted that job, and also opened a private law practice in my father's old medical office. At that time this was perfectly acceptable.

As a special assistant I had access to the Bureau of Criminal Investigation. That's where all the records are kept. One afternoon I looked up my family, and the only member I found was my uncle Jimmy, whose Prohibition speakeasy apparently was known to the law. Incredibly, those records have since disappeared, not that I would know what happened to them. No, not at all.

I prosecuted an extraordinary variety of cases while working in the attorney general's office. When I started I was scared to death. Like so many young prosecutors, initially I was assigned to menial cases in district court, I did a lot of preliminary hearings and pleadings, and I got a great introduction to the realities of the legal system from the older lawyers there. One day I had a case and, trying to save some time, I asked the defense attorney, "Will you waive the preliminary hearing?"

He looked at me and replied, "The only thing I wave is the American flag."

Eventually, though, I began trying important cases in front of juries. It turned out my personality was perfect for this job: Put me in front of an audience and I'm going to put on a show. The jury was a great audience—and they had to sit there and listen to every word I said. I discovered that in the courtroom the most effective tools are preparation, honesty, and humor, particularly self-deprecation. In that regard it was similar, as I later learned, to campaigning.

DeSimone actively went after organized crime. Like me, as an Italian American he resented the fact that the Mafia had been responsible for the creation of the stereotype that every Italian was a criminal, or at least tolerated a colorful criminal in the family. DeSimone, and later his successor Richard Israel, often assigned me to our high-profile mob cases, perhaps because he wanted to emphasize to any Italians on a jury that we were prosecuting criminals, not persecuting poor innocent Italians. In 1971, for example, I prosecuted an organized crime guy named Bobo Marrapese for car theft, but really for being a degenerate criminal who had to be taken off the streets. My main witness was his former girlfriend, who came to us after he had assaulted her. Several times. I knew exactly what she was going to tell the jury, and I knew the effect it was going to have on them, so I put her on the stand and led her directly to it. The whole thing started when she took the keys to several cars Bobo had stolen and hidden in various garages around the city, she admitted. She had stolen the keys to the stolen cars. In response, Bobo beat her up. That's when she decided to get even.

She prepared a large bowl of Italian soup for him. Every woman takes special pride in making the best homemade soup in the world, and none of them easily reveal their secret recipe. Bobo apparently accepted this soup as her apology. "You like the soup?" she asked.

It was delicious, Bobo told her, perhaps savoring his victory.

"Want some more?" she asked him.

He had another bowl, she told the jury. I glanced at the jury. They were with me, wondering where I was taking them with this testimony. And then she told him her secret recipe. This is a very good example of why most of the cases we tried would never be dramatized on television. "I'm glad you liked it, Bobo," she said. "Because I pissed in it."

Marrapese responded by breaking her arm. Eventually, he was convicted of the car theft and served three years.

There were times when I turned out to be the punch line. I was prosecuting an arson case and a witness for the defense, a fire department battalion chief named Sullivan, was demonstrating to a judge in his chambers how a fire could spontaneously detonate and the explosion would not be heard by people less than a block away. The defense was claiming the fire had been caused by a gas leak, and had built a large glass-enclosed floor model of the crime scene. It actually had gas running into it. The defense planned to ignite it in front of the jury to show them how the fire could have started. As I watched this I casually asked the judge, "Do you mind if I smoke while we do this?"

Chief Sullivan interrupted. "That depends," he replied, "on whether you just want to observe the demonstration or you want to be part of it?"

The case that put me on the front page of newspapers throughout New England for the first time was the prosecution of Raymond Patriarca for conspiracy to murder. At that time Patriarca wasn't simply perceived to be above the law; most people believed he made the law. Or at least owned the law, and the politicians. Patriarca's reach stretched across the entire country; when New York's five crime families had a dispute, it was Patriarca they brought in to settle it. He had his hand in the major unions, and he silently had a piece of the Dunes Hotel in Las Vegas; in fact, the mob used to say that you couldn't take a crap in New England unless Raymond Patriarca owned a piece of the toilet paper.

The murders for which he was indicted actually had taken place before I joined DeSimone's office. In April 1968 a bookie named Rudolph Marfeo and his bodyguard had been shot and killed in a meat market in Silver Lake, ironically the neighborhood in which I'd grown up. Apparently Marfeo had refused to pay proper tribute to Patriarca, in that world a capital offense. An armed robber named Red Kelly eventually turned stool pigeon, testifying that on Palm Sunday several weeks before the murders he'd met with Patriarca at a place called the Gaslight Lounge and Patriarca had ordered him to arrange the Marfeo hit. This was the type of direct testimony that can put someone even as powerful as Patriarca away for a long time.

I was assisting a very able prosecutor named Irving Brodsky in this prosecution. Admittedly, I was a little nervous. This was the major leagues of criminal prosecution. Basically my job was to do the research. I certainly knew Raymond Patriarca's reputation. He had grown up in the same neighborhood as my father, although I don't know if my father had ever met him.

To contradict Red Kelly's testimony, the defense team called Father Raymond Moriarty, a Maryland priest who had grown up with Patriarca. Believe me, at that time it was almost impossible to top a priest as a defense witness, especially when the priest was wearing his collar when he testified and there were Catholics on the jury. Father Moriarty testified he was the pastor at Saint Timothy's Church in Maryland and that on the day that Kelly claimed he'd met with Patriarca to plan the hit, "he was with Mr. Patriarca," that he "knew him from Worcester, where [they] grew up together." He had driven up from Maryland that day, he explained reverently, to accompany his old friend on a solemn visit to his wife's grave at the Gate of Heaven cemetery. And then they'd gone to Raymond's home together.

This was perhaps the single finest alibi witness in history: a priest swearing on the Bible that he had spent the day with the accused at the grave of the man's departed wife. Poor Mr. Patriarca was crying as he listened to Father Moriarty testify. And just to make sure the jury understood that God's representative here on earth was bestowing his blessing on Raymond Patriarca, when Father Moriarty finished his testimony, the two men hugged.

I was the one who should have been crying. But I had been an altar boy. I'd known several priests, and Father Moriarty's testimony just didn't have the ring of truth to it. What priest isn't in his own church on Palm Sunday? Besides, few of the priests I knew would drive all the way from Maryland to Providence for one day. I asked Irving Brodsky to let me check out the quality of the good father's memory.

At that time in legal proceedings we did not have what is called discovery, so Father Moriarty's testimony had been a complete surprise to us. We really were blindsided, and the judge granted us a one-day continuance to investigate Father Moriarty's claims. That afternoon I called the church secretary at Saint Timothy's Church in Maryland, where Father Moriarty had been assigned on that particular Palm Sunday in 1968. There was a lot of pressure on us; if we couldn't destroy Patriarca's alibi he was going to walk right out the door. The secretary at the church was aggressively unhelpful; my memory is that she actually hung up on me. I called the diocese in Providence to ask for some help. The appropriately named Bishop Angell put me in touch with a monsignor in Baltimore who was associated in some way with the FBI. He may have served as a chaplain. I don't think this monsignor liked the concept of a priest serving as an alibi witness for a mob boss. He invited me to come down and take a look at the church records.

I flew down to Baltimore that night with Detective Bobby Stevenson, and we were met there by members of the Organized Crime Division of the U.S. attorney general's office. I didn't even have time to get a cash advance, so I had to put all my expenses on my credit card. The monsignor brought us into the rectory and provided access to the church records. At first we couldn't find anything that would show where Father Moriarty was that Sunday. I took a deep breath; it was just another long shot that hadn't paid off. But then we asked to check the church baptismal register. "We don't usually do baptisms on Sundays," the church secretary explained, "but you never know."

A few minutes later we hit the jackpot. Father Moriarty had baptized a baby girl that Sunday afternoon! There was absolutely no way he could have been with Patriarca. As soon as I saw that I thought, We got you, you bastard, we got you. Patriarca's lawyers were stunned when they learned of our discovery. What happened next was more like a scene from *The Great Race* than from *The Godfather*. Patriarca knew that if we could produce the register and the witnesses, his alibi was gone. I decided we had to get hold of the parents whose child had been baptized that morning and bring them back to Providence to testify.

We raced to their house, and when we got there, who did we find sitting on their front porch but Patriarca's son, Raymond Junior, and his supposed chauffeur Joseph "Joey One Arm" Tomasso. Apparently they had chartered a private jet and beaten us there. The federal agents told them to get off the porch and stay out of our way. We went inside and met with these people. They were great. They handed me dated photographs from the baptism that showed the good father standing there smiling. It was the evidence we needed to prove he was either a perjurer or a time traveler. These people also agreed to fly to Providence to testify.

Later that evening we met with attorneys representing the diocese in the rectory dining room. They were from a firm like Stone, Stone, and fucking Rock. He knew he was screwed, because Brodsky hadn't dismissed him; we hadn't cross-examined him yet. But his lawyers claimed we couldn't compel him to return to Providence because we had no subpoena power in Maryland. I spoke with the diocese's attorneys. In return for allowing Father Moriarty to return to Providence with his memory refreshed, the diocese wanted an agreement that we would not prosecute him for perjury. When I told that to my boss, a terrific guy named Al DeRobbio, he laughed. Clearly he didn't think it should be necessary to make a deal with a priest in order to get him to tell the truth. "Does Stevenson have his handcuffs with him?"

Stevenson said he did. "Good. You handcuff one of his arms to Stevenson and the other arm to you and you bring that cocksucker back right now."

I pointed out to DeRobbio that he was asking me to kidnap a priest. Generally that's not considered a good career move.

"Maybe," he agreed. "But five to ten years from now when the Supreme Court decides it, then we'll know for sure."

Finally we compromised with Stone and Rock; we didn't guarantee anything, but we agreed that Moriarty would be permitted to recant his testimony. We spent the night in a motel with Moriarty and several marshals. Before we left the motel the following morning, the marshals traveling with us asked Moriarty to take off his collar. They felt it made him too much of a target. We met the baptismal couple at Washington National Airport. My credit card was fast running out. Just as we were about to board I got an emergency call from DeRobbio. "Don't get on the plane," he warned me. "We got word it's going to get blown up."

Jeez. That stopped me. There was no doubt in my mind that Raymond Patriarca was entirely capable of that. His freedom was at stake. But as I was deciding what to do, who did I see walking right toward us? Raymond Junior and Joey One Arm. Stevenson immediately reached for his weapon. I stopped him. "Stevenson, put the fucking gun away, please."

"We want to speak with Father Moriarty," Patriarca said.

I stopped this conversation. "Raymond," I wondered. "Are you going back on this flight?"

"Yeah? So?"

I smiled. "So? Then so are we." I knew the mob wasn't going to blow up a plane with Raymond's son on it. Those two sat in the back; my group sat in front. I sat in a seat facing the rear of the plane and watched them throughout the flight. That afternoon Moriarty admitted on the witness stand that he had not been in the cemetery with Patriarca that Sunday. Brodsky was kind to him, allowing him to claim he'd simply confused the dates.

In the end it didn't matter. Our main witness, Red Kelly, had his own memory problems. His credibility took a big hit when the defense pointed out that the Gaslight Lounge, the restaurant where he'd supposedly met with Patriarca, had been closed at that time because of a fire. Several other inconsistencies in his testimony bothered the jury, and after eight ballots they acquitted Patriarca of the charges.

While obviously I was very disappointed, I wasn't surprised. In those days convicting a mob boss was only slightly less difficult than convincing a city council member to give up a free parking pass. But one of the important lessons I'd learned proved particularly important during another high-profile trial, this one the largest payroll robbery in Providence history, which I tried myself.

I wasn't supposed to try this case. One day I came into the office a little late—truthfully, that was not unusual for me—and someone handed me a file and told me to go down to the courtroom and take a plea. Supposedly a plea deal had been arranged. Except when I got there, it turned out the defense was ready to go to trial. I had no idea what the facts of the case were, so I told the judge, "I'm going to waive my opening argument."

The judge looked at me and smiled. "Not in my courtroom," he said.

I asked for a recess and got briefed on the case. A psychopath named John Gary Robichaud, his wife, and a mob associate named William Cresta were accused of dressing as priests and robbing an armored car of $66,000. Their alibi was that they were in Miami Beach, sitting by the pool at the Fontainebleau hotel, when the robbery took place.

Although this was a state case, the feds were in the courtroom every day. They wanted Robichaud for murder. As it was explained to me, a Ford executive from Detroit had been in Boston for a meeting and was using a pay phone. Robichaud was waiting to make a call. Basically, when he asked the businessman how much longer he was going to be on the phone, the man replied arrogantly, as long as he wanted to be. Robichaud responded by grabbing a mallet and beating the hell out of him.

The executive survived and volunteered to testify against Robichaud. A couple of days before that trial was about to begin, the executive's wife tried to start their car and it blew up. The government had been unable to connect Robichaud to that murder, so they really wanted him put away for this armed robbery.

Robichaud and his accomplices' alibi was provided by the hotel pool boy, who testified that at noon on the day of the robbery he remembered serving them drinks. Maybe a pool boy isn't as strong a witness as a priest, but you put a nice-looking teenager who responds respectfully on the stand and every mother on the jury is going to fall in love with him. The only shot I had for a conviction was to break that alibi.

The pool boy was a student at Miami Dade Community College. In those days it was possible to get all the information on students you needed. That's no longer true. I spoke with the dean of students and asked every question I could think of, looking for some loophole in that student's testimony. And I discovered that this student got an A in an English course—a course in which the final exam was given on the day he supposedly was serving drinks poolside. I put the dean on the stand and asked him, basically, is this student registered at your school?

He was. Did he take this English course? He did. Was the final exam given on the day of the robbery? It was. And what was his grade in this course? An A.

It was beautiful. The defense had rested its case, so the judge wouldn't allow them to present surrebuttal witnesses. Robichaud, his wife, and Cresta were convicted. After the verdict was announced Robichaud looked me directly in the eyes and said flatly, "I'm going to get you." He wasn't the first criminal to threaten me, but I always pay a little extra attention to psychopaths. As a prosecutor I didn't have to worry about the mob associates. They understood that I was doing my job. It was only when a prosecutor allowed witnesses to lie or presented creative testimony that he had to be careful. But you did have to worry about the crazy ones, the John Gary Robichauds.

This case eventually went into extra innings. As I later found out, the witness had taken an English test—but not that day. It was a take-home exam. Even worse, while we had substantial information that Robichaud absolutely committed the robbery, Cresta was innocent. The guilty verdict came in on a rainy Friday night. Afterward a detective told me, "Cresta wasn't guilty."

"That's not what the jury said."

He shook his head. "He's not guilty." He had a good informer, he explained, who told him the whole story. This cop gave me the name of Robichaud's accomplice.

The next day I went to see the attorney general. "This one can't stand," I told him. But in reality there was nothing I could do beyond giving him my opinion.

A couple of months later John Gary Robichaud escaped from state prison. I was making a speech at a country club dinner when two state troopers interrupted me and literally escorted me off the podium. "Robichaud broke out of jail," they explained as we rapidly drove away. "We're taking you into protective custody." I saw no sensible reason to object.

They took me to the state police barracks, which actually was much closer to the prison from which Robichaud had just escaped than the country club. When I looked at the prison I saw that every light inside and surrounding the prison was shining brightly. "Jeez, I think it's a little late for that," I suggested. The next few weeks were very tense. Robichaud seemed to have disappeared. My close friend Detective Vinny Vespia, who'd also grown up on Federal Hill, and two state troopers lived with me in my home until the day Robichaud's body was found in Massachusetts. Apparently he'd been shot several times, probably soon after his escape. When Vinny heard the news, he told me, "I'm going to go up there and make sure he's dead."

"That's a fine idea," I agreed.

Eventually I would prosecute hundreds of cases, but there were a few that stand out in my memory. For example, I prosecuted one of the few birking cases in recent Rhode Island history. A defendant named James Pelliter was charged with murdering his estranged wife, who choked to death during oral sex. He claimed in his defense that he and his wife had decided to get back together and were having consensual oral sex on the banks of the Providence River. I understood the salacious aspect of this case, but I focused on the fact that a woman had died that night. His attorney asked him what happened that night and he said, basically, that she started to fellate him and she died. He was asked if he had returned to the crime scene and he replied that he had gone back there with the detective who'd arrested him. That detective happened to be sitting in the courtroom during this testimony. Pelliter said, "That detective asked me to tell him what happened. I told him what happened. Then he said to me, 'That's okay Jimmy, I've done that myself and I kind of liked it.' "

The defense argued that this was an unfortunate accident. I didn't believe that was true. I thought he had forced her to commit sodomy and she had died in the act. That's called birking and it is murder. But I also understood how difficult it would be to prove that beyond any doubt. Then I realized his confession had put him in a very difficult position.

There is in the law a doctrine known as felony murder, which means basically that if someone dies during the commission of a crime, even if it is an accident, the person committing the crime is guilty of murder. For example, if a bank robber slips and his gun goes off accidentally and kills someone during a bank robbery, it's still first-degree murder. Intent was not to be considered a factor. In Rhode Island at that time it was a criminal offense for two people, even if they were married, to engage in fellatio. Even if it was consensual. He had already admitted they were committing that crime when she died. I explained that to the jury, which convicted him of felony murder.

The judge didn't really buy my theory. He sentenced him to five years—and then suspended the entire five-year term.

In 1973 our new attorney general, Dick Israel, appointed me the chief prosecutor of the organized crime and anticorruption strike force. It was a very fortunate assignment for me. I don't know when I first seriously began thinking about going into elective politics. My mother always told a story that in first grade the teacher went around the room asking each student what he or she wanted to do. Apparently I responded, "I want to be president." And she would add, laughing, "And that teacher thought he meant president of the *class!*"

I was always fascinated by politics. As I was growing up, Winston Churchill was my political hero. The first books I ever took out of the public library were biographies of Fiorello LaGuardia and Theodore Roosevelt. But until I got to know several politicians and got close enough to the political process to see and understand how it was being used, and too often misused, for personal gain, I didn't take the possibility of running for office very seriously. That seemed like something other people did.

But then I got to see the reality of it. In both 1970 and 1972 I had been a volunteer in Herb DeSimone's unsuccessful campaigns for governor. It was then I discovered how much I loved politics—and became convinced that I certainly was capable of doing as good a job as those people already in office. To be honest, right from the beginning I knew I could do a better job than they were doing.

I certainly had the essential prerequisites for running for political office: a strong desire to help people and a very big ego. What I didn't have was the connections. I liked to say I wasn't a member of the Lucky Sperm Club. I didn't have a family background or the old-boy network connections to push me to the head of the political line. In

Rhode Island, for example, in 1969 then-Senator John Chafee nominated Lincoln C. Almond to be a U.S. attorney. In return, Almond proceeded to nominate Chafee's son Zechariah Chafee as an assistant U.S. attorney. In 1994 Almond was elected governor, and in 1999, when Senator John Chafee died, Almond selected his son Lincoln Chafee as his replacement. Lincoln Chafee was sworn into office by Al Gore Jr., whose father had been a senator. Also in 1994, Patrick Kennedy, Senator Ted Kennedy's son, was elected to the House of Representatives from Rhode Island. In 2004 Lincoln Chafee appointed Lincoln D. Almond, the former governor's son, a U.S. magistrate judge.

Notice there's not a single Cianci in the bunch. I suspect if I had participated in this type of political payback they would have called out the cavalry to investigate me, but for the establishment it's a way of doing politics. After DeSimone's failed second campaign I started seriously looking for an opportunity to run for office. I felt confident that once I got my foot in the political door I could push it wide open. But I had to start somewhere.

There really wasn't much to recommend me beyond intelligence and enthusiasm. Not only did I lack the proper political heritage to guarantee me a place in politics, I wasn't even an active member of the Democratic or Republican organizations that might have helped me. And I didn't have that singular high-profile case that could make me a viable candidate for any office. Since New York's Tom Dewey turned his role as a special prosecutor against organized crime into a political career that almost reached the White House, being a successful prosecutor has been seen as a viable path to a political career. I had a lot of solid convictions, some headline-making cases, but not that one case that I could ride into politics. In 1973 I was in my office when my political future walked through the door. Any prosecutor or attorney with ambition who looks you in the eye and tells you with great sincerity that they didn't recognize a politically important case when it appeared is probably a natural politician.

In 1972 one of the few bright spots in Providence was the brand-new Providence Civic Center. It was one of the major accomplishments of our then-mayor Joseph Doorley. Many years later I'd sell the naming rights to Dunkin' Donuts for $9 million and it would become known as the Dunk, but for a long time it was simply a big and too often empty building. Only a few weeks after it opened, a local music promoter named Skip Chernov showed up in my office accompanied by an American Civil Liberties Union (ACLU) attorney and told me, "The management of the civic center want me to pay to get dates there. I want to get them asking for a bribe on a wiretap."

Essentially, management was looking for a kickback to provide the better dates for Chernov to promote a concert. Chernov was pretty well known in the city. He'd opened a very successful rock-and-roll club called the Warehouse on the waterfront. Personally, I didn't think he was a very stable guy, although I certainly understood the potential political ramifications of his claim. He'd been feuding with Doorley for several years; when the city's Board of Licenses had refused to issue a permit to allow a pretty raucous band named MC5 to perform, Chernov had sued the city claiming his rights of free speech were being infringed—and won. So I knew where this ACLU lawyer had come from. But when Chernov told me he wanted to tape a private conversation, I looked at the lawyer and said, "Beautiful. You're a lawyer for the ACLU and you want to tape a conversation?"

Eventually I went to see Dick Israel, who pointed out to Chernov that Rhode Island law permitted people to tape a two-person conversation so long as one of them consents. Israel suggested to Chernov, "Get a tape recorder and get him on tape. Then we'll talk."

About two weeks later Chernov returned to the office with a recording on which the civic center's then executive director, Harold Copeland, could be heard telling Chernov that it would cost him $13,500 to book the venue for a Grateful Dead concert—and then very clearly asking for $1,000 for himself. Chernov had done a very good job. In the next few days he had spoken with Copeland at least twice more, and Copeland had reiterated the deal. I took the tape to Israel and suggested, "Let me see if I can make a friend here."

The following day I called the president of what was then the Industrial National Bank, John J. Cummings. He was a big Democrat and served on several committees; Doorley had appointed him chairman of the Civic Center Authority, which was the financial arm of the civic center project. I had decided to tell him that we were investigating his executive director for being on the take. But here Mr. Cummings made a serious mistake—he refused to take my phone call. Believe me, it's never a good idea to piss off someone who is young, ambitious, and aggressive, and has just enough power. And an Italian temper. Me, for example.

I called him several times. Finally, he got on the phone and told me, "If anyone from that office wants to talk with me, you have the attorney general call me."

Oh yeah? I told the attorney general that if he accepted that demand I would quit, and I wasn't going quietly. Dick Israel had no intention of embarrassing me. "No, no, just go ahead and do what you need to do."

I called the state police and asked them to subpoena the civic center's books. We discovered several serious problems with the civic center management. Almost fifty thousand dollars was missing from their accounts, and two hundred extremely hard-to-get tickets for a sold-out Frank Sinatra concert had been delivered to Mayor Doorley's office. But the most interesting thing we discovered was that all the money earned by the civic center was being deposited into non-interest-bearing accounts at the Industrial National Bank. If they grossed a million dollars on a Frank Sinatra concert it went directly into a checking account. It was a great deal for the bank, which was getting the use of a substantial amount of money without having to pay any interest on it. The minute we saw that, we knew something was wrong. There were many other banks in the city; why was all the money going there? It was either an extraordinary coincidence or it was because the president of the bank was also chairman of the Civic Center Authority.

It was also illegal. The law was clear: Any member of the civic center board, or the business he or she worked for, was prohibited from gaining any benefit from that association. I remember looking at the audit and thinking, I'll bet he'll take my phone call now.

I explained to his secretary, "I'd like to speak to Mr. Cummings, but if he doesn't want to talk to me I'd like him to appear in front of the grand jury tomorrow."

Five minutes later my phone rang, but it wasn't him. It was an attorney from the most expensive law firm in the city. "Oh, Buddy . . . ," he began.

I interrupted. "I think you should call me Mr. Cianci, because I'm not going to call you Knight."

He ignored me. "Well, listen, I'm sure we can work this out."

"There's nothing to work out. Your client's either going to be here at the grand jury tomorrow or he's not." Admittedly, I was enjoying this. "Oh, by the way, the way things have been developing, I don't even think I want to talk to you because I think we're going to get an indictment."

This attorney was not used to conversations like this one. "Oh no, Mr. Cummings has an important meeting in Houston tomorrow."

"It's his choice." But I did suggest I would be willing to meet with them—in my office.

A quartet of very well-dressed civil lawyers showed up in my office the next day. Before we began they looked around the office for a taping system. I made it easy for them; I put a tape recorder on my desk and turned it on. Then they began challenging our theory that a crime had been committed. And even if it had, they explained, it wasn't Cummings who did it. A man named Jay Sarles was Cummings's young administrative assistant. Sarles claimed he was responsible. I have always believed he took the rap for the whole thing.

Al DeRobbio looked at Cummings and said flatly, "I don't believe you." There were many times when I was mayor that I asked someone who worked for me to do something. I had a habit of telling them, before they responded, that they should carefully consider their answer, because it was a career move. For Sarles this was a career move. He made the correct decision and eventually had a very good career with the bank.

Eventually we indicted the civic center director, Harold Copeland. The attorney general decided he didn't want to indict the bank. By the time Copeland was tried I had resigned and was in the middle of my first campaign for mayor. Copeland was convicted—and fined one thousand dollars. Wow.

But the case received a great deal of publicity and established me as the anticorruption candidate. And while we never connected Mayor Doorley to any illegal activities, when I finally announced in April 1974 that I was going to run for mayor, I pointed out, "The operation of the Civic Center is a prime example of the kind of political hanky-panky and lack of judgment that the taxpayers can no longer accept. . . . It is time that we reaffirmed that the civic center belongs to the people, not the mayor."

In addition to the civic center case I had the essential qualities necessary to become a successful political candidate: I was young and energetic, I had a lovely wife and a beautiful young daughter, and I had a full head of Kennedy-esque hair. I was particularly proud of my hair—in fact, I'd picked it out myself at a barber shop across the street from my law office!

Two

lmost two decades later, when I began my campaign for mayor in 1990, I was definitely the underdog. In fact, it would have been almost impossible to be any more under. Six years earlier—after having been elected mayor three times—I had resigned from office in the middle of a scandal. I had pled guilty to assaulting a former close friend who'd been having an affair behind my back with the woman I was happily divorcing. I regretted it terribly and I was really sorry it ever happened, which, not surprisingly, was exactly the same way I felt about my marriage. But find me a man who will never admit to having made a mistake and I'll show you a successful politician.

The 1990 campaign was to be my big comeback, Buddy II, and I was running against two very decent men Fred Lippitt, the Waspy scion of one of Providence's most respected families and a man I'd beaten eight years earlier, and an Italian kid from the neighborhood whom'd I hired during my first term and who eventually became a city councilman, Andrew J. Annaldo. The incumbent mayor, Joseph R. Paolino Jr., was running for governor, so the race was wide open. In mid-September the polls had the three of us only a few points apart, and my private polls had me running third by about two percentage points.

I needed to do something to change the race. My opportunity came when in the final moments of one of our debates, the moderator said, "Yesterday afternoon the bishop of Providence said that any candidate who is pro-choice should not be supported by Catholics. What is your opinion about that?"

What was my opinion about that? My opinion was leave me out of it. Abortion is a highly controversial issue that I had successfully avoided for my entire political career. Mayors should be supporting construction, enticing businesses, and building parks, not making private moral decisions for people. That's not an issue for a mayor. I had never actually spoken about it, and honestly I didn't really have an opinion. By the luck of the draw I was last. Fred Lippitt said flatly that his position on the issue had long been known, and he was pro-choice. Andrew Annaldo was from Saint Ann's parish; he was a good Catholic. And even though he was Catholic, he said, he believed that a woman should have the right to choose.

This was interesting. Let me understand something, I said. Mr. Lippitt says he's pro-choice. Mr. Annaldo says he's pro-choice. Is that right? Both men nodded. Good, I'm pro-life.

Beginning at that moment, I had always been pro-life. Why not? Was it hypocritical? I prefer to consider it political. Anyone who doesn't believe that politicians choose at least some of their positions based on political expediency hasn't read the polls, some of which tell politicians what positions they should take. I was in a close race and I knew there were a considerable number of pro-life zealots searching for a candidate. I ended up getting a list of pro-life voters from the diocese. There were twenty-four hundred names on that list. That's a big number in a Providence election. These were essentially one-issue voters. I could be for anything else; it didn't matter. Raise taxes forty dollars per thousand? They didn't care; I was pro-life. Support a fund to give the zoo animals a two-week vacation? It didn't matter; I was pro-life. A few days before election day we mailed out letters to these people that would be delivered Saturday, so they could discuss it in church on Sunday. The letter emphasized the fact that I was the only pro-life candidate in the race; that's Cianci on the Independent line. On election day I was standing in line to vote with my then girlfriend, Wendy Materna, when two Irish nuns came up to us. I whispered to Wendy, "That's not our profile." But one of the nuns introduced herself and explained, "We came just to vote for you. We got your letter Saturday and made up our minds."

I won that election by 317 votes.

I had decided to run for elective office in 1974 because I believed I could make a positive difference in people's lives. Don't laugh; that's absolutely true. What's more, I continue to believe that most elected officials originally get into politics for that reason. Please, don't laugh. But admittedly there is always an alternative motive. If you haven't been bred for elective office—meaning your last name isn't Kennedy, Chafee, Bush, or Gore, for example—it takes a tremendous amount of audacity to enter politics. I would guess at some point most people believe they could do a better job than their elected officials, but they don't cross the line and run for office. I'd thought about it for a long time before I decided to run. In addition to my high-profile job as a prosecutor, I had a successful private law practice, I had just gotten married, and I had inherited enough money to provide a very comfortable lifestyle. So why would I choose to run for office?

Actually, there are a variety of reasons people get involved in politics. Some people run for elective office to satisfy their egos, and others want the power, prestige, and attention that come from it; certainly it can be an exciting and rewarding career, and truthfully, it also can be very lucrative. For me, it probably was a combination of ego fulfillment, the desire to be in charge, and a need to have fun. It was a simple equation: I fulfilled my ego and retained my power by helping people. I loved being mayor of the great city of Providence every minute of my six terms in office. I admit it, I loved being onstage, I loved being at the center of the action, I loved feeling the affection from the crowd. I loved it when people came up to me and thanked me for something my administration had done. And in the end I believe I did make a positive difference for the people of my city. I made their lives better.

Any elected official will admit that in addition to their natural charisma, extraordinary charm, and superior intelligence, being elected to any political office for the first time requires an element of luck. You just have to be in the right place at the right time. For me, that place and time was Providence in 1974. Under normal circumstances I wouldn't have had a prayer of being elected. The popular incumbent mayor, Joe Doorley, was a Democrat, which in Rhode Island pretty much guaranteed election. In the 1900s a wave of Catholic immigrants from Italy, Ireland, and French-speaking Canada had come to Rhode Island to find work in the mills, and turned the once-Protestant state strongly Democratic. The city hadn't elected a Republican mayor since 1938, three years before I was born, and, given the incredible unpopularity of Republican president Richard Nixon, who was then fighting to survive the Watergate scandal, there was little reason to believe I was the person who could change that. In fact, when I first was considering making the run I sought advice from several people, including a friend named Bud Counihan, who worked with me in the attorney general's office. "I think I may do it," I said. "What do you think?"

"You can't win," he said flatly. "There's never going to be an Italian mayor."

"What are you talking about? Why wouldn't there be?"

"Because it's just not going to happen. But you should run anyway. The publicity'll be great for your law practice when you leave this job."

I knew he was probably right—it would take some sort of miracle for me to be elected—but I was still considering it. Because the Republican candidate had almost no chance of winning, pretty much anyone who could raise or put up enough money to pay for his campaign could have the nomination. So I knew I could get it. And Counihan was right; the publicity would be beneficial for my private law practice or if I decided to make another political run in the future. On the other hand, I hated losing at anything and if I really had believed I didn't have a chance of winning, I probably wouldn't have entered the race.

As all politicians eventually learn, every election is unique. In 1973 the Democratic machine that had so successfully controlled Providence for decades had been splintered. Ten years earlier Democratic party chairman Larry McGarry had backed Joe Doorley. In return, after his election Doorley appointed McGarry head of the Public Works Department, and McGarry had dispensed patronage from that position, using Public Works jobs to reward political loyalty to the machine. Jobs are the currency of politics, with the exception of currency, of course.

The oldest political cliché is that all politics is local. But it's true. Every city has its own political structure, but the battles for power are amazingly similar. In Providence, after getting along for almost a decade, Doorley and McGarry were battling each other for control of the party. There were several reasons for this, one of them being that Doorley was too liberal for the conservative McGarry. He pushed school integration, fair housing regulations, and President Lyndon Johnson's antipoverty programs. He was a rising figure in the Democratic party; at the 1968 Chicago convention he'd run the important Credentials Committee and in 1970 he had almost been elected national party chairman. But it also had become common knowledge that Doorley was spending more time in bars than in his office.

McGarry was one of the last of the old-style machine politicians and was fighting to hold on to his power. He had been diagnosed with multiple sclerosis and probably wanted to put someone into the mayor's office he could control more easily than Doorley. But whatever his reasons, McGarry announced that Doorley would not receive the endorsement of the Democratic Committee. In fact, they were going to put up another candidate against him for the party nomination. Their feud broke the party wide open, forcing people to pick sides. Eventually four men entered the Democratic primary, including Doorley.

I remember the precise moment when I decided to go for it. I lived at home until I got married. Believe me, it was a great deal. My father had built an addition to the house, then put in a swimming pool and a cabana. I had my own separate quarters with a beautiful bedroom and a nice bar next to the pool. One beautiful summer day I was sitting by the pool reading *The Providence Journal*. There was a major story on the front page about the fight between Doorley and McGarry. According to this article, this was the beginning of the end of the Democratic machine. No matter who won the nomination, the reporter predicted, the split would not be healed. Well, I thought, that's interesting. It didn't matter to me who won, because the loser could be my ally. Although I was quietly hoping Doorley would get the nomination, as he had a ten-year record to run against. Suddenly the race made a great deal of sense.

There was at least a possibility I could win. It would take a lot of work and would require a lot of support, but it was possible.

As I had hoped, it was a very bitter primary race. Doorley won the Democratic nomination with about a third of the votes, or, as I saw it, he didn't get two-thirds of the Democratic votes. Those were the votes I needed to win. And rather than trying to mend political fences, Doorley made it clear to the Democrats who had supported his opponents that there would be payback. They had the option of sitting out the election or supporting me. They knew that no matter who won the election, the city council would remain Democratic, so they would have a much better chance of retaining power if they got rid of Doorley.

Let this be a lesson to all readers who do not believe in the power of prayer.

Every campaign has to have a theme. The country was right in the middle of Watergate. New revelations about the corruption of the Nixon administration were being published practically every day. So my theme was obvious: I was the anticorruption candidate, meaning that Doorley had to be the corrupt incumbent. As I said when I made my announcement, "This administration has taken the people's trust, and has turned . . . a government into a powerful, dictatorial, political regime." Naturally, I pointed out the corruption at the civic center, and just in case they didn't understand that I was accusing the mayor of being corrupt, I added, "In the midst of a serious energy crisis, when scores of gasoline stations were closing every day, the mayor responded by clearing the way for construction of a gas station, owned by his close friend, the head of his reelection finance committee."

Even with all the problems the Democrats were having, nobody really thought I had much of a chance. In fact, the first ad agency I tried to hire for my campaign turned me down. "You can't win," they told me flatly. They didn't want to risk alienating the mayor who would be doling out business during the next administration.

I'll tell you how tough it was nationally for Republicans. After my announcement I got a flyer from the national Republican party inviting all Republican candidates to a meeting with the then national party chairman, George Bush, at the Bellevue-Stratford Hotel in Philadelphia. That made sense to me; I figured I could meet other people in my situation and maybe learn something. I flew to Philadelphia and the entire gathering consisted of . . . George Bush and me. Literally, I was the only candidate to show up.

In 1973 nobody, absolutely nobody, wanted to be associated with the Republican party. I certainly didn't stress the fact that I was a Republican during my campaign. Steven Smith, who eventually became a state representative and a teachers' union leader I worked with, remembers meeting me for the first time during that campaign. This was probably very typical of the way I campaigned. Steve was eighteen years old and bagging groceries in a supermarket. I had no idea who he was, but he looked old enough to vote. I planted myself in front of him, smiled widely, stuck out my hand, and introduced myself. "Hi, I'm Buddy Cianci and I'm running for mayor. Are you registered to vote?"

"Yeah, I am," he said, and then added, "but I'm a Democrat. My father was a Democrat, my mother was a Democrat, and I'm a Democrat."

"That's okay," I apparently told him. "I didn't run in the Democratic primary. But I am running in November and you can vote for me then!"

I did have several things going for me. The local newspapers had come out strongly against the entrenched Democratic machine, and I was the only alternative. And in addition to being a tireless campaigner with a big smile and a hearty handshake, I had earned enough money in my legal practice that with the help of my family I could finance my campaign, I had a pretty wife, a new baby daughter, and of course my brand-new head of hair.

I honestly don't remember if I got my wife or my hair first. In those days politicians had to be married, because being "single" was generally considered to be a euphemism meaning "light in the loafers." My wife's name was Sheila Ann, and *The Providence Journal* accurately described her as "the made-to-order political wife. Blond, attractive, relaxed before a camera [choosing] her responses carefully and deliberately, offering little more than what was asked, but courteous in her manner."

Our marriage actually had come as a big surprise—especially to me. I learned about our engagement when I read the announcement in the newspaper. I'd met Shelia when I was home on leave after my father's funeral. One night I went out to the Copper Galley, a local restaurant. I knew the maître d', Caesar Brown, and he came over to me and said, "I got two hot numbers over there in the corner." So I went over there and introduced myself. Shelia was there with a girlfriend. Caesar was right, she was very attractive, but she was also married. She'd gotten married as a teenager, and her husband was the son of a very successful jewelry manufacturer. We exchanged phone numbers and I went back to my assignment at Fort Gordon. Basically, I forgot about her.

It was after I was transferred to Fort Devens that we started having an affair. We went out for several years; I used to tell people that I gave her a Saint Bernard and in return she helped me spend my money. By 1973 she was separated from her husband. We spent a weekend at the St. Regis Hotel in New York and she ended up pregnant. Several weeks later my mother called me angrily to ask why I hadn't told her I was engaged. I told her the truth, that I didn't know about it. Sheila had put the announcement in the paper without mentioning it to me. There was no question about what we were going to do. I knew I had to marry her; that's what men did in those days. I married her in a quiet civil ceremony and bought a beautiful house for us. We were the perfect young married couple, except I didn't love her and I don't think she loved me, although I'll never know that. In those days, though, I did think she was a good person, and she gave birth to a gorgeous little girl, Nicole. It was never a great marriage, but throughout that first campaign she certainly was supportive. And in the newspapers she was an asset.

My hairpiece lasted a lot longer than my marriage. I don't know why I started wearing it in the first place. I was a young attorney, just beginning my career, and I was losing my hair. There was a barber shop across the street from my law office that sold toupees and the owner suggested I put one on. I thought it looked awful; I looked like Napoléon's brother. I don't know why I continued wearing it for decades; it was pretty obvious it was a rug. It actually became sort of a joke. I used to say that I worked so hard that I didn't even have time to go to the barber. Instead, I just took off my hair and sent it there to be cleaned.

When my campaign started, every morning I kissed my wife and baby daughter good-bye, put on my hair, and went out to find votes. I can say with confidence that nobody campaigned harder than me. Having been through two campaigns with Herb DeSimone, I had learned that there is no substitute for hitting the streets and shaking hands with voters. Even with television and the Internet, there is no bond stronger than personal contact. That's really what I became known for. I was relentless, I never stopped. I used to say I retailed votes, I didn't wholesale them. I went to every conceivable event, I shook every hand. It was said about me that I would go to the opening of an envelope. Always smiling, always talking, I'll put a tree in here, I'll fix the sidewalk, what a beautiful baby, my mother knew your aunt, glad you were born, sorry you died; it never ended. The former mayor Joe Paolino, Jr. once said about me, "If he has to French kiss an old lady who's got a jelly donut in her mouth to get her vote that's what he'll do."

It was almost true. I once got into a heated discussion with my chief of police, Colonel Bernie Gannon, who told a reporter about some of his own ideas for the city. I called him after reading the interview and said, "I understand you want to make some changes. Tell you what, you want to be mayor, you go out and kiss the old lady with the mustache and I'll take your job."

But Paolino was right, I would go anywhere and do anything for a vote. I went to every graduation; every communion, confirmation, and bar mitzvah; every Little League opener; every breakfast, picnic, and banquet. I marched in every parade, I cut the ribbon at every store opening. Hi, I'm Buddy Cianci and I'm running for mayor and I'd really like your vote. I went to every ethnic event, it didn't matter to me, Irish, Italian, Jewish, African American, Polish, Puerto Rican, Dominican, a few Guatemalan; when the Hmong people moved here I went to their weddings. To me all people were equal; they were all potential votes. I never said no. Once, I remember, I went to a Portuguese Democratic Club event because I was trying to get their endorsement. At first it was alien territory, but eventually I could feel the winds shifting and thought, I'm beginning to win these guys over. They roasted a pig over an open fire and then proudly explained the old tradition, the guest of honor gets to eat the eye. I looked at this thing looking right back at me and I thought, Eat the eye? You gotta be nuts. But there were a lot of potential votes watching me. I gotta eat the eye. I took a deep breath and swallowed it. Then I looked at the crowd and said with as much disappointment as I could pretend I felt, "What? I only get one?"

If anybody invited me to an event I was there; even if they didn't invite me I'd be there. In fact, sometimes even if they didn't want me there I'd be there. Parades are to politicians as blood is to Dracula. We thrive on them. Hundreds, sometimes thousands of people standing there cheering. I can't even begin to estimate how many parades I've marched in. I even initiated and funded a Saint Patrick's Day parade, and was made the first grand marshal. As I learned, there's a science to marching successfully; most important is leaving a considerable distance between yourself and the people marching in front or behind you so the spectators on both sides can see you. Dignitaries are supposed to march behind the color guard, the flag bearers, but if you do that people can't see you, so I always marched in front of them. For obvious reasons never, ever march behind a horse. In fact, when possible I would ride on a horse; people can see you clearly when you're on a horse—and the other marchers will not get in your way. Never march behind a bishop, either, because he'll stop frequently to bless people, and they make the sign of the cross, so they can't clap for you. And don't march in front of the parade queen's float because no one is going to be looking at you.

The biggest parade in Rhode Island is Bristol's Fourth of July parade. It is the oldest continuously conducted Fourth of July parade in America, dating back to 1785, and draws several hundred thousand people from all over the country. At one point special legislation was passed to allow the town to paint its white road stripes red, white, and blue. I've marched in that parade since 1975, although theoretically I'm not supposed to be there. To prevent the parade from being overmarched by politicians, parade organizers long ago established a policy that prohibited all politicians—except elected federal, state, and local officials—from participating. So those first few years I was not permitted to march as the mayor of Providence. I could have marched with several groups—the Italian American War Veterans, the Vietnam Veterans; believe me, if I had to become a Jewish veteran to march I would have had a bris. Instead, I marched in front of the Matadors, a Providence drum and bugle corps. With those drums and bugles, you couldn't ignore us.

I was officially disinvited from that parade in 1980, during my campaign for governor. But my opponent, the incumbent governor Joe Garrahy, had been invited to march, so I had every intention of being there. I told reporters I intended to fly to Bristol in my helicopter and march in the parade. The fact that I was banned by Bristol made headlines. In late June the police chief announced that his officers would prevent uninvited guests from marching in the parade, then threatened to arrest anyone causing problems, "anyone" meaning me.

Now right around that time a man who could have been my twin brother walked into city hall. He was an insurance salesman from New Hampshire in town on business and, in fact, he looked so much like me that people kept coming up to him to say hello and were offering to buy him drinks. So he decided he had to meet me. When he walked into my office it was like I was looking in a mirror. It was uncanny how much he looked like me. I toyed with the idea of flying him down to Bristol on the helicopter and letting the cops arrest him. I allowed myself to talk myself out of it. I made a convincing argument to me. But you know what, I'm still sorry I didn't do it.

I had no intention of being arrested. I brought a security force with me that was larger than the Bristol police department. That turned out not to be necessary. When my helicopter landed in a school parking lot near the start of the parade route, the only person there to meet me was Miss Rhode Island. But just before the parade began a parade organizer came over to me and asked me not to march. "Why?" I asked. "I'm an American veteran and it's the Fourth of July. I'm entitled to march."

He said, "Okay, I got it. So where do you intend to march?"

"I'm going to march with the Matadors," I told him.

That's when he thought he had me. He waved a finger in my face and told me, "You can't march with them unless you play an instrument."

A band major standing nearby listening to this conversation tossed me his whistle. "I do," I said, showing it to him. "Watch." I am still probably the only marching band whistle player whose photograph appeared on the front page of *The Providence Journal.*

So the type of relentless, in-your-face campaigning for which I eventually became known started during my very first campaign. As every politician will tell you, and then tell you again, the most difficult and most disagreeable part of politics is fund-raising. The American people continually complain about the impact money has on government, but the reality is inescapable: raising money is required to run for any political office, and once you're in office, those people who gave you the money to get there aren't going away. Please do me a favor, call and tell me the next time you hear a victorious politician standing at a podium on election night telling his supporters, "I want to thank all of you people who donated your money and worked hard for me during my campaign, but I've decided to give all the jobs and contracts to those people who contributed to my opponent and worked hard for my defeat."

That's not the way politics works and everybody knows it. I didn't invent the system, but I did have to live with it. At the beginning of this first campaign I estimated I would need $250,000. It didn't seem that unreasonable; at that time television advertising still wasn't an absolute necessity in a campaign. I kicked off the campaign with a fund-raising cocktail party to which I sold only one ticket. Fortunately, I sold it to my mother for one hundred thousand dollars. I also put in a considerable amount of my own money. I had inherited several hundred thousand dollars from my father, and my private law practice was thriving, so I could afford it. I organized a committee of friends and people I worked with to do the actual fund-raising.

At that time there weren't a lot of restrictions on fund-raising. In fact, many U.S. congressmen actually had safes in their office. Until the 1960s people could walk into a congressman's office carrying a bag of cash and legally hand it to him. And even during my first campaign, corporations could legally contribute pretty much any amount to a politician as long as it was reported. That was some great deal for incumbents; a corporation could do business with the city or the state and then at election time send a contribution. Believe me, if some of the political icons of the 1960s and 1970s had to live under the fund-raising rules of the 1990s, they would be doing a hundred years in jail.

My committee raised funds mostly by holding cocktail parties for small contributors. It was very difficult to raise money because nobody thought I had much of a chance of winning. That's one of the ironies of politics: A politician who is heavily favored to win a race and doesn't need to raise substantial funds can generally raise as much as he wants. But if you need the money because you're running behind it's very difficult to raise it. I was running as the anticorruption candidate, so I emphasized the fact that my campaign depended on small contributions from real people rather than large donations from the corporations and wealthy people who supported the Democratic machine. The truth was that I wanted those small donations because I couldn't get any large donations. The large contributors were all connected to the machine; they didn't want to hear from me. I also believed that once a person contributed to my campaign, even a dollar, I had their vote. For them that contribution was an emotional investment in me.

I raised about half a million dollars—unfortunately, my campaign cost substantially more than that. What I couldn't raise my mother contributed or I loaned to my campaign. We ended up several hundred thousand dollars in debt. But the relationship between money and politicians was made very clear to me after my victory. As soon as my election was certified, we held a fund-raising party at the Colonial Hilton in Cranston. That night we raised slightly more than two hundred thousand dollars—and that's in 1974 dollars. Almost every penny came from people I had never met, and they were either people who were thrilled that I had won and believed this was a victory for good government or people who wanted to do business with the city. Obviously I'm kidding about the good government people. Hundreds of people showed up to personally congratulate the new mayor that night—of course, many of them hadn't even received an invitation—but if the new administration was keeping a list of its new friends, they wanted to make sure they were on that list.

That's the way the system works and I don't know how to reform it. There are many people who believe that all political campaigns should be publicly financed. But that would work only if every candidate in an election agreed to participate. I don't believe that's possible; there is always going to be a candidate who can raise a great amount of money who refuses to accept a public limit. If I were a challenger I'd probably want it mandatory. But why would any incumbent accept it? An incumbent has his entire term in office to raise campaign funds, while a challenger generally has only a few months. When Rhode Island passed laws limiting campaign contributions and prohibiting corporations from donating to candidates, I referred to it as the Incumbency Protection Act. Rather than reducing the influence of wealthy contributors and corporations, all that it did was make it harder for a challenger to raise sufficient money to compete. Fund-raising isn't difficult for an incumbent who is going to run for reelection. As the years went on, we became very successful at fund-raising, but during that first campaign it was difficult. If my dear beloved mother hadn't honestly believed that I was the best candidate in the race, I might not have been able to finance my campaign.

Most people believed that Mayor Joe Doorley's hard-fought victory over the Democratic machine in the primary guaranteed his election in November. In fact, reporters were speculating that in two years he probably would run for governor or even the senate. But I kept looking at the numbers, and as far as I could figure they didn't add up for Doorley. He had gotten slightly more than a third of Democratic voters while successfully alienating two-thirds. Not one of those disaffected Democrats had anything against me; they didn't even know who I was. If I could add some of those unhappy Democrats to my Republican base, I knew I had a chance. Doing that, though, put me in a somewhat awkward political position. I was running as the anticorruption candidate, running against the entrenched corruption of Larry McGarry's Democratic machine. But the only way I could win was to convince

McGarry to put that machine to work for me. That's what is known as Providence politics. I didn't have a choice; I didn't have any organization, just me, some friends, and a lot of good ideas. I needed bodies to hang posters, make phone calls, and get people to the polls.

Shortly after the Democratic primary I ran an ad in the newspapers announcing the formation of "Democrats for Cianci." It was a myth. At that time there were exactly no Democrats for Cianci, although the Democratic voters didn't know that. Once I had established Democrats for Cianci I had to recruit some actual Democrats.

It was a tough decision for a lot of these people. These were lifelong Democrats who had never voted for a Re ... Re ... some of them couldn't even say the word. There is an old saying that is often applied to politics, "Keep your friends close but your enemies closer." Joe Doorley forgot this. After the primary, rather than trying to heal political wounds, he was vindictive. I had heard that he told Sharkey Almagno, the president of a Democratic organization and a candidate for city council in the Seventh Ward, that because he had supported another candidate in the primary he could forget about receiving any patronage, any anything. A councilman who can't generate jobs and other perks for his district has what's known as a serious political problem.

Now, I have my own political saying, "You can't buy your enemies— but you can rent them!" I knew I couldn't convert these Democrats into Republicans but I could get them to work for me. Sharkey had known my family my whole life; as a kid he would literally walk a mile to deliver packages from his father's grocery to my parent's house. He knew my grandmother, and he had watched me grow up. Sharkey ran the bingo at Saint Bartholomew's church, so one night I went over there and asked his permission to work his crowd. Knowing I was a Republican, Sharkey told me he would ask the priest. I wasn't looking for confession, I was looking for votes. But he got permission and I began introducing myself. There was only one important political principle I had to remember: Don't get between a voter and their bingo card.

Eventually, I went over to Sharkey and told him, "Shark, do me a favor. I want you to support me."

He laughed. "How can I do that? I'm a Democrat. I'd get killed." I asked him if I could meet the Democratic leadership to try to convince them. Sharkey spoke to his people and agreed to set up a secret meeting. If word got out that they had met with a Republican, any chance of reconciliation was done. We met at 9 A.M. Columbus Day morning. Sharkey was there with four other important Democrats. The five of them had agreed that whatever decision they reached had to be unanimous, so I had to convince all five of them to support me or I got none of them. The parade started at one o'clock, so I had about three hours to convince them that this was a good career move. Maybe my political career was at stake, but I wasn't going to miss the parade. I'm a politician, I never miss a parade. It was a rough meeting; these guys were not easily persuaded. I offered what I could legally offer. I understand that few readers will believe this, but there were no secret deals. I told them I'd pick up the garbage, plow the streets, fix the sidewalks. But I never promised them anything except access to the mayor. If they had a problem, they could come and talk to me and I would remember that they were there when it took courage—which was a lot more than Doorley was offering. These guys were washed up on an island and I was offering them a rowboat. That's legitimate hardball politics.

Eventually, they decided to get into the boat. Democrats for Cianci actually had some Democrats. But getting additional Democratic leaders to join my campaign remained a struggle. Each time Democratic leaders found out who I was talking to, they applied enormous pressure on that person to prevent him from going public with his support. They pointed out, accurately, that even if I won, the party would still control the city council, which meant I would have a title but little real power.

Joe Doorley also knew how to play this game. The Democratic primary had been very close until the labor leader who had organized the city's labor force, Arthur Coia, endorsed Doorley. His support was considered the key to Doorley's victory.

Two days after the primary Doorley signed a new contract with the union, which included a new benefit—if city workers needed legal services, the lawyers' fees would be paid by the city. The estimate was that it would cost the city about $125,000 a year. I am not saying any deal was made. I wasn't in that particular smoke-filled room. But that is some amazing coincidence. Even more amazing, after I beat Doorley in the general election he was appointed the first administrator of the Rhode Island Public Service Employees' Legal Services Fund. I continued to be very critical of this contract right up until the 1978 election, when I doubled the city's contribution to the plan.

The 1974 campaign was very difficult. I didn't have any real experience, so I listened to my advisers and made it up as we moved along. Certainly one of the key factors I had working for me was Doorley's overconfidence. Though there are always a few high-profile issues in every campaign, there are also many smaller issues that most people never hear about. These are issues that personally affect a specific group of people and can influence their votes. In this campaign, for example, our elderly population was concerned about the fact that our fire rescue service did not have telemetry in their trucks. Basically, this was a system that allowed hospitals to monitor a patient's condition in a rescue truck, which is particularly important for heart attack victims, and to be ready to go to work when they get there. Doorley was against it, explaining it was too expensive for the limited use it would get, so naturally I was for it, pointing out, "No life is too expensive."

The police department wanted to equip its officers with a certain type of cold-weather coats, and when Doorley refused to buy them, the cops began referring to him as "No Dough Joe." Naturally I wanted those officers to have those coats. Coats? I guaranteed that when I was mayor they would never have to pay for their own clothing again. In fact, when those poor shivering officers set up a picket line to protest Doorley's lack of support, I marched with them. The police department had a concerted effort to vote against Doorley. Who knows how many votes that was worth? We had five hundred cops, plus their wives and relatives. But almost no one outside the department was aware of that issue.

A campaign consists of numerous small decisions, but you also must have a vision; you have to sell voters on your vision of their future. And your future has to be better and less expensive than your opponent's. It's Herbert Hoover's campaign promise, "A chicken in every pot and a car in every garage." The best thing about vision is you're not limited by reality. You don't have to worry about the cost or whether it's even possible. At that time professors at the Rhode Island School of Design had created Interface Providence, an overall plan for turning Providence into a walking city. It didn't envision moving rivers or railroad tracks, but it was the seed that would grow into a new city. Joe Doorley didn't endorse it, so naturally I did. But I also believed in it. It enabled me to talk about my plans for revitalizing the city. Basically, as mayor I was going to breathe life into the city by revitalizing downtown Providence and the neighborhoods, cleaning up the parks, modernizing the port to bring in jobs, utilizing the historical landmarks to create a tourist industry, and, as every urban politician has promised every worried parent, providing the best public school system in the nation!

In addition, I took five thousand dollars in campaign money and hired architect Lester Millman, who previously had been a Republican candidate for mayor, to develop a viable plan to restore the once great port of Providence. This was more than the city had done. Millman's plan included the construction of a modern marine facility and dredging the river so that larger cruise ships and cargo ships could dock there. We unveiled the plan and *The Providence Journal* supported it. Eventually, I went down to the docks and spoke to the longshoremen and stevedores, most of them Portuguese people from the Fox Point neighborhood, who traditionally voted Democratic. I showed them a plan that would produce jobs, and before I left they were endorsing me.

I wasn't kidding about these projects, either. I had a plan for downtown with Interface. I had a plan for the port. I had embraced historic preservation. I was creating a vision for the future that I actually believed I could deliver.

Unfortunately, dreams don't win elections. There is a political theory that the first candidate to go negative wins. Well, I don't know about first, but it's difficult to fight a campaign without dirtying your opponent. The primary theme of my campaign was a promise to rid Providence of corruption. I promised an open government, conflict-of-interest laws, and civil service protection for city workers. The Democratic machine would no longer be running the city! I proclaimed loudly, "The Providence River is like the Democratic machine that has been running this city—namely, it stinks!" Running against corruption immediately puts your opponent on the defensive. What's he going to do? Run *for* corruption? So Doorley had to spend considerable time defending himself. In politics that's not where you want to be. I was helped tremendously in the middle of the campaign when Harold Copeland was convicted of soliciting a bribe from Skip Chernov for giving him better dates at the civic center for concerts. It reinforced my theme that everything in the city was for sale.

To prove my own honesty I revealed my total worth, which was mostly what I inherited from my father, and then became one of the first political candidates to release my tax returns. I called upon my honorable opponent to do the same thing, and when he refused, it created the impression that something just wasn't right.

With a week left in the campaign Doorley finally realized that I was climbing in the polls and that he had to go really negative. The expression I've always used is that "he had to put some gum on my shoes." He was scheduled to speak at a major state Democratic party dinner, and informed the media that in his speech he would reveal why I wasn't qualified to be the mayor. Well, that certainly raised my curiosity. I went over to Herb DeSimone's house to watch the news. At that Democratic dinner Doorley waved a sheet of paper over his head, which he identified as an affidavit from an insurance adjuster claiming that I had given him a cash payment in return for falsifying records after an automobile accident. In an angry voice, Doorley cited this as evidence, "that Mr. Cianci, after he settled the case, gave him a cash kickback." He added, "This seriously reflects on the integrity and character of my opponent."

A week to go in the campaign, and this was their smoking gun?

"What's he talking about?" Herb asked.

"It's nothing," I told Herb. I knew exactly what he was talking about. I'd had a kid working for me part-time as a driver. I was paying him fifty dollars a week, although he was also collecting workmen's compensation for an injury. Three years earlier he had been driving my future ex-wife in my car when another driver hit him. Doorley claimed I'd paid this adjuster to file a false claim so that my future ex-wife could continue to get unemployment benefits after going back to work and so this kid wouldn't lose his workmen's comp. The insurance company paid my future ex-wife eleven hundred dollars for medical expenses and lost wages and seven hundred dollars to repair the car. And I had never paid a dime to anyone to change any information. I knew that, but with a week left before the election the public didn't.

This was my introduction to hardball politics. One thing I knew without having been taught was that you can't let an allegation hang in the air without responding to it. You have to make certain your denial is included in every story reporting the accusation. So I immediately denied it. Then I went further, eventually offering to take a lie detector test.

Within two days we discovered that the insurance adjuster who made the claim had been under indictment on three charges of insurance fraud. Doorley had refused to identify him—so I did it for him. Turned out he was a former state trooper who had been fired because he was dirty, a former insurance adjuster, and was currently working in a liquor store. Probably not your most reliable witness. I attacked Doorley for bringing up these charges five days before the election, pointing out that they should have been made four years earlier to a law enforcement agency. My campaign responded, we overresponded, which is what you have to do in that situation. We just continued to punch holes in the accusation. I invited prosecutors to inspect all of my financial records for any evidence that I'd paid a bribe.

I didn't let Doorley take the offense. I forced him to respond to my offer. He said, in turning down this offer, "I am positive that not one record in his possession will reveal what is contained in the affidavit." Well, no kidding. Of course they wouldn't—because it never happened.

After the election the attorney general, my former boss Dick Israel, presented the charges against me to a grand jury. In the process it was revealed that Doorley supporters had promised this adjuster that in return for his testimony they would pay off his mortgage. The grand jury agreed that their accusation was nonsense. But I went even further; I went to the police barracks and told them to "put me on the box." I passed the test.

This charge backfired completely on Doorley. He should have known that if you're going to throw something at your opponent, you need to make sure it isn't a boomerang.

From the beginning he had refused to debate me. I understood his reasoning. Incumbents want as few debates as possible, since they mostly help a challenger become better known. What is an "extremely important exchange of ideas" for the challenger quickly becomes "nothing more than a rehash of old campaign promises and slogans" for the incumbent. Naturally I challenged Joe Doorley to debates and naturally he turned me down. However, in early September he had agreed to appear with me on a local Sunday morning political show to answer questions from a panel. I realized for the first time that my campaign was working when he pulled out several days before the show. His spokesman said Doorley withdrew because "he didn't see any purpose in subjecting himself to the same type of, and this is a quote, 'repetitive, broken down questions'" about the corruption at the civic center and the mayor's personal finances. Meaning his refusal to release his tax returns. The aide added that Doorley certainly wasn't afraid to answer questions about his bribery charge against me.

Here's a fact of politics: When a politician says he or she is not afraid to answer questions and then doesn't answer those questions, voters believe the politician is afraid to answer them.

Doorley's spokesman did say that he would be willing to meet me in an "open debate" without some panel asking questions. All of it just added to the growing impression that Doorley was afraid to respond to the charges I'd made. At this point the polls had him comfortably ahead, and I've always believed he was certain he could coast to victory. But we knew those polls were questionable. Polling in 1974 was far from the science it is today, and we knew there were a lot of lifelong Democrats who were not about to tell a stranger on the telephone they were voting for a Republican. At least we hoped so. The only thing that was preventing Doorley from shooting himself in the foot was his poor aim. He certainly was trying. And there also were reports that he had started drinking heavily, which had caused him to miss several campaign appearances.

Under normal circumstances there was no way a thirty-three-year-old unknown Republican who had never held political office should have beaten the incumbent Democratic mayor of Providence in the middle of the Watergate scandal, but I was on the verge of doing it. Obviously, I had a lot of help. I actually didn't even know how smart I was until I read it in the newspapers. The Providence papers wanted Doorley out. After I'd had a press conference or appeared at a political event, I would read the stories quoting me in the papers the next morning. Boy, I'd think, am I eloquent! The truth is that the papers would creatively quote me. They would clean up language and refine my ideas to make me sound almost poetic. I couldn't wait to read the papers in the morning to read my magical words. I figured they must be magical, because I would read quotes that I would have been proud to say, but I didn't recall actually saying them.

The love affair between the Providence media and me didn't last very long. Eventually they came to dislike me. Dislike me? I used to tell people that if I had gone outside and walked on water across the Providence River, the next morning the headline of the *Journal* would have been CIANCI CAN'T SWIM!

But in this election the papers endorsed me, which was very important for my campaign. It gave me the credibility I needed. They called me "energetic, articulate and aggressive," and wrote, "We are impressed not only with Mr. Cianci's courage in facing political odds, but more with the fact that he sees the potential and opportunity to make Providence a great city in which to live and work."

The beauty of a political campaign is that it is usually just long enough for the truth about a candidate to be revealed. If you know what you're doing, you can fool a lot of the people a lot of the time, but the day-to-day grind of a campaign and the incessant attention make it difficult to fool enough voters. They get to know who you are, and they get to know your opponent. The fact is that even with all my shortcomings in this campaign, I really did believe I could make Providence a great city in which to live and work. And I knew I had convinced a lot of voters to give me the opportunity to do that the Saturday night before the election when, very late in the evening, I walked into an East Side diner with my director of advertising, Norm Roussel, and everyone in the place stood up and clapped. But on election day we weren't confident that I had convinced enough voters.

I won by 709 votes. Contrary to the prevailing wisdom, there was no great surge of ethnic pride for me. I actually won only four of the city's then thirteen wards. The only Italian ward I carried was Silver Lake, where I'd grown up, and I carried that only by a few hundred votes. I carried the black and minority communities who had been ignored by the Democrats and the liberal East Side, but I stayed competitive enough in those wards I lost to make up the difference.

I knew for sure I'd won when Doorley's chief of police, Walter McQueeney, reached out to me on election night, calling me on an unlisted number at my mother's house where I was watching the returns. Nobody was supposed to know where I was, but he had the phone number. Okay. He cut right to the chase. "I heard you're going to fire me."

I didn't hesitate. "I don't know where you heard that. It isn't true." The reason it wasn't true was because it was still a very close election, he was chief of police, and his department had control of the voting machines. The election was close enough for the result to be overturned if Doorley could come up with enough absentee or shut-in votes, or could show there was an error, so the board of elections had ordered the police department to guard the machines. A couple of hours earlier we'd heard a rumor that cops were throwing voting machines off the backs of the trucks to break their seals and then adding votes. Even if it was true—and there was never any evidence it was—we didn't know for whose benefit they were adding those votes. But I reassured him, "I am absolutely not going to fire you."

Later we met in an office apartment in a hotel. "My daughter is in nursing school," he told me. "I have to stay."

"I'll give you one year," I told him. And that was our deal. He was a fine police chief, but he was too political. In 1976 I replaced him.

When the returns were official at the end of election night, I turned to my mother and asked, "So are you proud of me now?" It is almost impossible to adequately express what I was feeling that night. When I spoke to the media I gave them all the politically correct answers, but inside me there was this kid jumping up and down screaming, "I won! I won!" Maybe some politicians take victory for granted, but that night I was euphoric. This was the most exciting night of my life. Nothing would ever be the same again, and I knew it. I certainly remember that among the first words out of my mouth were, "I am so proud to be the first Italian-American mayor of Providence."

The Democratic machine was stunned. These people hadn't lost a major election in more than three decades and they didn't know how to react. They assumed I was a fluke that they would have to put up with for four years until the world was right again. And that's the way they treated me.

I was inaugurated on January 6, 1975. Among the people who were at my house that morning were Uncle Charlie the diaper man, and my barber, who told reporters he was responsible for my distinctive "Napoleonic look. It's franchised, how do you call it, it's exclusive style."

Among the people who joined me at city hall were Democratic city chairman Larry McGarry, who still controlled the core of the Democratic machine, and Ronnie Glantz, a highly visible leader of Democrats for Cianci, and a charming man who I eventually discovered was one of the most sophisticated con men I'd ever met. As I was to learn eventually, Glantz was the type of man who could never lose—because he was playing on everybody's team.

I ended my first working day in office by attending a performance of *Peer Gynt* at the Trinity Square Repertory Theatre. Early in an administration symbols are important, and I picked this one not because I was desperate to see a play including trolls, but because Joe Doorley used to boast that he'd never seen a play in that theater. I knew that working with the artistic community in Providence was going to be very important in my administration—and that it was a highly visible way of pointing out to people that we were going to do things a new way. There is a cliché often used to express this, "A new day was dawning in Providence." Unfortunately, it was overcast, with a real big chance of storms.

As I had complained during my campaign, the city was in terrible shape. Obviously it wasn't all Doorley's fault, but he certainly hadn't done much to prevent it. Our infrastructure was old and falling apart, our industrial base—the textile and costume jewelry industries in particular—was gone, storefronts downtown were boarded up, many buildings were half empty or had been abandoned, our rivers were both covered by cement and polluted, our parks had not been properly maintained, and there was no support for our arts community. Our population base was fleeing to the suburbs, so our retail industry was collapsing; our biggest department stores—Shephard's and the Outlet—were either out of business or headed in that direction, and those few restaurants still in business were struggling. Our tourist industry consisted basically of people waving as they passed by on their way to New York or Boston. As our tax base had declined, our school system had deteriorated, we had racial and ethnic problems, the Biltmore was closed, and the zoo was so awful the animals were embarrassed to be living there.

We didn't have the money in the budget to even begin making the changes that were necessary. When I looked at the budget, I realized almost all of it had already been obligated. Under our union contracts we had to pay the teachers this much, the cops that much; the fire department wanted more than the cops, the sanitation men wanted more than anybody. We had to pay interest on our bonds, and fix the potholes and pick up the snow. After I went through our revenues and our budget, it became obvious to me that once all these mandated expenses were paid I could do anything I wanted to do to improve the city with the eleven dollars I had left.

Worse than all that, there was a sense of hopelessness pervading it all. There was just no reason to believe things were going to get better.

On my inauguration day I had intended to throw open the massive front doors of city hall to symbolize the fact that I was going to run a completely open and honest administration. Everyone was welcome. It turned out that those doors had been shut for so long that the workers couldn't get them open. We were upstairs getting ready to take the oath of office when we heard this banging downstairs. Finally, they literally had to kick them open.

That turned out to be even more symbolic than I had anticipated.

Three

There are certain pieces of legislation that in addition to being worthwhile are also very useful political tools. At one point, for example, I proposed a far-reaching antidiscrimination city ordinance. This ordinance pretty much outlawed any type of discrimination for racial, religious, ethnic, gender, or sexual preference reasons. It meant you had to treat everyone—Caucasians, Southeast Asians, homosexuals, Italian Catholics and Irish Catholics, Jews, African Americans, Portuguese, little green men from New York City, everyone—as absolutely equal. The proposal made me popular with every minority group in the city, which added together constituted a majority, but it created a problem for some of the old-time Democratic city council members. To vote against me, they had to vote *for* discrimination. Go ahead, pal, try to explain that vote.

At that time Providence was still a relatively conservative city, so the ordinance was very controversial. The night it was to be debated by the city council's Ordinance Committee I was in my study at home and I turned on the eleven o'clock news. A reporter had interviewed the chairman of the Ordinance Committee, a veteran member of the council named Vinny Cirelli, just before the hearing. Vinny was a no-nonsense politician, with a thin gold chain wrapped around what there was of his neck, and he was smoking a cigar. The reporter asked him,

"I understand you've had a conversation with the mayor about this. How do you think the vote is going to go?"

He took a thoughtful puff on his cigar, then replied, "It's going to pass the council. This ordinance is okay and I think I might vote for it myself. I think this is good. But like I already told the mayor, I still don't want no fags on the police department."

And that is what I was up against when I became mayor of the great city of Providence, Rhode Island. See, I had made a mistake. When I was elected I had assumed that as the mayor of the city I actually had some power. That's where I was wrong. While every city has a mayor, the powers of that office vary wildly. Some mayors have tremendous power, while others are nothing more than figureheads. Because of the way our city government had evolved, I was basically just a pretty face.

Okay, I admit it, that was a bad situation.

The mayor of Providence derives his power from the city charter. Before 1940 the mayor's office was mostly a ceremonial position; the real power was exercised by the Board of Aldermen and the Common Council, which controlled the budget and the patronage—the jobs. Jobs equal power, period. In 1940 the new mayor, Democrat Dennis Roberts, led the movement for a new city charter that gave some power to the mayor, but eliminated the Board of Aldermen and gave the real power to the Democratic-controlled city council. What those people never envisioned was that one day Providence would have a two-party system. While theoretically I had the right to appoint department directors, commissioners, and members of the numerous boards that make the city run, from tax assessment to licensing, in reality the fact that the city council had the right to approve my appointments prevented me from hiring or firing anyone. It required a majority vote of the city council, for example, for me to appoint my own director of the Department of Public Works. That was bearable, but to fire a director I needed two-thirds of their votes, which was almost impossible to get. There were twenty-six Democrats on the city council and two Republicans. So what power did I really have? Who was I the mayor of? I couldn't fire anyone. The city council controlled the Director's job. A couple of months into my administration I tried to fire the city's director of recreation. I sent my own guy down there—and the assistant director locked him out of the office. I sent the police there and they arrested the assistant director. The only way I could get rid of that assistant was to start an investigation into his handling of department funds—and that's when we discovered that he had embezzled lunch money during a field trip to the Bronx Zoo. He was stealing lunch money from kids going to the zoo. It's amazing that *CSI* hasn't done that case yet.

I had a nice limousine and a chauffeur and a nice office, but every department at that time was being run by a Doorley appointee who was not accountable to me, and there was nothing I could do to change that. The city council refused to vote on my nominations. But as mayor, I also had full responsibility for their actions. They could do whatever they wanted to do; it was my name that was going to end up in the headlines.

The Democrats on the city council, or "The Gong Show," as I began referring to the council in honor of the TV show that celebrated a total lack of talent, considered me a temporary problem that they would have to live with for four years. Joe Vileno, one of my aides, remembers being told by a council member that "Cianci is a usurper," meaning I had seized power without any legal rights. Joe told me, "Mayor, they think this is Shakespeare. You're the usurper to the throne." I've been called many names during my career, but this was the only time I have been accused of usurpery! I enjoyed playing with that, though; at one point during negotiations with the council I told them I didn't make deals with "people who are trying to usurp my power"!

Any chance that the city council might be willing to work with me for the good of the city ended about twenty minutes after I was sworn in. In preparation for taking office I had named the new directors of the various city agencies, the Department of Parks and Recreation, for example. The city council met and, rather than approving them, sent them to a committee for review. In city government, committees are where new ideas and tired politicians go to die. Committees are like movie trailers for horror movies, "Legislation goes in, but it never comes out!" When I heard that, I said to one of my aides, "Well, that was a short honeymoon." Knowing me, I probably added something like, "They didn't even have the courtesy to kiss me before they began screwing me." It wasn't only the city council that created problems; Rhode Island's Democratic-controlled state legislature had its own agenda. For decades Providence had emptied its sewage into Narragansett Bay. About three days after I took office, the state legislature passed a resolution demanding that the mayor clean up the feces in the bay. Three days in office and I was being blamed for decades of crap—figuratively and literally.

Two weeks into my administration, after I had tried to fire several department heads and midlevel supervisors and put my own team in place, the city council declared war, announcing "a full investigation" of my administration. I had been in office two weeks, what were they going to investigate?

Francis J. Darigan Jr., a councilman who had been defeated by Joe Doorley in the primaries but had been elected the new Democratic city chairman, had already started positioning himself to run against me in four years. So he wasn't going to give me any easy victories. To get anything accomplished we had to play games. For example, when I fired the recreation director I had to use an obscure law adopted twenty-five years earlier that required the director to have a four-year college degree "or its equivalent" in field experience.

Darigan responded that the director had been a high school and Catholic Youth Organization coach for many years and therefore was qualified to run the department. This is how petty it got almost immediately. The city council fought me on every move I tried to make. If I had the power to bring back Jesus Christ but it had to be approved by the city council, Jesus would have lost 16–11. When I tried to replace the chairman of the Zoning Board with my selection, Darigan told reporters that it was evidence that I lacked "the maturity to deal with the high position of mayor of the city of Providence."

Darigan didn't realize it at the time, but his election as party chairman was the best thing that happened for me. That made him a visible target. I could blame anything the Democrats or city council did on him. And I did, believe me I did. For example, as part of our battle the city council reduced my emergency management budget to one dollar. One big dollar. After the great blizzard of '78 Darigan was extremely critical of the job we did responding to the storm, and naturally he blamed me. I replied, "I guess you could say that. But I think we actually did accomplish a lot in that blizzard considering the fact that you led the fight to give me one dollar for emergency management. What did you expect me to do with that buck? Should I have spent forty cents on snowplows or fifty cents on blankets?

"You were responsible," I said. "You didn't want to give the mayor the money or the authority."

If the city council had any doubts I was going to play hardball with them, that ended when the newly elected city council president, Robert Haxton, was arrested for picking up a sixteen-year-old boy and charged with committing an indecent act. That's a big felony. It's also the end of a political career. This really was a difficult situation for me. There were people who felt this was a very convenient way for me to get rid of a potentially powerful enemy, and they hinted loudly that I had something to do with his being picked up. I didn't. I was informed of his arrest and met with Chief McQueeney and several other people in my office. The city council had good friends on the police force, and there were several high-ranking officers who just wanted this arrest to go away, to just let him walk. It wouldn't be the first time a politician walked away from a mess. In fact, it was suggested to me that I could sit down with Haxton and work out some sort of arrangement to ensure his political cooperation in the future if that happened. But I didn't have a choice. If I allowed him to walk and that ever came out, which might well have happened, my anticorruption reputation would have been trashed. I would have been seen as just another politician willing to play political games. I didn't put Haxton in a compromising position; he did it himself. Who knows what a Democratic mayor might have done to help the Democratic city council president? I did the only thing I could have done, nothing. Haxton remained council president, but after that night he lowered his rhetoric and his public profile. In 1976 he was found guilty of transporting a boy for immoral purposes and given a year's probation. After his conviction my chief of staff, Ronnie Glantz, with my approval initiated a legal effort to force the council to remove Haxton, citing a statute in the charter that stated if a council member is convicted of a felony or a crime involving moral turpitude he must forfeit his seat. The city council eventually voted to unseat Haxton, and his appeals to the judiciary failed.

The Democrats on the city council did everything possible to sabotage my administration. The previous September the Doorley administration and the council had passed legislation giving the labor unions a fourteen-dollar-a-week wage increase—but that pay raise didn't take effect until the following July, when the next fiscal year began. Obviously they did it to make sure the unions would back Doorley in the election. Well, to fund that raise I had to come up with an additional $1.2 million. But when I put that money in my first budget—the council refused to approve it! You actually sort of have to admire them for that. They refused to approve the money to pay for a raise they had approved.

I also had to find an additional $125,000 to pay former Mayor Doorley and a relative of the International union's vice president to run that Public Service Employees' Legal Services Fund. That was beautiful; the former mayor had successfully figured out a way to stay on the public payroll even after being defeated. In the newspapers I described it as "testicular fortitude."

Eventually I reached an uneasy truce with the city council. After I had named several acting directors, using a law that allowed acting directors to serve on a month-by-month basis until a permanent director was nominated—which was going to be precisely never—they finally relented and allowed some of my choices to serve. My battles with the city council lasted until I was able to successfully start a campaign to revise the city charter two terms later.

Rather than wasting my efforts fighting with the council, I began looking for initiatives I could take without their approval. My first week in office I sent my limousine to bring seventy-year-old architectural historian Antoinette Downing to city hall for a meal and a meeting. I made a big deal about it. Antoinette Downing had been the leader of Providence's preservation movement since 1955, when she organized a group to prevent Brown University and the Rhode Island School of Design from tearing down a block of eighteenth- and nineteenth-century row houses in a slum and putting up dorms. Since then, every time the city had tried to knock down a building, she and her wealthy friends were there trying to stop them. The Doorley administration hadn't exactly banned her from city hall, but she hadn't been welcome, either. I embraced her. She was a symbol that we were trying to bring those people who cared deeply about the city into my administration.

And it didn't cost me anything. Yet. She was a lovely, genteel woman who could be as tough as the cement covering the Providence River when it came to saving the city's architectural past. And she was known to like her bourbon. She and her group of older women became my allies in saving the city's heritage.

It turned out that we had been fortunate that so few new businesses were moving to Providence. There had been no rush to replace our old buildings with modern towers when there were no tenants to fill them. We had successfully avoided progress! For a politician, this is the definition of optimism. When I took office, cities across the country were knocking down their old buildings. There were all these futuristic thinkers who insisted it was necessary to tear them down and replace them with sleek, modern glass-and-steel towers. Big boxes like that would give the city the modern image it needed, I was told, and it would generate revenue and create a lot of good construction jobs. Cities like Hartford and New Haven believed these new buildings would be their salvation. I didn't. I had learned from Mrs. Monahon at Moses Brown to appreciate our historic architecture.

I believe that the very first expense we authorized was a grant to Antoinette Downing's organization to compile a monograph identifying those buildings with architectural historic value in all the neighborhoods of the city.

I also immediately stopped the demolition process. There were plans to tear down the Shepherd's department store building. I stopped that. There was a beautiful but dilapidated building called the Casino in Roger Williams Park that they wanted to tear down. I stopped that. They wanted to tear down hundred-year-old houses and churches.

Our magnificent movie palaces and legitimate theaters built in the early part of the century were already mostly gone, replaced pretty much by parking lots. B. A. Dario, the owner of the once-gorgeous Loew's theatre, had applied for a demolition permit to knock it down so we could have another vacant lot. I stopped all of that. There were even plans to tear down city hall and replace it with a sleek, modern edifice. That's the way those people talked. I said "building," they said "edifice." Right. I used to tell them that they had an edifice complex. I told them right away that none of those buildings were coming down.

We began our renovation program at city hall. There is a room inside city hall known as the Alderman's Chamber. If you looked around its edges you would find indications that at one time it had been a gorgeous room. But the Doorley administration had covered up the floors, walls, and ceiling to turn it into cold, functional office space. We began referring to them as the Philistines. They had broken up the entire room into office cubicles separated by particleboard walls. They had smashed floor tiles and nailed two-by-fours into beautiful mahogany wall paneling. They had installed a dropped ceiling with fiberglass sections and fluorescent lighting. So our first project wasn't precisely groundbreaking, it was ceiling breaking. I literally took a crowbar and began ripping down all those horrible partitions. We uncovered the rich mahogany-paneled walls. We got rid of that fiberglass ceiling and exposed a magnificent vaulted ceiling with fine stencil work, and light started pouring through the leaded windows. We could have rented additional office space if we had needed it, but it would have been impossible to reproduce this room.

I didn't want to tear down anything. Old was new again. There was an old public comfort station—okay, a urinal—in the middle of the city. I knew there had to be something we could do with it. It was difficult because we couldn't take down the copper pipes and we couldn't change the design—so we ended up turning it into a police substation.

At the beginning of my first term I was just winging it. I didn't have specific plans; I had ideas and campaign promises. Until the day I was inaugurated I had been in city hall only once before in my life, and that time it was only for the five minutes it took me to register to run for election. This was basically on-the-job training. There is no rule book for mayors. I had very little concept of how to use those powers that I did have. But I learned, and I had good teachers.

I had to start someplace. The day I took office you could have rolled a bowling ball down the center of Westminster Street at 5 P.M. and you wouldn't have hit a soul. So I focused on the most visible symbol of what had happened to downtown Providence, the empty, lifeless Biltmore Hotel. I always believed that it was absolutely essential for the city, both economically and psychologically, to get the Biltmore Hotel back in business. One of the first things I did was begin searching for somebody, anybody, who might help bring the Biltmore back to life. Several developers wanted to buy the building and use federal subsidies to turn it into a retirement home for the elderly. I turned them down; two thousand people with walkers was not exactly the symbol I wanted for the new exciting downtown I intended to create. I was committed to reopening the Biltmore as a great hotel.

To figure out how to make that happen, I worked with a Providence group that had been formed to revitalize the downtown area. The group was composed of *The Providence Journal,* the Outlet, a worldwide conglomerate called Textron, and our banks. We worked out a deal to provide a ten-year tax abatement and other benefits to encourage the group to renovate and reopen the hotel. The Biltmore was owned by the Gotham Hotel Group, so the first thing this group had to do was buy it. Textron's chairman, Bill Miller, who several years later became chairman of the Federal Reserve and secretary of the Treasury, sent his associate John Henderson to meet in New York with Gotham's representatives. Henderson offered, I believe, a million dollars for the building. That was a fair offer for an empty building in a decaying downtown, but Gotham turned it down. Bill came to my office and explained, "You know what you have to do here, don't you, Mayor?"

I didn't, but Bill was about to teach me Mayor 101.

Gotham had asked the city for several reasonably standard waivers from our city ordinances while the hotel was closed. For example, rather than having to heat an empty building, they requested permission to shut off the heat and the sprinkler system. "You can't give them that," Bill advised.

I agreed, "I don't think I want to allow that."

Instead, as Bill suggested, I sent an army of inspectors into the building. I told the director of Building Inspections, "I have complaints that this building is not properly following the safety regulations. Go over there and look at it." Later there would be situations in which I told a director what results I expected, but I didn't know enough about that yet. In this case, though, the inspector got my message. It was made clear to Gotham that the city was going use all its resources to make the company's life miserable if they couldn't reach a fair agreement with my buyers. My job wasn't to fight with Gotham; my job was to get the hotel reopened. I knew I wasn't being fair, but so what? This wasn't supposed to be a fair fight. They were playing on my field and I owned the referees. For Gotham, it was like going to a gunfight with a water pistol. They figured out quickly that they were not going to win. They sold the Biltmore to Bill Miller's group for $925,000—and agreed to pay as much as $300,000 in back taxes to the city from that sum. It was an education for me, and the beginning of the revitalization of downtown.

I was learning how to use those powers that I did have. For example, renovating the hotel was going to cost several million dollars, and the developers said flatly they would not exercise their option to buy the hotel if they didn't get a tax break. So I agreed to give them that tax break.

Next thing I knew, city council members were complaining to reporters that I gave tax breaks to "multimillion-dollar corporations" while imposing tax revaluations on "the little people." Whatever I did, the council was against it. As I pointed out to a reporter, the empty building generated no taxes to the city, provided no jobs, depressed the value of all downtown property, discouraged new investment, and deprived the city of the lodging and meeting facilities we needed to attract tourists and conventions. And I did point out that the councilman making the most noise about this tax break had received more than $190,000 from 1963 to 1974 for running a training program for Rhode Island residents preparing them for jobs in the dry-cleaning industry.

Nearly $200,000 from the city to train dry cleaners? Oh, you can be sure the fine citizens of Providence would appreciate knowing where their tax dollars were going. Eventually, the city council supported the tax breaks for the developers.

With experience, I got very good at forging the necessary deals. I was accused many times of abusing my power, but I admit that at least one time I really did—and maybe I should have gone to jail for this one. I had been in office for about a year when I got a call from one of the wealthier citizens of Providence. "Mayor," he asked, "do you know Mr. Bacciocchi?"

Mr. Bacciocchi? Oh yeah, but I knew of him as B. A. Dario, which is what he had begun calling himself years earlier. B. A. Dario was an Italian immigrant who eventually owned Lincoln Downs racetrack and many other properties throughout Rhode Island. I said, "I think I met him once when I was a kid, but I don't really know him. Why?"

"He owns the Loew's and he wants to knock it down. We've got a group here that would like to buy it and refurbish it, but he wants too much money."

The Loew's State Theater was the last of the magnificent movie palaces left in Providence. When it opened as the opulent Loew's Movie Palace in 1928 it was a perfect example of the Loew's philosophy: Make people buy tickets to see the theater, not the movie. But it really was in awful shape. The basement had been flooded since the 1938 hurricane. That's not hyperbole; that was a fact. Maybe the theater was an architectural masterpiece, but Dario was a hard-nosed businessman. In addition to the Loew's, he had owned the equally elegant Albee Theatre, which had opened in 1919 with Providence native George M. Cohan as the first act. If anyone doubted Dario would knock down the Loew's, all they had to do was look at the vacant lot on which the Albee had stood until 1970. "Why are you calling me?" I asked.

Sometimes people are too honest for their own good. There had long been rumors in Providence that Dario was loosely connected, meaning he knew people who knew people in the mob. And the caller didn't hesitate to make that accusation. "Well, we figured, you know, he's Italian, you're Italian . . ."

The old secret handshake charge. You prick, I thought, but I didn't say it. "Okay," I said. "I'll be very happy to call him for you. But what about your plans; what are you gonna do with it?" This group had real plans; they were willing to put substantial funds into the building to turn it into a first-class theater. It was exactly the kind of project I had been pushing for. I called Mr. Dario and made an appointment to have dinner with him on the Saturday night of Easter weekend.

I drove up to his beautiful home. As I got out of the car, these two huge German shepherds came bounding at me. I got right back in the car and told my driver, "Go knock on the door."

He leaned back over the seat. "What, are you nuts, Mayor?"

Suddenly the front door opened and Dario was standing there. He called off his dogs and invited me into his home. Inside, his house had all the grace and elegance of a Las Vegas casino—except it had more mirrors. He escorted me into the living room, where these two dogs were waiting for me. Dario told me his wife would be right down. Good, I thought, looking at those dogs; maybe she could hurry. The dogs started sniffing those parts of my anatomy that I'm very concerned about. If I had been forced to wait a few minutes longer, I would have decided that the theater was destined to become a vacant lot.

Finally, his wife came sweeping down the curved stairway wearing a long gown. Okay. At dinner I spent twenty-five minutes explaining to him why he shouldn't tear down the theater. The city's going to get better. We can help. We're going to build a tourist industry. I tried to paint a beautiful portrait of the future. At times I can be very persuasive, and I felt I was making a strong argument.

Dario was sipping his soup as he listened to me. From time to time he nodded, and finally said in broken English, "Mr. Mayor, you want to do me this favor?"

Apparently I had gotten through to him. This was often the way negotiations begin. "Well, if I can, Mr. Dario."

"Gimme a demolition permit." Then he went into this soliloquy as to why he would never sell this theater to that group. "Those no-good bastards," he said. "Ten years ago they have this big Italian festival. I brought for them horses from Italy. Thoroughbreds, the best. I had the thoroughbreds race for them. And those bastards, they never invited me once to their parties."

"Dario," I said. "I was in the army then. I had nothing to do with that. I was serving this country we both love so much." The more we talked, the more I realized his determination to tear down the theater came from a combination of anger at these people and his business sense. He really didn't believe the theater would ever be financially viable. Finally I just told him, "Dario, you just can't demolish that beautiful theater."

He shrugged. "Mayor, you remember the Albee Theatre? They told me the same thing about that one, too."

I made it quite clear to him that I was never going to give him a permit to knock down the building, but we both knew he could get permission from the court. I convinced him to let me speak with his lawyers. For several days I continued going back and forth between the two sides, and eventually we set up a meeting. I knew I could never put Dario in the same room with the Waspy group trying to buy the theatre, so we arranged to meet by phone. The group that wanted to buy the theater gathered in Textron headquarters. Dario came into my office. The negotiations were difficult and eventually to get it done I had to commit a million dollars from the city. It was a fair deal for everyone. I was thrilled; the refurbished theater would serve as the anchor of our arts community. This was a big win for the city. But at the very end, when I went to shake hands with Dario, he smiled and said, "So Mayor, what about my other forty thousand dollars they owe me?"

"What forty thousand?" I had no idea what he was talking about.

"Those bastards, they promised me they'd pay me a thousand bucks a day to negotiate. That's forty days. I want my money."

As usual, I called Bill Miller. "Uh, Bill, there's just one more little thing we got to tie up. That's this forty thousand for Dario."

"What the fuck are you talking about?" I told him what Dario had said. I had never heard Bill Miller swear like that before. Never. But he made it very clear he wasn't going to give Dario a penny.

When I told that to Dario, he was very gracious. "Fuck 'em, then. Deal's off."

"Just wait a minute." I was part of this now. "Listen, I can give you half, Dario. How about that?"

"What are you talking? How can you do that?"

I was thinking pretty fast. I was the mayor. I knew there had to be some way I could do that. "How about I make you the artistic consultant to the city of Providence for a year at twenty thousand a year."

He thought about that. "You can do that?"

I didn't see why not. "Absolutely," I said.

"All right," he agreed, then hesitated. "But make it twenty-five."

Now that is the kind of deal that I should have gone to jail for.

In October 1978, three thousand people squeezed into the refurbished Ocean State Theatre to hear Ethel Merman, the Brian Jones All-Tap Revue, and the Quantico Marine Band officially reopen the theater. Since then, the Providence Performing Arts Center, as it is now known, has been expanded and modernized, while keeping its classic splendor. It provides Providence with a full season of Broadway shows, concerts, and events. It has been added to the National Register of Historic Places.

I have heard people say that the scariest words in the English language are "I'm from the government and I'm here to help you." But in fact, a key element of the Providence revival was the 1974 federal Community Development Act, which awarded a $9.1 million block grant to the city. In 1974 $9.1 million was like $40 million today. It was a huge amount of money. I had hired a former federal Housing and Urban Development consultant named Joe Vileno to help us get federal grants for urban planning. Although Joe Vileno originally was from Providence, he had been working in Detroit for eight or nine years, so he had plenty of experience in working in a blighted city. When I first learned about this grant I asked him to explain it to me. Most federal programs came with cookie-cutter instructions, with pages of regulations restricting how the funds had to be used. But Joe told me this was different. "This is a mayor's program," he explained. While it had to be used for community development, the real decision-making authority was left to local authorities. "You can break it up any way you want."

Oh really?

This was a bonanza. The question was, how should we spend it? What should it be used for? Should it be used to rebuild our aging infrastructure, to build new community centers, maybe for historic preservation or as seed money to help new businesses develop? I'm going to admit something now: I didn't have the slightest idea how to spend this money. A few months earlier I'd been trying to balance my checkbook; suddenly I was supposed to know the best way to spend 9 million bucks? We had so many good projects that needed funding that I didn't know where to start. Remember, I had no experience running a city government.

But I did have a lot of common sense. I had grown up in the neighborhoods; I knew that the people who really knew what each neighborhood needed were the people who lived in those neighborhoods. I knew that because they told me that. Every single day. I had run my election campaign on the promise that I would open up the government. Well, here was my opportunity.

To get the grant we had to submit a plan detailing how we were going to use it. Joe Vileno brought in a consulting team from Boston to help us put together the package that had to be submitted to HUD for approval. We knew we needed strong citizen participation, so those consultants eventually recommended we put together a citizens advisory board consisting of twenty-seven people. Even twenty-seven people was considered a large board; the city of Warwick, for example, appointed eight people to its citizens advisory committee, and three or four of them were members of the administration.

Eventually, I put 107 people on that 27-person committee. I couldn't help it. I can't begin to tell you how many neighborhood association meetings I attended to hear what the people had to say, or sometimes had to shout, about this money. I would often go to three or four meetings a night. I found myself in an interesting situation. People in Providence had been left out of the political process for so long, they didn't trust any politician. So when I invited them to participate rather than simply accepting the invitation, they became very wary. A politician asking people for their opinions? What's the catch? They figured I had to have a motive. As one community organizer warned, "We have to be worried about being used." But once they realized we were listening to them, they wanted to be heard. They all wanted to participate. "Okay," I would respond, "you want to be on the committee?" One hundred and seven times.

It was quite a diverse group. We had representatives from every local organization, from the West End Senior Citizens to the more radical PACE (People Acting through Community Effort). We had representatives of every race, every ethnic group, every neighborhood in the city. I set up numerous task forces; I created more task forces than Eisenhower did when planning the Normandy invasion. We had several meetings in large auditoriums. Everybody knows about organized chaos; this was disorganized chaos. It was unbelievable to see those aging society doyennes from the East Side preservation movement negotiating with the hard-core street reps from the poor neighborhoods, but eventually they got together and decided what the priorities should be. It was a beautiful thing to witness, democracy in action, and their requests made great sense. And when we added up all those requests for that $9.1 million, it came to slightly more than $17 million.

Now this definitely was a problem. I'd gotten a lot of people involved in the process. Somehow I had to figure out how to fulfill $17 million in requests with only $9.1 million in grants—without infuriating too many people. So how do you allocate the money? How do you decide which project gets how much money? This was the first time I did it, but it became an annual problem. I had the same problem with the budget. Each year I would get big books filled with detailed statistics reporting how much each neighborhood association was requesting, how much it had received the previous years, and what its success rate had been. Some of those requests would tear my heart out. These were very difficult decisions. Do you buy schoolbooks for kids or increase the subsidiary to help senior citizens pay their heating bills? Do you give a grant for a playground or a drug program? How much goes for housing assistance and how much to support a high school where gay students wouldn't be harassed?

Most politicians want their constituents to believe that there is a very sophisticated decision-making process and that these decisions are reached based on a dispassionate formula that takes every aspect into consideration to reach a fair and compassionate conclusion. Who knows, maybe in some situations that's the way it's done. Maybe in some cities the mayor delegates the decision making. I didn't. I would receive a list of recommendations from my staff, but the final decision was always mine. I would put off making these decisions until the last possible hour. Then I would take all the requests and all my staff recommendations home with me and get into bed and stay up all night reading them. These were Draconian decisions. How many people did I want to starve? Do I cut a hundred thousand dollars from this request to give it to that group? Are AIDS patients more needy than retired nuns? I'd often go against my staff recommendations, thinking, I'm the guy who spends those beautiful summer weekends marching in parades rather than being on Block Island, I'm the guy whose carefully retouched photograph is on the campaign poster. So I get to make the decisions. And I did. I took everything into consideration and then I gave the money to whatever groups I wanted to have the money.

There were no easy answers. I'd just make my picks. I'm giving this group a million for a new building and I'm taking $250,000 away from those guys. In the end my secret formula was that I did what made me feel best.

I would always hope that partisan politics and personalities didn't sway my decisions, but who knows. One election year, for example, a wealthy couple gave me a large campaign donation. The only thing they asked for in return was that I visit a school with which they were involved, Community Prep, a private nonprofit school that took poor kids with special talents off the street and worked with them to try to get scholarships to fancy schools like Country Day or my alma mater, Moses Brown. I went there because these people contributed a substantial amount of money; truthfully, I probably wouldn't have gone there if they hadn't. But I loved the school, and the next time I was lying there in my bed making grant decisions I thought about the school and decided to give it three hundred thousand dollars. Politics? Maybe. I wouldn't have been there except for politics, and what I saw there impressed me.

Winston Churchill once said that the difference between a politician and a statesman is that a politician gives the people what they want but a statesman gives them what they need. What I always tried to do was give the people what they needed—but first I'd try to make them want it.

Most of the funds from that first Community Development block grant went to highly visible projects that would service the largest number of people, spread as evenly as possible throughout the neighborhoods of the city. We allocated almost a third of the money for housing rehabilitation—which included giving low-interest loans or grants that enabled people to fix up their homes; we even bought them paint to brighten their houses and their blocks. We built nine multiservice community centers so people had a place to go to receive social services, and we handed out grants to several existing settlement houses to expand. We also put a lot of money into cleaning up our parks, fixed some streets, created more than a thousand temporary jobs, and used some of the money for "discretionary purposes." One discretionary purpose, for example, was the five-thousand-dollar grant I gave to a Silver Lake marching band for instruments and uniforms. That was one HUD did not like. Hey, those dry cleaners we trained for $190,000 had to have something to clean.

Our parks, in particular, were in terrible shape. There is nothing that serves more people and is more visible than a city park. Politicians should love parks. I remember when, the night before the election, after I had finished campaigning, I stopped by the Old Canteen restaurant to see its owner, Joe Marzilli. We sat together on the front step of the restaurant. "You did fine," he told me. "Whatever happens tomorrow, you ran a good campaign."

Across the street from the restaurant was an old abandoned public bathhouse. Before people had running water in their apartments, they would go there for a shower. It had long been out of use and was falling apart, but it sat in a beautiful area. "You know what, Joe," I said. "If I win the election tomorrow I'm going to knock down that wreck and turn this into a park." That was the first park we built, and it served as a message to the people of Federal Hill that we were sincere when we said we were going to rebuild the city.

Eventually the renovated park was renamed for an Italian military hero, Giuseppe Garibaldi. We named it for Garibaldi for a very good reason; we found an old statue of him that wasn't being displayed in a park in Fox Point. The Portuguese residents of that neighborhood had no association with Garibaldi and didn't care at all that we moved their statue. They had no other use for it.

The fact is that people want parks in their neighborhood, and they want them clean and safe. A few months after I took office a member of another neighborhood community association called my office to tell me that his group had decided to name a neighborhood park for me. Well, that certainly was a great compliment. "Thank you," I replied modestly, "but you shouldn't do that. I've only been mayor a few months."

"Oh no, you don't get it," the caller said. "If you saw the shape this park is in you wouldn't want your name on it!"

At that time Rhode Island Democratic senator John Pastore had announced he was not going to run for another term, so I thought it would be a nice gesture to name another one of our parks for him. But at the annual dinner of the National Association of Christians and Jews, Pastore said, "I see the mayor is here. He wrote me a letter telling me that he intended to name a park the John Pastore Memorial Park. Maybe he doesn't know it, but I'm not dead yet. In fact, I've known the mayor since he was a baby. I know his mother, a beautiful lady. His father was my doctor. I used to bounce him on my knee, and I must have bounced him too hard because he became a Republican."

Ha, ha, ha. Big laugh. And in response I explained, "Senator Pastore, of course I would never, ever think your career is over. In fact, I'm so much a fan of yours that I know all about you. I know, for example, that you were born on Saint Patrick's Day and your name actually is Giovanni Orlando Pastore, so if you don't like the name John O. Pastore Memorial Park I'm sure that in your honor we can change it to the GOP Park." Bigger laugh!

Not everything that was old in Providence was beautiful or historic or worth salvaging. We actually did use some of those Community Development funds to knock down some houses. There were a lot of abandoned houses that simply were dilapidated and dangerous. They were never going to be rehabilitated, and as long as they were standing they made it impossible to rebuild neighborhoods. We had a survey done and identified 250 houses in such terrible shape that, as I said, "Ninety-two percent of them are not going to make the cover of *Better Homes and Gardens*. They're attractive nuisances. Kids'll get hurt." We used the Community Development money to knock down those houses, but then we did something pretty creative. Rather than leaving vacant lots, we established a homesteading program that gave the lots to the adjoining landowner, which put the land back on the tax roll.

Naturally, the Democratic city council was furious that I was spending the $9.1 million without its input—or its fingerprints—on it. To prevent me from getting any credit, the council passed a resolution giving itself the right to approve any development contracts. Darigan called it "a safety valve" to assure the good people of Providence "that the money will be spent where the people want it spent." Meaning not where that Republican mayor Cianci wants it spent.

By this time I had a pretty good idea how municipal politics work. I invited each member of the council into my office and showed them a map that included the projects planned for their wards. "Look at this," I told them. "Look what we're using that money for in your district." You probably won't be surprised to learn how quickly that reduced a lot of the opposition. Few politicians want to have to explain to their constituents why they fought against a new neighborhood community center or why they voted against funds to clean up the local park.

On the night I had to publicly present the plan to the council, I asked Joe Vileno if he could "gin up the folks," meaning arrange a supportive turnout. We invited every agency or community organization that owned a piece of this plan to come to the meeting. We packed the room with several hundred people. When the council tried to fight me on certain aspects of the plan, these people began screaming and yelling and eventually we got it passed.

Those first months I was basically playing whack-a-problem, running from one place to another trying to knock down each problem before it could get bigger. The only thing Providence had in abundance was problems. There was so much that had to be done. In the 1970s mayors were basically social workers. Every municipality was broke. Gas prices were rising. The middle class had left the cities, leaving behind the elderly and the minorities and reducing the tax base. We were so desperate that we took a deep breath and closed about eight schools—politicians do not want to close schools—that we didn't need, and absolutely nobody complained. We were worried about people surviving. As if poor people didn't have it tough enough, during the campaign the chairman of the Industrial National Bank, John J. Cummings, had announced that his bank would no longer sell food stamps the first ten days of each month—when people needed them most—supposedly because those people were creating long lines for the bank's customers. Other banks in the city followed Cummings's lead and also refused to sell food stamps. That forced poor people to go to distribution centers, which were located in high-crime areas. Several of these places were robbed and people were hurt. Another one of my campaign promises was that when I was mayor, these banks would once again participate in the food-stamp program throughout the entire month.

Within the first weeks of my administration I asked the banks to reinstitute the food-stamp-distribution program. Trying to pressure them, I told reporters covering the story that in the future the city would deposit its money in banks that were interested in community participation. "There's no pressure here," I said, as I applied the pressure, "no pressure at all. I just want to see which banks are going to respond to this emergency situation." Basically, the banks ignored me.

John Cummings had been a powerful man in the city for a long time and spoke for the Rhode Island Bankers Association. I called him and asked him what he intended to do, and he put me in my place. In a patronizing tone he explained to me how things really worked in Providence and why his bank would no longer be selling food stamps in the city the first ten days of each month.

I listened to his brilliant lecture for about five minutes, and then I politely told him, "That's fine, but I want all my money out of the bank." As befitted Mr. Cummings's reputation, Industrial served as the city's fiscal agent. The bank managed the city's pension system, so we had millions of dollars on deposit there. "And," I continued, "I want it all by three o'clock today. In cash."

"That's impossible."

"Maybe. But at 3:05 I'll be sure to tell the press that you can't give the citizens the money that we put in there."

Eventually he told me, "I'll get back to you."

"Fine, but you'd better make it pretty quick, because at three o'clock I want my money."

Cummings despised me. But he understood he had no options. The city was certainly among his largest depositors. Following his capitulation a total of nine local banks agreed to distribute the food stamps at forty-two branch offices. In addition, they leased an armored car to the city for one dollar a year to deliver food stamps to elderly and handicapped citizens. A representative of the Bankers Association said flatly that my threats had no affect on the bankers' decisions, to which I also lied by claiming that I had not intended my remarks to be a threat. I added that at some point in the future a task force I appointed would recommend where the city should deposit its funds.

My relationship with Cummings never got better. In fact, when he died, a representative of the family called and specifically informed me I was not welcome at his funeral. As I replied, it wasn't on my agenda.

I was once advised that I should run the city as if it were the family business, the idea being that I would then be cautious about spending money. "Right," I responded. "What family business do you know that has two giraffes and three elephants?" Running a city is not a business, it's an art. The only thing it has in common with a business is that it is all about money. As every mayor will tell you, the amount of money you need to run a city will always be substantially more than whatever you have. Where I got lucky was being a Republican in 1974. It's very possible that I'm the only person who can make that statement, but it's true. Nationally, the Republican party was in disarray. I was one of very few Republicans elected to any office that year, so I received considerably more attention from the national Republican party than I ordinarily would have. I was considered one of the most promising young Republican officials in the country, and the party wanted to do as much as possible to help me succeed.

For that reason, my second month in office I was invited to Washington, D.C., to meet with President Gerald Ford. Now, I was about to learn how party politics get done. While I was in Washington I went to see a friend of mine named Arthur Sampson, who was at that time the head of the General Services Administration (GSA). The GSA is the federal government's logistical supply branch, in charge of everything from making sure an office has enough copy paper to allocating buildings. I had met Arthur through a woman he was dating, a woman I'd met a couple of years earlier when she was involved with my commanding officer at Fort Devens. We'd stayed friends after that relationship ended, and she had moved to Washington and started seeing Arthur. After my election Arthur had asked me if I could take care of his nephew. Sure, why not? I'd hired him to be the city photographer. There was nothing wrong with that; he was a good photographer, I needed a photographer, and I didn't know another photographer in the world. And oh yeah, his uncle was the head of the GSA, a federal agency with a multi-billion-dollar budget. It couldn't hurt.

Before meeting with President Ford I met with Arthur in his gorgeous office. As head of the GSA, he had one of the best offices in Washington. We were sitting there, enjoying a drink, when I noticed a little memento from a federal building in Cincinnati sitting on the table. "Arthur," I said. "How come I don't have a federal building in Providence?"

"You want one?"

"Yeah," I said. "Definitely."

All right, he agreed, we'll see. The next morning I had an appointment to meet the president. This was the first time I had ever been inside the White House. I was thirty-three years old and I was thrilled. I'm told the most common request made by people invited to the White House for the first time is that they be permitted to call their parents to tell them where they are. I understand that. It got even better than that: I was sitting in the waiting room with Henry Cabot Lodge, Jr. Henry Cabot Lodge! He was one of America's most respected statesmen; he was a former senator from Massachusetts, a UN representative, an ambassador to Vietnam, and at that moment our ambassador to the Vatican. We spoke for a while and he made it pretty clear that he enjoyed being the respected statesman Henry Cabot Lodge. But finally a Secret Service agent opened the door. Ambassador Lodge stood up and nodded somewhat condescendingly to me, just as the agent said, "Mr. Mayor, the president would like to see you." Ambassador Lodge sat down.

I shall never forget that moment I walked into the Oval Office and saw the president of the United States, the most powerful man in the world, standing next to his desk wearing a red plaid suit. Gerald Ford was a wonderful man who became a friend, a man I continue to admire, but he was wearing a red plaid suit. But that day the thing he really wanted to talk about was how a Republican managed to get elected in Providence. It took a lot of money, I told him, a lot of effort, and a divided Democratic party.

After we'd spent about an hour together, he asked me to represent the United States at the International Conference of Mayors in Milan, Italy. I replaced San Francisco's Democratic Mayor Joe Alioto, who later became a good friend.

I actually hadn't taken Arthur Sampson's offer of a federal building that seriously. I mean, who just hands out $32 million buildings? But two weeks later I was informed that the federal government had put a freeze on all existing leases in Providence. No agency was allowed to sign a lease or renew a lease without GSA approval—because the government was going to construct a $32 million building in the city. I remember thinking it was a real shame that Arthur didn't have two nephews, because maybe I could have gotten a bridge thrown in. The proposed federal building would bring together employees from several federal agencies who were scattered in rented offices all around the city. Naturally, the owners of those buildings renting space to the federal government were not happy with me, but they were all Doorley people, so what did I care?

This was potentially a huge project for the city. In addition to the money pouring into the city and the construction jobs it would create, it was a major symbolic gesture. Providence was on its way back! Now all I had to do was get the construction money included in my new friend President Ford's budget. Over the next eighteen months I made numerous trips to Washington trying to nail down the funding for that building. But James Lynn, head of the Office of Management and Budget, just wouldn't put our building in his budget. And after more than a year spent running around Washington trying to fund this building, I had lost confidence it was ever going to be built.

During the 1976 campaign President Ford and I had become close. I campaigned hard for him. After he lost the election to Jimmy Carter, I went to see him in the White House one last time. His administration was packing up and handing out last-minute favors. I brought my wish list with me, knowing the next four years were going to be pretty bleak for Republican mayors. It was snowing outside, and the president was leaving the next morning for a ski trip to Vail, Colorado. I knew this was my last chance to get a federal building. When I walked into the Oval Office, the president came around from behind his desk and gave me a big hug, then thanked me for my efforts during the campaign. "What do you need?" he asked. "What can I do for you?"

I told him I needed a five-hundred-thousand-dollar loan guaranteed by the Small Business Administration to rebuild the Wilcox Building, a beautiful hundred-year-old building that had been left as a shell after a fire two years earlier. Most people wanted to tear it down. I needed money to rebuild it. I told him about several other projects for which I needed money. And finally I reminded him about the federal building. As always, he was very amenable. "Go see Jim Lynn," he told me.

I shook my head. "No thanks; you've sent me there a hundred times. He's just gonna tell me no. Listen to me, just put it in your budget. Even if you can't give me the whole $32 million, just give me enough to get it started. That way even if the Carter administration takes it out, you can say you tried to do it." My real hope was that if he put it in his budget, the Democratic representatives from Rhode Island might be able to convince Carter to fund it.

Things had to be done surreptitiously because the Carter people were already moving in. But several months later Senator John Pastore announced that a new federal office building in Providence had been assigned priority status. President Carter eventually received the credit for the building, which really helped anchor the downtown, but it was Arthur Sampson and Jerry Ford who made it possible, primarily as a reward to me for being elected as a Republican and because I knew the woman Sampson was dating.

In addition to the number of problems I had to deal with, I guess what surprised me during that first term was the variety of those problems. My first Christmas in office, for example, they put up a nativity scene, a crèche, in front of city hall. As far as I knew this was traditional. I didn't know who put it up—probably the same person who put it up every year. I didn't care; put up whatever you want. Put up a menorah, put up flamingos; I had too many other problems to deal with. But apparently the American Civil Liberties Union did not. The ACLU sued me for putting the poor baby Jesus in a manger on city property.

Just what I needed. In a city that was about 80 percent Catholic, they wanted me to boot the baby Jesus. Imagine those headlines: CIANCI EVICTS JESUS! That is arguably the worst possible headline for a politician. Unfortunately, this issue got a lot of publicity. When a reporter from *Time* asked me why the ACLU was suing me, I told him, "It's because they're jealous."

Jealous?

"Absolutely," I said. "They're jealous because in their ranks they can't find three wise men or a virgin!"

Throughout my whole first term there was one thing I knew I could count on: Whatever I did, whatever I tried to do, the Democrats were going to be against it. They just wanted to limit the damage I did until they could replace me the next election. They never accepted me as mayor. For example, in 1975, in my role as mayor of the city, I was invited to the annual St. Patrick's Day party at the Colonial Hilton. This was one of the major political events in the state. But when I got there I found out I was not seated at the head table. That was intended to be an insult, and that's the way I took it. But I quietly took my assigned seat at one of the tables on the floor. I will never forget Kenny O'Donnell, who had been an adviser to President Kennedy, giving a speech in which he departed from his planned remarks and pointed out that the mayor of the city was not seated on the dais. He didn't say it was because I was a Republican or, far more likely, an Italian, but he did say, "That's not what America is about."

There were lessons I had to learn, too. Believe me, I hadn't become perfect yet. America was changing rapidly at that time, and really for the first time mayors had to deal with newly empowered minorities. In 1976, for example, a gay organization demanded the right to march in the city's bicentennial parade. Admittedly, in those days, I was not supportive of the homosexual community. Listen, I was a product of my upbringing; in the atmosphere I grew up in they were "queers" and "homos." They were "in the closet," and I didn't want to know what was going on in that closet. I didn't care if they marched in the parade or not, but my police chief, McQueeney, was adamantly against it. I did know that there were a lot of voters in Providence who didn't want gays marching openly where their children could see them, and I wasn't going to alienate those people. Eventually we ended up in court, where a liberal judge ordered us to allow them to march. I'll never forget that the head of our bicentennial celebration came out of the courtroom and told reporters he wasn't surprised at the judge's ruling: "What else would you expect from a former dancing academy instructor?"

It took some time for me to understand that if I was going to be mayor of a city as diverse as Providence, I couldn't be the mayor only for straight people. The issue wasn't whether or not I approved of their sexual orientation; my job was to deliver city services to my constituents. All of my constituents. I grew up. Many years later I was the first mayor of a major city to put a liaison to the gay community on my staff. His name was Fitzgerald Himmelsbach, and he convinced me that simply appointing a gay man wasn't enough, that I actually had to attend gay events. Sure, I told him, I'd be delighted, it wouldn't bother me at all, I don't care what people think—as long as I can bring my girlfriend.

I started attending gay events. I started meeting with gay business groups. I went to a couple of clubs and people would buy me drinks. Next thing I knew I was standing on the stage giving a speech about gay rights. Among the most popular of these events was gay bingo. Being invited to call numbers at gay bingo was considered a great compliment, it meant you were accepted by that community. You should have heard me, "Seven, under the O," like a professional. Eventually, the gay community became an important support group for me. I didn't realize it at first, but I soon discovered that they had money, that many of them didn't have kids to spend it on, and that they actively supported those politicians who fought for their rights. It took me a while, but I went from challenging the rights of gays to march in a city parade to being the grand marshal of the gay rights parade. I also ended up hosting the annual convention of gay political officials. In my home. Naturally, of course, with my girlfriend next to me.

But my position in the gay community was guaranteed when we lured the Gay & Lesbian Leadership Conference to Providence. This was an organization for the top gay officeholders in the country, many of them very prominent people in their communities. I hosted the party for about one hundred people in my house. And eventually we became one of the first cities to offer full health benefits for same-sex partners. That was not exactly received by the rest of the city with a tremendous amount of enthusiasm—actually, none—but it was the right thing to do. It required employees to sign an affidavit, and I believe they had to be living together. We had to fight to get it, but eventually we were able to include it in our contracts.

Conventions are vital for the economic stability of a city. At one time in our history Providence had been a popular tourist destination, but that had ended. There was very little reason for tourists to visit. What could we show them—this is our yak? On this vacant lot the Albee Theatre once stood? Rebuilding the tourist industry was an important part of our renewal effort.

The very first convention I was able to lure to Providence was the Fraternal Order of Police. I had to go to Nashville, Tennessee, where they were meeting, to make our pitch. Rather than selling them on

Providence, I spoke about Rhode Island, especially Newport. We were competing with Phoenix and one other city. After we won the vote we celebrated at an Italian restaurant in Nashville. It was not exactly a gourmet place. I ordered spaghetti al dente—and when they brought the spaghetti they explained politely that they had run out of the al dente.

That trip was notable for another reason. It's where I began to hone my negotiating skills with the union. Accompanying me on that trip was the head of the police officers' union. In those days the police and fire departments were not well paid, but they had good benefits. In their next contract they wanted to extend their Blue Cross coverage for life, which naturally I did not want to give to them. The head of the union continued to badger me for Blue Cross, give us our Blue Cross for life. Finally, we were in Nashville pitching the convention and one night we ended up in a bar that had a pinball machine. I offered to negotiate right then and there: We would play pinball and if I won he would never mention Blue Cross again, but if I lost I would give it to them.

That's how the police officers' union got Blue Cross for life. Obviously, I had already decided to give it to them. We'd run the numbers and it cost a lot less than I had expected. Later that night I called the head of the firefighters' union and told him, "This is your lucky day."

The Fraternal Order of Police convention came to Providence and had a very good time. That was the beginning of our new tourist industry. I became active in trying to bring conventions to Providence, which became a lot easier once we moved the rivers, renovated our historic neighborhoods, and helped create an incredible restaurant industry.

Another minority group I became involved with during my first term was the Cambodians. In my first election I didn't actively pursue the Cambodian vote. Cambodians in Providence? There was no Cambodian vote. But soon after my election I got a call from the White House telling me they were sending several hundred Cambodians to Providence. These were people who had supported American troops in Cambodia and had escaped when the war ended. They originally had been sent to Indiantown Gap, Pennsylvania. When they got to Providence, they had nothing; they barely had clothes, and no place to live. I related that back to my grandfather arriving in America carrying only his clothes, and the people of Providence had taken him in and given him the opportunity to succeed. Maybe that's one of the reasons I have always loved this city. The politics may be rough, but its people have always had a heart. So I wanted to do for these people what was done for so many other people for so many years.

These particular immigrants knew nothing about American life and culture. Less than nothing. I remember one day the second floor of an old building collapsed. We discovered that the Cambodian family living there had planted a garden in their living room. They had covered the entire floor with about eight inches of topsoil, but interestingly, that wasn't the reason it collapsed. It collapsed because they watered the garden every day. When the fire department got in there, they discovered the refrigerator had been unplugged, and whatever clothes these people had were stored there. They didn't understand refrigeration. The churches worked with the Cambodians, opening the Genesis Center to help serve their needs, allowing them to assimilate into the community. I gave them substantial financial support through community development grants.

I went to all their festivals and for several years I even had a Cambodian house man named Sovan Chhouk. The first night he was there, he got up in the middle of the night and started walking around outside the house. That made me very nervous. "What are you doing?" I asked him.

"I make sure no bombs outside."

I assured him that there probably weren't any bombs outside the house. I tried to teach him to speak English, with somewhat mixed results. He had trouble saying the days of the week, so when I asked him about an appointment he would always respond, "After two tomorrows." It turned out that everything in my life was taking place "after two tomorrows."

He was a wonderful person and we became good friends. He used to play a lovely instrument, sort of a Cambodian guitar. I would come home at night and he would say, "Mayor, I play song for you."

"Great, kid," I would tell him. "Do you know 'My Melancholy Baby'?"

He eventually married a lovely young Cambodian woman, and we held their wedding ceremony in my house. I knew for sure I had done a good job helping these Cambodians settle in America when I ran for reelection in 1990 and the Cambodian American Chamber of Commerce threw a very successful fund-raiser for me. They had truly become Americans—because what could be more American than raising money for a politician?

By the end of my first term I had learned how to be the mayor of a large city. I had successfully started the rebuilding program that eventually would transform Providence. I'd learned how to use the political power that I did have to compensate for the powers I didn't have. I'd discovered that, as in all big cities, a certain level of corruption was ingrained in the system. Thousands of people were employed by the city and, unfortunately, not every one of them was honest. And I'd learned that the secret to success in the job was that there was no secret: There was absolutely no substitute for being out there in the streets, marching in every parade, showing up at every street fair, attending every possible meeting, shaking hands, kissing babies, telling jokes, going to the Little League games, putting on a pair of coveralls and joining a neighborhood cleanup effort. The most important thing I had going for me was me. By the end of my first term I was on a first-name basis with the city. I was a high-profile, in-your-face politician. Nobody was shy about approaching me to tell me they needed their sidewalk fixed or that they were having trouble with a city agency, or to complain that their taxes were too high, to offer me advice, to ask for a job for their kid, or to tell me about their crazy neighbor.

There were a lot of people who loved me, and, admittedly, there were quite a few people who didn't—but nobody, absolutely nobody, could ignore me.

Four

One evening I hosted a wine-and-cheese party at city hall for members of one of our departments. During this event a man I didn't know came up to me and said pleasantly, "Mayor, I want a tree." No problem. I took tremendous pride in our constituent service program. We had a street tree program going on, and if a citizen of Providence wanted a tree planted on his or her street, we'd get it done. I said to one of my aides, "Write down his name. Make sure he gets a tree."

Ten minutes later this guy came up to me again and this time said, not so pleasantly, "What do you tink, I'm an asshole? I don't want no tree. I want to *be* a tree."

I didn't know what he was talking about. "What do you mean, you want to be a tree?"

"A tree," he repeated loudly, frustrated that I didn't understand a simple request. "I wanna be a building inspector tree!"

"Oh," I said, getting it. He wanted a promotion. "A three."

Some days I would attend anywhere between six and fourteen different events. I'd wear out three drivers a day. I attended that many events only because I didn't have time to get to more than that. But if there was a gathering of citizens, I wanted to be there. I'd show up and rip right through the place. In and out, say hello and good-bye, get to the next place. This was seven days a week; I'd get up Sunday morning and think, *even God said you were supposed to rest on Sundays,* but then I'd remember God didn't have to run for reelection. I'd go to a communion breakfast or a ward committee annual breakfast. Then in the afternoon there was always a picnic. On beautiful weekends I'd see people out on the bay in their sailboats or barbecuing in their backyards while I was shaking hands and agreeing to try to find a job for somebody's brother-in-law who wouldn't get off the couch. I was a Republican, and eventually an Independent, in a strongly Democratic city. I had to build my own political party vote by vote.

The single most important aspect of my job was to deliver services to the voters. There is nothing more important for an elected official, nothing, than providing constituent service. Every local election eventually comes down to quality of life. In local politics, the popularity of an elected official usually can be determined by the number of potholes per block or the number of days it took to clear the streets after a snowfall.

I have always said that there are only five things you have to do to run a city. And I've been adamant about that, even when I listed seven or eight things. Basically, people want to be safe in their homes and on the street, they want their neighborhoods to be clean and the snow cleared within a reasonable amount of time, they want to have good housing, they want their kids to have the opportunity for a good education, they want to have good recreational facilities ranging from public parks to restaurants, they want good jobs available within reasonable commuting time, and they want to pay as little as possible for all of it. There's no magic to it. If you can provide enough of that, you win elections.

But in addition to it being good politics, there was another reason we emphasized retail politics, as it became known: It made me feel good. It's actually intoxicating. You wanted a tree planted on your street, I could give you a tree. There was a pothole on your block, I could get it filled. Your nephew needed a job, I could get him an interview. A cracked sidewalk needed to be fixed, a traffic light wasn't working, someone's kid is in the wrong class at school or needs a recommendation to Harvard Medical School; whatever it was, we would write it down and follow up. We couldn't get everything done, but we took everything seriously. This was old-fashioned ward healing, local politics in action. For most people, I'll bet it was one of the few times in their life that they actually got something they wanted done in return for the taxes they paid. It made a difference to them, and I loved doing it. I know how cynical we have all become about politicians and the political process, but the truth is, I loved that feeling. I had big plans—I intended to rebuild an entire city—but I can't begin to explain how good it felt to be able to deliver a simple quality-of-life service to one person.

We established a sophisticated system to deliver these services. At times I had as many as eight advance people working with me. These were kids I took right out of college and gave their first exposure to traditional politics. I liked to refer to it as providing real-world training for them—which is the nicest way of explaining I worked them harder than plow horses. It was always a diverse staff that represented the diverse neighborhoods of the city, and I prided myself in putting these kids in what I would charitably refer to as "learning" cultural environments. I had a young African American kid named Wil Fleming, for example, whom I would send to the Jewish community on the East Side or the old North End Italian neighborhood. He would call and beg, "Mayor, you got to get here quick. They're all Italians here. They're going to kill me." Or Freddie Passarelli, whom I'd send up to Brown University to deal with the professors. It was the job of my advance team to prepare a briefing sheet for me for each event: how many people were going to be there, whom I should acknowledge, whether it was a community organization or a ribbon cutting, a ground breaking, a celebration, an ethnic festival, an organizational picnic, a parade—I lived for parades!—or some other reason for the event. They always got to these sites before I was scheduled to arrive, and on my way there I'd contact them for the details; What's the setup? What door do I come in? And when I got there they stayed right by my side and wrote down every promise I made. Every single promise.

We covered every neighborhood in Providence. Once, for example, a gentleman living in Olneyville, sort of a rundown area, complained that pit bulls were running loose around his neighborhood. Pit bulls running loose is definitely a quality-of-life problem. Scott Millard, who was then a member of the advance team, went to meet him to determine the extent of the problem. Just as he pulled up in front of the address, a chicken ran across the street, pursued by a pit bull. The chicken ran under Scott's car and the dog attacked the car to get underneath it. Scott watched this in disbelief. This definitely was not what he had expected when he got involved in the exciting world of politics. Suddenly the chicken made a run for it, but the pit bull was quicker and caught it, then paraded around holding it in its mouth. After the dog ran away, a man approached Scott's car and said, "See? See? This is what I'm talking about."

The way we worked was that wherever I went, whatever I was doing, I had an aide at my side. When a constituent came up to me and made a request, that aide would write it down, making certain he had that person's address and phone number. I was often tough on my aides; it was trial by Buddy, and admittedly I wasn't always the charming, folksy person I am today. One afternoon, for example, I was working the crowd at the annual Welcome to Summer hot dog festival in the scenic parking lot of the United Food and Commercial Workers Union when someone with badly cracked sidewalks in front of his house asked me about getting them repaired. I was breaking in a new advance person and I said to him, "Sidewalks."

The advance person stood poised with his pen and asked, "New ones?"

"No," I said, admittedly sarcastically, "old ones." I was constantly yelling at those kids, as they would be happy to tell anyone. When they made a mistake, they'd hear the usual refrain from me, "That's twenty votes you just cost me, that's definitely a bad career move for you." I admit it, working for me wasn't easy, but every one of those kids who survived eventually graduated to much better jobs. I made sure they got placed. But I never asked for or expected more from them than I was willing to do myself. And I was proud of the fact that when I gave my word to a constituent, I expected my aides to keep it. And I gave my word. My advance kids used to commiserate with each other,

"I hope he doesn't make any commitments tonight, because if he does it'll be our problem."

As a result we had the most efficient constituent service system in the country. Things got done in Providence. The first thing we did every morning was put each of my commitments into the system. Usually there were about two dozen of them, and they would all be routed to the proper department. Streetlight requests went to Public Works, for example. Quality-of-life concerns went to the police department. Garbage problems went to Sanitation. "Routed" probably isn't the proper word: The heads of the departments were notified, both by phone and then on paper, and they were expected to follow through on it. Manny Vieira, who eventually worked his way up to become the director of communications, explained, "I'd always get calls from the advance people. Buddy wasn't the type of mayor that you could call back and say, 'Shucks, I can't do that.' If you had to go out there with a shovel yourself to get it done, that's what you did."

I held my staff and department heads accountable. They knew I wasn't going to forget too many things. Every ten days or two weeks I would hold a staff meeting. I scheduled these meetings because I wanted my directors to understand the ramifications their decisions might have on other departments. I didn't think the police chief knew what the director of public works was really going through, or that my communications director understood the problems the director of human resources was trying to deal with. I thought if I could mix them up and bring them to the same table for a couple of hours, our ability to work together would be greatly enhanced.

The head of every department would be there, and they knew they'd better have done their homework. We'd discuss policy decisions and try to coordinate between departments. I'd also question them on these constituent requests. At each meeting I would call on one or two department heads and grill them on a variety of subjects from their budget to getting these tasks done. It was only one or two of them, but every one of them had to be well prepared because they never knew who I was going to pick. Trust me, nobody wanted to be caught without an answer. I was rough on them. They understood that if I was willing to embarrass the police chief, I wouldn't hesitate to also embarrass the director of Public Works. I was a big believer in equal department embarrassment. One of my police chiefs, Bernie Gannon, used to like to hide way in the back, hunkered down behind the biggest person he could find, but I'd find him. At one meeting I called on him and when he stood up, I really started attacking him. Finally, as I was asking another question, he sat down. I said, "Colonel, did you hear me tell you to sit down?"

"No, Mayor," he explained. "But every fight I've ever been in, we rest after three minutes."

That made sense to me. "Okay," I agreed, "but when the bell rings we're gonna get going again."

I was persistent. One meeting I asked Manny Vieira to stand up. "I'm going to call the 911 emergency line," I told him. The emergency line was his responsibility. I wanted every emergency call answered on the first ring. "How long is it going to take your people to answer?" No more than three rings, he said, but without a lot of confidence. I dialed 911 and put the phone by the speaker. *Buzz. Buzz. Buzz.* Poor Manny was dying, standing there listening to that phone ring. After seven rings an operator finally answered. I know that Manny left that meeting and let his staff have it. Good, that's what I wanted.

At our next meeting Manny was ready for me to test him again. If ever there was a night in Providence to have an emergency, this was that night. So naturally I didn't call on him. Instead I waited a few months, then called on him again.

My team made sure we got political credit for this. We would respond to every request with a phone call to let the person making that request know exactly what we were doing, and eventually we would send a letter out with a complete explanation of what we'd done. And at every city project, every rehabilitated house, every pothole, every fixed sidewalk, we would put up a big sign reminding people that it was the Office of Mayor Cianci that got it painted, repaired, fixed, cleaned up, washed, rehabilitated, rebuilt, or whatever else we had done. EXCUSE

THE INCONVENIENCE, our signs read. THE INCONVENIENCE IS TEMPORARY, THE IMPROVEMENT IS PERMANENT. We maintained a database of every job we did that included the address of the person who had requested it, and during election campaigns we would use that information to remind those people of what we'd done for them. There's nothing wrong with that; that's just local politics at work.

Without a doubt, though, the single thing that every northern mayor is judged by is how quickly the streets get plowed after a snowstorm. Every mayor who has ever dealt with it will tell you that "snow" is a four-letter word, in the worst possible meaning of that word. It's odd, people talk about "snow jobs," meaning to try to convince people of something that isn't true. I can't imagine where that phrase originated; there is nothing more real than fifteen inches of snow on the street. There is no way to convince people their street is cleared when they can look out their window and see piles of snow. Snow is apolitical; there is no Democratic or Republican way to clear the streets, but there are few things more important in municipal politics. You can make the streets safer, improve the schools, revitalize the downtown, build roads, but none of that matters if you don't get the snow cleared quickly. I knew I was going to be judged by how we handled snowstorms. There is a phrase used in politics to describe those people who failed this particular test: "former mayor." New York City mayor John Lindsay's political career pretty much ended when it took him a week to clean the streets of Queens after a storm. Chicago mayor Michael Bilandic lost his job when he couldn't get his streets cleared.

I had a very public policy that my street would be the last street plowed in Providence. When people called our office to complain that their streets hadn't been plowed, we would tell them that neither had mine. Actually, that was what I refer to as a philosophical truth rather than a literal truth. If it was possible, my street would have been the last to be cleared, but it wasn't practical to plow all the streets in my neighborhood except mine, or to clear my street except for the snow in front of my house. The city had a route schedule that had to be followed—we opened the hospital roads first, for example—and it would have been more difficult not to plow the snow in front of my house than it was to just push it out of the way.

Difficult, but not impossible, as the publisher of *The Providence Journal* once learned. I had nothing to do with this, honest. Among the worst things a mayor—or, as in this case, a publisher—can do is to pick a fight with the union during snow season. After an early 1970s snowstorm, the *Journal* printed an article criticizing the city's response and calling Public Works employees incompetent. The next snowstorm, the plows did a great job clearing all the streets near the publisher's house—and using the snow to build a wall around that house. It was piled up to the second floor, blocking every door. And because the other streets were so clear, people were able to come from all over the city to see it.

They don't teach the fine art of snow removal at the Kennedy School of Government at Harvard. When I was mayor, preparations actually began in April, when we held a meeting between city officials and those private vendors who operated the snow-removal equipment that would be involved in the process to review our plans. These vendors were primarily private construction companies whose trucks were idled during a snowstorm. We'd put a plow on the front and pay them between fifty to eighty dollars an hour per truck. Unfortunately, during previous administrations the city had had a notoriously bad record for paying vendors on time. We instated a policy to get them paid within two weeks, which ensured that they responded quickly the next time we called them.

When a storm was forecast, we positioned sand and salt trucks around the city and made sure the generators in city buildings and the zoo had plenty of fuel. When it was appropriate we closed the schools—which was always a difficult decision because we risked angering parents who then had to leave work early—and got cars off the streets. Even before it started snowing we pretreated the streets with a layer of sand and salt, which melted the ice and snow as it came down and made it easier for the plow blades to move it. Then I got my department heads out in the streets. In fact, whenever any type of bad storm was forecast, we put all of our people on alert, ready to clear fallen trees so power could be restored, secure the safety of an area if power was lost, get through blocked streets to fires, deliver medicine and food if necessary, and provide communications between agencies.

I expected my department heads to be out in the streets during the storm so we had a pretty good idea of what needed to be done. If I was out there, I expected them to be there, too. I constantly checked with them on the phone. During one storm my communications director, who had been working the entire day, had decided to sneak home for a few hours' sleep. He figured I'd never find out. Of course, I didn't know that when I called him. "Where are you?" I asked. He made up some location. "Great," I told him. "I'm only a few blocks away. Stay right there, I'll meet you there." As I later found out, he turned around and raced back to the meeting point. On the way he slid on ice and blew a tire, but he didn't even slow down. He knew he had to beat me there. I was waiting for him when he got there, and I knew exactly what had happened. "Where're all your people?" I demanded. Many of them were home in bed—well, at least until he called and got them back to work.

Unfortunately, I learned all these lessons during the worst natural disaster that I had to deal with during my years in office, the blizzard of 1978, when everything possible went wrong.

We knew a storm with "impressive potential" according to the weather service was coming; but no one was predicting it would become the largest snowstorm in Rhode Island history. It began snowing about eleven o'clock Monday morning, February fifth. But rather than dumping the forecasted few inches of snow we were prepared for and then moving through the region and out to sea, it got trapped by the wall of a Canadian high-pressure area and didn't move. For more than a day it just continued dumping snow. Late in the afternoon, hurricane-force winds that would eventually gust to more than 90 miles per hour began screaming through the city, creating whiteouts.

That Monday morning I hadn't been overly concerned about the snowstorm. By this time my people had worked through enough storms to be able to anticipate most of the problems. We'd already suffered through a rough winter, and a lot of our snow-removal equipment was being repaired, but I was confident we could fight our way through this one with what we had available. Once the problems began, though, they cascaded faster than our ability to deal with them. It was like watching dominoes fall in a straight line, except that this was my city coming to an absolute and complete stop. None of the buttons I was used to pressing worked. My experience with past storms was of no help; there was no training for a storm of this magnitude, and we weren't prepared for it. And in the middle of it, I found myself fighting a battle for my political survival.

My initial mistake was not closing the city in the morning and ordering everybody to go home. I did discuss that possibility with my staff, but the weather forecast just wasn't that bad yet. Closing the city is an important economic decision. When you do it, every business in the city—the department stores, the restaurants, the parking lots—they all start screaming that you're trying to put them out of business. Fortunately, many schools closed early and sent the kids home so they didn't get marooned on buses. The snow started coming down hard early in the afternoon. There were about two hundred thousand commuters working in the city, and unfortunately too many of them decided to leave work at about the same time. Our normal rush hour turned into chaos as cars and trucks began sliding on the icy, wet roads, causing numerous fender benders; everything began backing up. The ramps on and off Interstate 95, the fastest route out of the city, became blocked very early in the storm, and because we were disputing with the state whether the ramps were city streets or state highways, they never got cleared. The highways didn't get cleared because the state was having a contract dispute with the unionized plow drivers, and those drivers showed their unhappiness by staging a slowdown. Traffic quickly came to a complete halt, and within an hour those stalled vehicles were buried under a mountain of snow. Unable to move, all over the city people began abandoning their vehicles and trying to find safe shelter. People squeezed into the civic center and diners and bars, all the hotels filled up and people moved into their lobbies, and we had people sleeping on pews in the churches and synagogues. The police rescued hundreds of stranded people and brought them to our police training academy building—to feed them, cops were given permission to take food and liquids from some of the stores that had been looted, though we did ask them to leave a note so we could settle up later.

Those abandoned cars and trucks made it impossible for those plows we did get out to keep any roads cleared, which meant that police cars, fire department trucks, and power-company repair trucks couldn't move. We got every tow truck we owned or could beg or borrow on the streets to yank fire trucks out of snow drifts or push cars out of the way for the plows, but whatever we had, it wasn't enough. Neighborhoods began losing power and there was nothing we could do about it. And the snow kept falling throughout the afternoon and into the night. Eventually we would get an estimated thirty-five inches of snow, but the drifts were easily more than seven feet high.

Just to make an already impossible situation worse, I had been considering running for governor of Rhode Island against the Democratic incumbent, Joe Garrahy. There had been a lot of speculation in the press about it, and this storm pitted us against each other in a fight for the limited available resources. Luckily for the governor, the NBC station in town had only one mobile truck and it was sent to the statehouse rather than city hall. Once it got there it couldn't move, so the governor was on TV throughout the entire storm, which gave him a huge political advantage. He had the cameras and the microphones and it looked like I had disappeared.

Though I know many people will dispute this, in my opinion the snow cleanup became a political issue for the governor. He certainly was a good politician. I believe he directed cleanup efforts to begin outside the city to place as much blame as possible on me. He was going to bury my reputation under this snowstorm. And truthfully, I had to admire him for it. Had our positions been reversed I probably would have done the same thing.

For a while I was trapped at home. I had to use a snowmobile to get to the emergency headquarters we'd set up in a conference room in the communications center building. Even if we could have gotten every piece of snow-clearing equipment available to the city on the streets, it wouldn't have been enough. We had to clear the streets vehicle by vehicle. We were towing hundreds of cars and trucks a day. When it finally stopped snowing on Tuesday, the governor declared the entire state a disaster area and asked for federal assistance. President Carter mobilized the National Guard and ordered construction Seabees and equipment from Biloxi, Mississippi, to get to Rhode Island. We cleared thirty inches of snow from the airport runways so their massive planes could land. The problem was that all the snow had been dumped too close to the runways, so the wings didn't have sufficient clearance. We had to pack down all the piles of snow before the planes could land.

The biggest conflict I had with the governor took place when I discovered more than seventy pieces of heavy snow-clearing equipment, owned by the federal government, sitting in a lot at Fields Point and claimed them for the city. These were the trucks and plows and frontloaders we needed to open the streets—but after I announced that we had this equipment, Garrahy tried to grab the vehicles for the state. Finally, I exploded. I was furious. In an effort to embarrass me, the state was trying to screw the city. I could take care of the political fallout, I wasn't overly concerned about that, but this was a life-and-death situation for the people of Providence. I called the governor's staff at the statehouse and started screaming at them. The last thing they wanted was a war; it was important for everybody that it looked publicly as though we were working together. So finally they gave in and agreed the equipment would be sent to Providence.

I didn't sleep; nobody slept. We had to make all our decisions on the run. For a time just about the only way of getting around was by snowmobile. We had volunteers delivering medicine and emergency supplies, ferrying sick and injured people to the hospitals, or getting medical help to people who needed it. There were many stories of extraordinary heroism, of police officers and firefighters risking their own lives trudging through the blizzard to rescue families trapped in cars with no heat, and of city employees using snowmobiles to deliver food, medicine, and in several cases babies. But still, people died. And when they did, there was no way to move their bodies to funeral parlors, so we stored them in rows in the cell blocks of the police station. There was a large holding cell, a drunk tank really, in which the floor slanted down so it could be easily hosed down in the morning. We lined up the corpses there and covered them with snow so they wouldn't decompose.

By the third day we had fallen into a kind of a routine. We were functioning, just barely, but functioning. I went up in a helicopter to get an overview of the city. It was an astonishing sight. Almost no vehicles were moving—and the world was just all white. The military help we needed had finally arrived, though Governor Garrahy had ordered the equipment to start clearing the smaller towns in the northern part of the state rather than clearing the capital city and moving upward. It was pretty amazing to look out the window of my office at the staging area and see rows of trucks and equipment lined up. We blocked the few cleared roads into the city with police cruisers and trucks to keep sightseers out, and I declared a curfew. With power still out in large sections of the city, we just didn't want people walking around at night.

By the fourth day other areas of the state had been cleared, while in Providence we were still fighting the snow street by street. But people just kept working at it. It was amazing, and in many ways the community came together. You could feel the spirit of the city come alive, and people actually began finding some enjoyment in the unusual circumstances. Everybody had a story to tell, about how far they walked to get home, whom they helped, what they did, how they coped with the situation. In fact, although people were very angry, many of them understood that this was a natural disaster beyond the resources of the city to handle and that we had gotten little support from the state. Within a few weeks we even began seeing I SURVIVED THE BLIZZARD OF '78, T-shirts.

It took us almost a week and a half before the city was close to normal. We towed nearly two thousand cars and trucks that had been abandoned, and it took several more weeks to get them all returned to their owners. Getting rid of tons of snow was not difficult; at that time we just dumped it into the Providence River, although several years later the Environmental Protection Agency made us stop because apparently we were polluting the river by dropping water into it. Figure that one out.

After the storm I knew I had a lot of work to do to restore my reputation. This was an election year, and had the snowstorm occurred closer to the elections it might have been disastrous for me. Two years earlier I had been so popular I had considered running for the United States Senate and, if I had run, I am very confident I would have won. Not running was the biggest mistake of my political career. But after this storm my popularity rating was somewhere between very low and "don't let the door hit you on the way out." Fortunately, this storm took place in February and I had sufficient time to heal the damage.

If clearing snow is the short-term measure of a mayor's success, the success of the police department is the yardstick. In any type of emergency the city's first line of defense is its police department. In terms of day-to-day contact with the public, the cop on the street—or, as it turned out in my administration, on the horse—is the most visible representative of any elected official. So picking the right person to lead the police force is always a difficult decision.

After being elected in 1974 I had to make a lot of appointments very quickly. Usually when a politician takes office there is a long line of people from his political party standing outside his door ready to take control of the government. It's the spoils of political warfare, the waiting list for power. But I hadn't been part of the political machine, so I had few political debts to pay. I honored my deal with Chief McQueeney that he would keep his job for a year. He was a fine police chief, but he was very political. One day I got a call from a member of my administration asking me for a favor. A friend of his had been arrested during a sting operation, he explained. Supposedly this man was simply stopped at a traffic light when a policewoman posing as a prostitute jumped in his car and propositioned him. The whole conversation was on tape. "This is a real family man," I was told. "An all-American football player, a hardworking guy, and if this gets out it's going to ruin his life."

Ruin his life? I didn't know about that, though obviously it wouldn't help him. But it did seem like a pretty heavy penalty to pay. I called McQueeney. I expected him to tell me there was nothing he could do about it. Instead, he asked, "You want me to take care of it? I can bring you down the tape."

It was political business as usual. That was exactly what I didn't want. Eventually I did nothing, I didn't get involved. The last thing I needed was to give Chief McQueeney an obstruction-of-justice case to barter for his job. So when McQueeney's year ended, it was time for me to appoint my own chief of police.

There were several very good candidates for the job, and each man had his supporters. I had a line of people telling me whom I should appoint. In fact, I wanted to appoint my old and close friend, state policeman Vincent Vespia, who was perfect for the job, but when I asked the governor if I could get him released from the state police—with his pension—the governor refused. Finally I selected an outstanding twenty-five-year veteran, Captain Robert Ricci. It was a completely nonpolitical choice, Ricci was the most professional appointment I could have made. He had been recommended to me by the extremely well-respected head of the state police, Walter Stone. There were a lot of reasons for this choice. Ricci certainly was well qualified; he was known to be very tough and totally honest. He was a dedicated family man, and it was said that on his way to work each morning he would stop at his sick mother's home to give her injections of insulin. He'd worked his way up the department ladder from patrolman to becoming head of the elite C-Squad, the crime squad, a detective squad that targeted drugs, prostitution, and gambling. Ricci was known as a cop who would never back down; supposedly he'd go up to our Italian neighborhood, Federal Hill, and literally glower at the bookies standing there. Some people claimed I'd picked him because he was an Italian American, and, truthfully, that did have something to do with my decision. I wanted to make a statement that the police department was going to change. Like many departments around the country it traditionally had been pretty much all white and excluded blacks, Hispanics, and women. Most of our chiefs had been Irish. I remember sitting at my desk and telling my chief of staff, Ron Glantz, "I decided I'm going to appoint Bob Ricci."

Ronnie was surprised and probably disappointed. There was nothing to be gained politically from this selection. "Why?" he asked.

"Because nobody wants him," I said. "No politician paid for him."

Ronnie shook his head. "You know what, you're going to be the first person he arrests." I assumed that was supposed to mean Ricci was such a straight arrow that he wouldn't even let me get away with anything.

Ricci did a fine job, reducing crime by almost 10 percent his first year in the job, but as it turned out, he probably wasn't the right choice for me. He was a great cop, but he didn't fully embrace my intention to change the complexion of the department. Like every city in the northeast, Providence was racially divided. The first recorded race riots in America had taken place in Providence in 1824. And while we'd managed to avoid the type of riots that had destroyed parts of New York, Detroit, and Watts, I knew we had to change. I believed in affirmative action, that we had to add minorities to the department even if they did not test equally to whites; he believed in following the same path the department had always followed. The Providence Police Department had hired its first black officers in 1947, but the department wasn't really integrated. Colonel Ricci and I discussed it several times. Though I never put political pressure on him to hire people who were not qualified to be police officers, I was always very clear with him that we were going to add blacks and other minorities to the department. "You have to have minorities in the police department," I told him. But anybody who knew Ricci would agree that trying to put pressure on him would have been a waste of time; he wasn't the type of person who would respond to such tactics. He loved the police department, and he would have quit first. In fact, when reporters asked him directly if he was being pressured by city hall, he said flatly, "I didn't ask for this job. I don't owe anything to anyone."

I knew he wasn't happy about adding minorities, though. I remember once when, after we'd discussed it thoroughly, he turned and looked out the window and said, "I'll hire them, but you civilize them first."

I was stunned. It wasn't a secret that I was adopting affirmative action policies to make the department more closely resemble the population of the city. In fact, several years later a female *Providence Journal* reporter asked the serving police chief, Bernie Gannon, "Did the mayor ever ask you to hire anybody?"

"Yes, he did," Gannon responded.

Apparently she got all excited at the scent of a story proving the mayor had ordered the chief of police to hire specific people. "Do you remember who?" she asked. "Can I come over there and talk to you?" "Sure, come on over," he said. "But don't you want to know who?" And when she said she certainly did, he told her, "Minorities and women." That reporter never showed up.

I did the same thing with Chief Ricci. My office gave Ricci a list of candidates we wanted to be considered for the next police academy class. Many of them were minorities. Ricci apparently forwarded that list to the department selection board, which approved fifteen and rejected five of them. Supposedly those five had failed background checks. For instance, one of these candidates was rejected because he had a minor criminal record. That crime turned out to be that he'd left the scene of a car accident in which there had been some minor property damage. Later we found out he did have a drinking problem and probably shouldn't have been appointed, but at the time I strongly suspected that if the then-active members of the force had been subjected to this same type of intensive checking, a lot of them wouldn't have become police officers. When we objected and asked the board to review its decision, three of the five applicants who had been rejected were approved for the next class.

There was also a provision in the regulations that excluded applicants under five-eight-and-a-half, I believe it was. I felt that provision was there to keep many Latinos and Italians, who tended to be smaller, off the force. It was ridiculous. We weren't picking models, we were hiring cops. No one could explain to me why someone five-six couldn't be an effective cop. Ricci was a by-the-book officer, and this was the book. I had to convince him it was time to turn the page.

Eventually the two white men who had been rejected sued the city, claiming they had been the victims of reverse discrimination. (Several years later one of them did become a Pawtucket, Rhode Island, police officer and had an exemplary career.) In January Chief Ricci was called to give a deposition. We had a severe ice storm a couple of days before he was scheduled to testify, and I stopped by his office to see what was going on. We talked about his testimony and I told him, "Robert, you tell them that I told you to hire blacks. That's not a secret. There's no lying here, we didn't do anything wrong." But there was something very wrong, and while I don't remember the details, I do remember wondering what was bothering him. A few of the things he said made very little sense. Whatever it was, I figured, it would pass. I made a note to check on him the next day. Then I went out to dinner with Herb DeSimone and his wife. I even mentioned to them that something was wrong with Ricci.

About 5 A.M. the following morning my phone rang. My public safety commissioner, Leo Trambukis, said urgently, "Mayor, I have a mortally wounded police officer."

Nothing, absolutely nothing, wakes you up faster. "What's going on?" I was already getting dressed.

"It's the colonel," he said, meaning Ricci. "He's lying in his office. He shot himself. He's dead."

"Let me call you back." I hung up and called Glantz. "The colonel just killed himself," I told him.

Waking out of a deep sleep his first question to me was, "Did he leave any notes?"

"How do I know? I'll meet you there."

When I got to the police station most of the department's top brass were standing in the outer office. I walked into Ricci's office and he was lying on the floor, his .38 caliber revolver at his side. I'd seen dead bodies before, but this was tough. I'd been sitting in that office speaking with him only a few hours earlier. This certainly was an unprecedented event; nobody quite knew what to do. I immediately appointed Major John Eddy, the night commander, the acting chief. Eddy took control, telling his officers, "All right, as far as anybody is concerned, nobody knows nothing about what happened here tonight."

Nobody knows nothing? As he said that I glanced out the window. It was just about dawn but the satellite trucks from all three TV networks had already arrived. What are we going to do, I wondered, take the body out the back door and bury it somewhere? Nobody knows nothing. Eventually we issued a statement. Ricci had left a note for Leo Trambukis and Major John Leyden, writing, "Leo—everything is too much. John—take care of my family."

Nobody could understand what had caused Ricci to commit suicide. His administrative assistant, Captain Walter Clark, who'd last spoken to him at most a few hours before he'd put the gun to his head, told reporters Ricci seemingly had been fine: "He gave me no inkling at all that anything was wrong." But a few days later the department's personnel director, Lieutenant Edward Collins, told the media that it was my fault. Collins had been a member of the board that approved or rejected candidates for the department. He claimed Ricci had committed suicide because I had forced him to admit at least three unqualified candidates to the training class—and he feared having to testify under oath about it. "Bob Ricci died because he couldn't get up on the stand and lie" about the fact that I supposedly was "jamming [unqualified] men down his throat." Collins said that Ricci had called him several times that night to discuss how he should respond when questioned about the political pressure that I had exerted on him to approve my list.

That was an outrageous statement. I was being accused of killing Ricci. I was beyond furious. One of the two other men who worked with Collins in evaluating candidates responded that he wasn't aware of any pressure being applied by my office. Leo Trambukis said the same thing: "It is inconceivable to me that it could have happened that way." The truth, whatever it was, didn't matter. My reputation was badly damaged. This was an incident some people never forgot about and continued to blame me for.

While I was fighting this slander, I had another problem. I got a call one night from an officer who told me, "Mayor, your acting colonel just wrapped a police car around a tree on Elmwood Avenue. He was coming from the Elks Club and he'd been drinking. What would you like me to do?"

The truth is, I would have liked to forget about it, to tell everybody to go home, but the risk of eventual exposure was high. I told him, "Just handle it the way you usually handle colonels who are drunk and hit a tree." I didn't get involved, and they successfully kept it out of the newspapers.

It was many years later that I finally learned the entire story. I was at a party at Walter Clark's home and I noticed a miniature rocking chair sitting on his mantle. I picked it up and was looking at it when Walter said, "You like that rocking chair?"

"Yeah," I said. "Where'd you get it?"

He smiled. "Oh, Mayor, that's a great story." And then he solved the mystery. "Remember when the colonel [Ricci] and I would come to your parties and you'd ask him if he wanted a drink and he'd tell you 'ginger ale'? And you thought he was such a Goody Two-shoes?" He shook his head. "That wasn't ginger ale in there. I used to get him the drinks."

I smiled at that. I never would have guessed.

Then Walter added, "Remember his mother was sick and he used to go see her all the time in the hospital?" I remembered. "I'd pick him up. He'd see his mother in the hospital for about fifteen minutes and then he'd go to his mother's house. He had a girlfriend. You'd never think of that with that guy. He'd screw the girlfriend in a rocking chair. So this little rocking chair was a gift from the girlfriend that she gave to him."

"Really?" I was surprised.

"Oh yeah. Mayor, you know why he killed himself, don't you?"

"No."

"The woman was going to turn him in. She demanded that he leave his wife and if he didn't, she was going to turn him in."

I just stood there, really stunned. The poor guy. That poor guy.

After Ricci's death I appointed another veteran officer, Angelo Ricci—no relation—as chief of the department. It was a politically convenient pick. The department needed a morale boost, and this Ricci was well liked. He was a very smart street cop, a very tough guy. I knew when I picked him that his strengths were not administration or dealing with the media—he wasn't particularly articulate—but we'd been through a really rough situation and I needed the support of the department.

One senior officer who did not like that choice was the acting chief, who began complaining loudly about not getting the permanent job. I invited him to my office and closed the door. "Let me ask you this," I said. "How would you like me to have a press conference right now and tell everybody that while you were serving as acting colonel you were driving drunk and wrapped your police car around a tree?" End of problem. And for slightly more than a year Ricci did a fine job. Early in 1979 he mentioned to me that a reporter from *The Providence Sunday Journal*'s *Rhode Island* magazine section was running with him to do a story. If I did think about it I probably would have asked myself, what could go wrong with that?

I had a ritual. Late Saturday night I'd get the Sunday papers and sit in a restaurant reading them. One Saturday night a pair of handcuffs was pictured on the cover of the magazine. This must be that story Ricci was telling me about. Oh, good for him, I thought. Then I began reading the article. For a few minutes I wondered if it was some kind of elaborate joke. I kept reading. It couldn't be a joke, it just had to be a very bad dream. Whatever it was, I knew it couldn't possibly be for real. Ricci, the chief of police I had selected, was quoted saying things like, "I believe that if you have to take a guy around the corner and give him a couple of shots, maybe that's what we should do."

Oh really, Colonel? It just got worse and worse. "Everybody is trying to rehabilitate. They want to rehabilitate these people. How can you rehabilitate an animal? You take a lion in the zoo they can't do anything with, what do they do with him after a while? They shoot him. That's realistic."

I read it and reread it and reread it, but the words never got any better. "If a guy commits murder and we know he committed a murder, why don't they string him up the following day? That's my theory." And just in case people didn't know who he was talking about, "In Providence, we have the Puerto Ricans, we have the blacks, we have a lot of minority groups and they're the toughest to control."

I put down the paper and just began imagining the racial damage that this article was going to cause. When I woke up Sunday morning, I checked; the article was still there. But that whole day nothing happened. I didn't get any phone calls about it. Wow, I thought, maybe we got lucky, maybe nobody saw it.

There's the definition of an optimist. Monday morning it began. Within a day the organization of black churches asked me to "reconsider my appointment" of Ricci. Ministers were holding press conferences to call for his resignation. The minority population of the city was furious—with the exception of one person, a black councilman named Lloyd Griffin. Lloyd and I were friends, he had supported me, and we mostly got along very well. But Lloyd never walked away from an open microphone. I was trying to quell this potential disaster, and he came out in support of Ricci's tough enforcement concept—admittedly, I'm being generous in that description—telling reporters he wanted the minority neighborhoods to be as safe as white neighborhoods and that this was one means of accomplishing that.

I tried to save Ricci's reputation. At first I told the media I had no intention of firing him. I thought if he apologized and I suspended him there was a small chance he could come back. When I met with him, he told me that he had never said those things. And rather than allowing the heat to dissipate, he decided to fight back. He made a tour of the city, accompanied by Lloyd Griffin, visiting community centers and retirement homes, and he was well received. People were applauding him. Apparently there were many people in Providence who believed that same crap.

In the middle of all this insanity, who showed up in Providence but Muhammad Ali. His arrival had absolutely nothing to do with this situation; it was just a coincidence. But he did get involved. One morning he walked into my office with several local ministers and walked out with one of my secretaries. I never saw her again.

Meanwhile, rather than apologizing for his remarks, Ricci gained confidence from the support he was receiving. Finally it became obvious that Ricci had to go. He had agreed to take a vacation to Florida, and I informed him while he was there that he was finished. In response, he told me he had checked with a city attorney and I couldn't fire him. He was absolutely right; police officers had tenure. So instead I sent him an official letter in which I thanked him for his service to the City of Providence Police Department, and then informed him that when he returned from his vacation he would revert to his permanent rank of lieutenant. That I could do.

He never came back.

After I fired Ricci, several of the small group of city council members who usually supported me came to my office to lobby for a particular candidate. We sat at a conference table and one by one, each of them gave me a reason why I should support this particular police officer. Finally I came to one member and when I asked him that question, he stood up, walked over to my desk, and put his hand on the phone. "I'll tell you why, Mayor," he said, and the scary part is that he was being completely serious. "Because any time you want to, you can pick up this phone and he'll arrest anybody you want him to."

So much for that candidate.

Though we were successful in adding minorities to the department, for a long time we were less successful in getting them into command positions. Decades earlier there had been two black lieutenants, but they were long gone. This finally came to a head in 1995. I was trying to get a budget passed and I didn't have enough votes. A white councilwoman named Patricia Nolan told me flatly she wouldn't vote for my budget until I appointed a black person to a leadership position on the police force. She didn't care who it was as long as that person was qualified, but it was time, she said. She gave me great cover: that it was the only way I could get my budget passed. As the mayor I had the legal right to make this promotion. I called the colonel, Barney Prignano, and asked flatly, "Which black officers do we have in the department?" He mentioned Cornel Young, an experienced detective I'd worked with in the attorney general's office. "Get Young," I said. "Bring him up to my office."

"Sit down, Cornel," I told him. "This is your lucky day. I want you to go and get a new uniform. Pick up your wife and family and bring them back here by one o'clock, because I'm going to make you a major."

He had hit the lottery. He was going to jump rank. His pension was going to skyrocket. "Really?" he asked.

"Really," I said. And as he was walking out of the office I stopped him. "One more thing. I want you to do me a favor. On your way home stop at a drugstore and buy us two lottery tickets, one for you and one for me, because this definitely is your lucky day." That's how I got the vote I needed to pass the budget.

Unfortunately, this is a story that didn't have a happy ending. Major Young's son, Cornel Young, Jr. eventually joined the department. In January 2000 he was off-duty, dressed in civilian clothes, wearing a baseball cap, standing on line at a diner when there was some kind of disturbance in the parking lot. Officer Young didn't hesitate: He went outside to try to help. He saw a man later identified as Aldrin Diaz sitting in his Camero pointing a gun out the window at two white, uniformed officers who were behind cover. It was clearly a very dangerous situation, so he pulled his own gun. When things happen as fast as this happened, the facts get confused. As Aldrin dropped his weapon, Young came outside holding his weapon. Apparently the two officers did not realize Young was a cop and ordered him to drop it. There is a discrepancy about whether he identified himself as a police officer, but he didn't drop his gun. The officers fired, killing him. For a mayor this is the worst possible situation; a black Providence police officer shot and killed by two white officers. The fact that this was a tragic accident made it even worse.

I was at a mayors' conference in Washington, D.C., receiving an award from the Americans for the Arts and U.S. Conference of Mayors for fostering the arts community in Providence. I'd spoken to two thousand people that night and I was elated—until I returned to my hotel and received a phone call with this news. And while I felt just terrible for Major Young, I also knew that this was the type of racially charged situation that could rip a city apart. I got back to Providence as quickly as possible. All kinds of accusations were being made about improper procedures being used, about cops not being properly trained. As I had learned from experience, a tragedy like this encourages a lot of people and organizations to try to use it for their own benefit. Several neighborhood groups had already begun making demands. Meanwhile, I was doing everything possible to hold the city together. In this situation, the first thing I wanted to do was to gather the religious leaders of the city to try to get them to defuse the situation.

Several days later I hosted a luncheon at my home. We invited several ministers from black churches as well as a Catholic priest, Father Dan Trainor, and Sister Angela Daniels, a community activist. Some of those ministers served only part-time, and held regular jobs the rest of the week. After everybody sat down, one of those ministers stood up and announced that to protest the shooting of Officer Young they were fasting. Fasting? They came to my house to tell me that. I thought, admittedly in a not especially ecumenical fashion, You c——, you're fasting on me? But before I could say anything, the Catholic priest stood up and said, basically, screw you, I'm eating. And he sat down and began eating my catered lunch.

Oh boy, I thought, this is not good. I was attempting to bring the communities together, but they saw it as an opportunity.

A resident of Providence who was closely connected to the Democratic party leadership also had a good relationship with Jesse Jackson. "You need some help here," he told me. "Let me see if I can get Jesse Jackson here to help out." Jesse Jackson? While in the past I had not been the Reverend Jackson's greatest fan, I thought, if he can help me keep a lid on this city, I want him here as quickly as possible.

Eventually I spoke with him on the phone. He told me, "You've got to get to the father, the major." It was an exploratory conversation and nothing was decided. But then the close friend who'd made this introduction asked me if the city could pay Jackson a fee—I believe the figure mentioned was a hundred thousand dollars but I'm not certain—to get involved as a consultant. A hundred grand to come to town and tell everybody how terrific we were? There was nothing I could do but laugh at that. I certainly couldn't pay it. Let me be clear: That demand did not come directly from Jackson, and I have no idea if he even knew about it. I also don't know to whom that money would have gone. My belief is that it was for him, but I have absolutely no evidence for that. It didn't matter where it was supposed to go, I turned it down flat.

The family supposedly hired Johnnie Cochran to represent them, although he was actually brought into the case by a black council-woman, and sued the city for $20 million. The claim was that Cornel Young, Jr. was shot by inadequately trained officers because he was black. As it turned out, Cochran had a conflict with another case and couldn't handle this one; instead his associate Barry Scheck took over. We made what I considered a fair offer to the family to settle their claim—but we refused to pay any legal fees. It could have ended right there, but it didn't. Eventually, the court ruled for the police department, deciding that the officers had been properly trained.

Without question the most wrenching moments I dealt with in office were the deaths of police officers. It's a completely helpless feeling. But there was one instance that I will never, ever forget. This took place in 1994. I was always concerned about the appearance of police officers while on duty. Police officers represented my administration; they represented me, to the public. I wanted them to look first class, so I was a stickler for small things that other people probably overlooked. For example, I insisted that our police cars be regularly cleaned, and I wanted them to have all their hubcaps. I made a big deal about that; it could have been a joke, Buddy and his hubcaps. I was in my car one afternoon when I saw a dirty police cruiser with no hubcaps on the street. I stopped that car and chewed out that officer. His name was Steven Shaw. I gave him the full Buddy. My secretary used to keep a set of colored flags on her desk to signal to everyone what kind of mood I was in: Red meant don't come near me, yellow meant she wasn't sure yet, and green meant if you needed a favor, that day was the day to ask for it. That officer had a double red flag day, and I reported him to the chief of police, Colonel Gannon.

What I did not know was that Officer Shaw had just returned from a vacation in Italy and wasn't fully aware of my hubcap crusade. His regular car had broken down and he took another car, the car without hubcaps that I saw.

It wasn't too long after that confrontation that he walked into a house looking for a robbery suspect and the guy came out of a closet and shot and killed him. Colonel Gannon called me. I rushed to the scene. I saw them racing him out of the house and we followed the ambulance to Rhode Island Hospital. We walked into the morgue together and I took a look at this brave kid, lying on a table, and realized who he was. "That's the kid with the hubcaps, isn't it?"

"Yeah," Bernie said. There is no way I can describe my feelings. When I had to resign from office after admitting that I had assaulted my wife's lover, I didn't cry. When I was sentenced to prison, I didn't cry. But the night I saw the body of Officer Shaw, I cried.

I didn't need anyone to tell me how brave our police department was; I'd seen it up close several times. I was involved in several hostage situations. Once, I remember, I had been at a retirement party for our chief of the fire department when we were notified that an armed man was holding Cambodian hostages in a house. I went to the house with Gannon. It was a miserably cold, wet night, and we were standing outside in the mud. The entire area had been cordoned off by the police, and the house was ringed by police cars. I took one look around and thought, Jeez, this is costing me a fortune in overtime. I knew I had to do something about it, that the situation could last for days, so I decided the best way to end it was for me to go upstairs and talk to the gunman. I was the mayor, I was Buddy.

There is no sensible explanation for that decision.

Gannon tried to talk me out of it, but I didn't accept the reality that I was in danger. When it became obvious that I was going up those stairs, a female police officer named Rhonda Kessler volunteered to go with me. Just as we started climbing the stairs I heard a shot. Officer Kessler turned to me and said, "Mayor, we're gonna get the fuck out of here. Follow me."

No kidding. If there is an Olympic record for getting down a staircase, we set it. I felt like the Road Runner. Fortunately, the police managed to defuse the situation without anyone being hurt.

On another occasion I really did climb that staircase. One Saturday afternoon I was on my way to a wedding with my girlfriend at the time. I had a police radio in my car and I heard the dispatcher announce a hostage situation in progress. We took the limo right through the police perimeter. I sent my date to the wedding and went into the house. An armed man was holed up by himself on the third floor; he didn't have any hostages but he was threatening to shoot anybody who came in the room. Basically, this guy had hit the lottery but had blown all his money on a girl and she wouldn't talk to him. The police finally got his psychiatrist on the phone and suggested I speak with him. As soon as I picked up the receiver, the gunman picked up an extension and immediately recognized my voice. "Who is this? Is this the mayor?" he asked.

"Yeah," I said. "Listen, what are you doing up there?"

He started telling me his sad story. It became clear pretty quickly that this whole situation had escalated much faster than he anticipated and he didn't know how to get out of it. "I don't want to go to jail," he pleaded.

"I can handle that for you, but you got to stop this nonsense right now." I didn't complain to him that he was costing the city a fortune, but that's what I was thinking.

"Okay," he decided. "I want to talk to you, but only you."

I'd successfully managed to get myself invited into a room with a gunman. I had learned my lesson; there was no way I was going in that room as long as he had that gun. "I want you to throw that gun out the window and I'll come up." It took him a little while, but finally he threw the gun out the window. I knew I had to go upstairs.

The head of our hostage rescue unit did not want me to go. "I can't let you go up there, Mayor. We're trained in this."

"Let me ask you this, if you're trained in this, how come he's still up there?"

It was a very narrow staircase. As I walked up I remember thinking, This is really stupid. The door opened and I walked inside. He came over to me and hugged me. For a moment I felt relieved. And then I looked in a mirror and I could see he was holding a knife. "All right, I'm here. What's the problem?"

He'd fallen on his job and received a big settlement and spent it all on his girlfriend and she'd dumped him. Finally he'd lost his temper. Now the house was surrounded by police—on overtime—and he was terrified that he was going to be arrested. I convinced him that we would take him to the hospital, but he refused to come down as long as the cops were surrounding the house. "You have to get them to go away."

That was something we could agree on. "They'll be gone in two minutes," I said. I got the commander on the phone. "Get rid of all the cops."

"Are you crazy?"

"Get rid of them all." We had a beer together and stood by the window watching them leave. I don't know who was happier, him or me. "All right," I said when they had cleared the area, "now we're going to the hospital." The colonel and I took him to the hospital for observation. He wanted me to stay, but I had to go to that wedding. But several weeks later he called my office and asked to see me. We set an appointment and he came in—although I made sure security was there and the door to my office remained open. He had come in to thank me, he said—and he wanted to make a $5,000 donation to my campaign.

That certainly was one of the larger campaign contributions I turned down.

I also worked with the police department in several suicide attempts. In one of them a man stood on the third or fourth floor ledge of a parking garage, threatening to jump. I talked him to safety from the ground. On another occasion a man threatened to jump from the roof of a building. I went up there with the colonel. Believe me, this time I was scared. None of us should have been up there. But in both cases the police risked their own lives to grab these people and drag them to safety.

Even though the police department is more visible, they're not the only city employees who put their lives on the line. In fact, the fire department also gets high marks. Providence has the second-oldest continuously operating fire department in America, behind only Cincinnati. I always appreciated the professionalism and the skill of the fire department, but I did have my battles with them. As far as I was concerned, the fire department and the teachers' union were tied at being the most skillful political organizations in the city. It certainly isn't the mayor, or the city council. When you try to go up against those guys you're in for a political fight.

When I was elected, the city had fifteen engine companies, eight ladder companies, a special hazards unit, an oxygen company, and all types of special units, and I knew nothing about any of them. To me they were all firefighters. But by the time I left office I knew every detail, from the cost of apparatuses to the penny, to response times to the second. My first decision was to keep the fire chief, Mike Moise. This is a job that is based almost completely on competence and the support of his men. Moise had a terrific reputation and was loyal to the city and his men rather than to the mayor. He was a strong advocate for his department, but he was realistic enough to understand the reality of a budget.

I tried hard to modernize our department. When I took office, most of our fire equipment had been in use about eighteen years; by the time we were done the average age of our trucks was four years. Fire equipment is expensive. Running a modern fire department is a large budget item, but there isn't much you can do to cut costs. We were always searching for ways to reduce our expenditures without reducing the department's effectiveness. At one meeting in my office a city councilwoman came up with a bright idea. "I know how we can cut their budget," she said with great enthusiasm. "Let's make sure we send our reserve equipment to the false alarms."

One way of cutting the budget is to reduce the size of the department. People don't want to admit it, but we don't need as many firefighters today as we did in the past. Their equipment has improved tremendously. We demolished old housing that was susceptible to fire. We changed fire codes to make buildings safer and forced landlords to install sprinkler systems. We emphasized fire-prevention programs. Our fire trucks were equipped with computers that showed firemen the design of a building and where all the hose hook ups were located. Improved communications have made it possible to respond more rapidly and to enlist the firefighting capabilities of several nearby cities; sometimes their units were even closer to a call than ours. In fact, about the only thing about the department that hasn't changed is the level of manpower. That isn't because the same number of people is still needed, but rather because the firefighters' union is so strong.

I remember once when I decided to close a single firehouse. I had hired a consultant in this field, and this consultant recommended that this particular station be closed. Basically, the only thing this station had done in three years was rescue a cat from a tree, and it was costing the city more than $1 million a year to keep it open. It was a retirement home for firefighters. But you would have thought I'd tried to kill Bambi. Close a fire station? How many people do you want to kill? The firefighters' union fought back. Believe me, they know how to mobilize the community, warning them, "The mayor wants to put your lives in jeopardy by closing this firehouse." Now, most people will never call the fire department, but they love the security of knowing that in an emergency the fire department will respond in minutes, even seconds.

While this debate was raging, I turned on the six o'clock news. The lead story was that I wanted to close a neighborhood fire station—and they showed old footage of a decrepit mill in Massachusetts burning; people were jumping out of the windows, flames roaring through the roof. The footage had absolutely no connection to this firehouse or the city of Providence. When the station reported the story, it put a female broadcaster in front of the station, and as she explained that I intended to close the station, a truck raced out, presumably to fight a fire. Son of a gun, I thought as I watched it, they got me. People aren't going to realize that's old film. But the story certainly wouldn't have been as effective if they had showed the department racing to save a scared cat and told viewers how much that had cost.

I called the commissioner of public safety and told him I wanted to know specifically where that truck had gone that afternoon, and I wanted a printout of each call that truck had responded to in the past months. The previous month that truck had gone out three times, three times in a month, and none of those calls were serious. There had been no call that day; it was a cruise to nowhere to create news footage.

I knew they were going to repeat that story on the late news, when the audience was larger. So I called the police department and found a man who had been arrested for breaking into a house. There may have been a minor sexual assault charge involved. It was not a major crime, but I was fighting fire with . . . nothing. By the time we were through, it was as if we had arrested a serial rapist. I immediately called a press conference to announce that the criminal who had been terrorizing Providence had finally been caught. An imagined serial rapist trumps a phony fire alarm. My press conference became the lead story on the nightly news. After it ran, the president of the union, Stephen Day, who knew how to play the game as well as I did, called me. "You screwed me!" he said.

"That's right," I said. "You are fucking with the master. They're not gonna remember your fire trucks, they're gonna remember my serial rapist."

I may have won that battle, but not the war. That particular station was kept open. The one fight I did win was my attempt to reduce the number of firefighters on a truck from four to three when weather conditions made it safe. It was perfectly reasonable; we were one of very few, if any, Rhode Island cities that operated four-person trucks. While this sounds like a relatively simple cost savings, getting it done was complicated and controversial. The department actually did not have sufficient firefighters to keep four people on each truck at all times, so to make that possible firefighters got extra duty and earned considerable overtime. The union did not want to give up that extra money for its members. I understood that, so I tried to put them on the spot: I offered to hire additional firefighters, which would still cost the city considerably less than paying overtime, but the union rejected that concept. Publicly, the union insisted it was concerned about protecting the endangered citizens of Providence, even though we had changed procedures to ensure that more trucks and therefore more people responded to calls.

Unfortunately, this became an issue in December 1977 when we had a devastating fire at Providence College. About 2 A.M. a coed was apparently using a hair dryer in a closet to dry her clothes, something sparked, and a fire started on the upper floor of a four-story dorm. The girls were trapped. The entire fire department responded, but seven young women died and fifteen others were injured. Two of the students died when they jumped from a window only seconds before the firefighters could reach them.

The best thing I could do was stay out of the way. I stood there in the freezing cold night, watching this disaster unfold. The whole event seemed surreal. The fire department did a tremendous job; who knows how many lives they saved that night—but the death toll was so high. What came next was awful. That's when the blame game began. The president of the firefighters' union suggested that lives might have been saved if four men had been on the trucks. He was careful in his accusations, telling reporters that the two young women who leaped to their death died "in a matter of thirty seconds. I'm not saying that the two women would have lived, I am saying that with adequate manpower we would have stood a better chance." Then he added, "It's impossible to operate with only three men on a truck."

There was no way I could respond to that. Maybe he really believed that, but I felt he was using this tragedy politically. But Chief Moise disagreed with him publicly, pointing out that he would have been complaining more loudly than the union president if he believed the safety of the city was in jeopardy.

What was equally sad was the attempt by some city officials to place the blame on the president of the college, Father Thomas Reginald Peterson. We had a meeting in my office, and all these old Irishmen who'd been running their departments for years were looking desperately for a scapegoat. Anybody but them. Father Peterson was the easiest target. All of a sudden they started talking about indicting him for failing to install a sprinkler system in the dorm. I couldn't believe what I was hearing. I pointed out to them that it wasn't this priest's fault, that he'd only been president of the college for a short time. And although the state had changed the laws to require new buildings to have sprinkler systems, the dorm, Aquinas Hall, had been built in 1939 and was grandfathered in. These people didn't seem to care, they wanted to walk out of that room with a scalp to show the media. I didn't know Father Peterson very well and I didn't owe him anything, but that was ridiculous. Finally, I stopped the meeting and told them, "I don't like the way this is going. Anybody here wants to place the blame on Father Peterson, just raise your fucking hand and then you can resign and leave. All right, who's first? Who wants to move to indict Father Peterson?" Not surprisingly, no one raised his hand. That was the end of that.

As a mayor you can try countless things to improve your city. But the foundation for it all is constituent services. There is nothing more important than keeping people safe in their homes and on the streets, and every mayor is completely dependent on the police and fire departments for that, and for getting the streets cleared after a snowstorm.

Generally, throughout my time in office I had a good working relationship with my police, fire, and sanitation departments; well, except for that one time when I had to put guards armed with shotguns on our garbage trucks.

Five

n 1973 I had been an assistant prosecutor barely known in Providence. Less than two years later I was being promoted nationally as the future of the Republican Party, the fair-toupeed boy touted as the bright new face of the GOP. In fact, slightly more than a year after I became mayor, the Republican Party asked me to run for the United States Senate. I met in the Oval Office with President Ford and Senator Bob Packwood, who was in charge of recruiting Republican candidates for the 1976 election. Rhode Island's Italian American senator John O. Pastore had announced his retirement, leaving the seat open. Who better to replace him than another Italian American—me? While it was well known in the state that John Chafee, a former governor who'd lost a race both for a gubernatorial election and for the Senate election in 1972, wanted to run again, Gerald Ford didn't believe he could win; he thought I would be the much stronger candidate.

After meeting in President Ford's office, Packwood took me on a tour of the Senate and tried to convince me to make the race. He promised me that the party would help me raise some of the money I needed. It was a strong recruiting pitch and it was very flattering. Later the chairman of the Rhode Island Republican Party, Jim Field, told me the same thing.

I had absolutely no doubt that if I ran I would win. That was more than ego speaking, that was reality: I was very popular in Rhode

Island and there was no strong Democratic candidate. Just as in the mayor's race, the Democratic Party was splintered. The Democratic governor, Philip Noel, had announced he was seeking his party's nomination for Pastore's Senate seat. But in response to a question he was asked about busing, he had made some awful remark that basically you could take a black kid out of the ghetto and send him to school in a white neighborhood, but when he came home his father was still a drug dealer and his mother was a hooker. He certainly didn't mean it the way it sounded. I've known Phil Noel for decades, and he is a thoroughly decent human being. There is no possible way he meant it the way it sounded. But this was politics, and it was hung around his neck.

Tell me I couldn't have beaten him. Noel eventually lost the Democratic primary to a car dealer; an inexperienced politician named Richard Lorber. Lorber was a good guy but he had no political experience, and the Republican Party would have made sure I had enough money to bury him. Don't try to tell me I couldn't have beaten him, too. Where do I go to take the oath? If I had decided to run, in addition to solid Republican support, many Providence Democrats would have voted for me. It was a good political strategy for them. Providence Democrats didn't care about the United States Senate; they wanted city hall, where all the money was, where all the jobs and patronage came from. With me out of the way, they easily would have replaced me as mayor with a Democrat. Senator Cianci. It still sounds good.

While I knew I had the endorsement of the Republican party leaders, the only real question I had was, if it came down to a primary fight, would those old Wasp voters support an Italian over the beloved patrician John Chafee? Italians didn't vote in big numbers in the Republican primary. The answer was that I didn't know.

Not too long after I got back from Washington, Chafee called and asked to see me. He drove up to my house in a little Volkswagen and we sat down for breakfast. He wanted to run, he told me. I said, "Well, you know, I'm thinking about running, too. I haven't made a decision yet."

Eventually, Chafee started tearing up. It was at that moment I realized without any doubt that he knew I could beat him. "I deserve it," he said. Then he basically pleaded his case, reminding me that I was considerably younger than him and that I would have other opportunities. "This is my last chance," he said. "And I've earned it."

Earned it? How, by losing the governorship and a race for the Senate? At that time people thought of him as a loser. "How many shots do you get?" I asked him. Nothing was settled that day. I told him that I hadn't decided what I wanted to do, but that if I didn't run, I would be pleased to support him.

I spent a lot of time considering it. Unfortunately, I made the mistake of listening to the people around me, the people who knew their jobs would be in jeopardy if I ran for the Senate. They reminded me that I was only thirty-five years old and had a tremendous political future ahead of me. Governor? The Senate? Even . . . Anything wasn't just possible, it was probable. Why should I risk a possibly divisive primary? My time was going to come. The more I listened to people telling me about my exciting future, the more I believed them. I finally decided not to run. I was politically noble about it, telling reporters that the people of Providence had elected me and I intended to serve out my complete term. "I just didn't feel I should leave," I said, adding that I was going to support "my friend" John Chafee.

The *Providence Journal* called it "a wise decision," not because I wouldn't have been "an effective member of the Senate" but because I still had to "prove my potential." In fact, this was the dumbest decision I ever made in politics, the biggest mistake of my career. I handed John Chafee a seat in the U.S. Senate. I still regret that decision. I learned that in politics when the brass ring comes sailing by, you'd better grab, hold tight and not let go; but by the time I learned that lesson, it was too late.

Chafee was so grateful he waited four years before he screwed me.

Ironically, several years later I hired the pollster he had used in his race, and this person told me that had I run, Chafee would not have opposed me in the primary.

Instead of becoming a U.S. Senator, I was invited to speak on national television at the 1976 Republican National Convention in Kansas City, Missouri. The party wanted to put me in the spotlight. They asked me if I preferred to second President Ford's nomination or introduce the keynote speaker, Texas governor John Connally. Naturally, I considered the most important aspect of that choice before making my decision: "What time would I be on TV with each of them?"

The seconding speech would take place at some ungodly hour. The introduction was scheduled for prime time. Ladies and gentlemen, I'd like to introduce Governor John Connally.

This was a huge opportunity for me. I was getting all the political buzz, and this would be my first major exposure to the country. I had a beautiful speech that was intended to broaden the party by attracting people who identified themselves as hypenated Americans, the ethnic community that until then had been the property of the Democratic party.

Truthfully, as I began climbing the stairs to the podium I was considerably less nervous than I had anticipated I might be. I was a very effective public speaker, I knew it, and I had a good speech to read. All I had to do was let myself go and feed off the energy of the crowd. The arena was packed; this was the largest crowd I'd ever addressed. This was the first night of the rest of my political career that might take me . . . anywhere.

Before I reached the podium there was a small landing, and Governor Connally was waiting there, sitting quietly on a chair reviewing his speech. As I was being introduced, he looked up at me and smiled. "You all ready?"

"Absolutely," I said confidently.

"Great. Let me give you a word of advice, son."

What could it be? I wondered. John Connally had had a storied political career, and was considered an American statesman. He'd been in the convertible with John Kennedy when the president was assassinated, and he was considered a very serious candidate for vice president. Whatever his advice was, I knew it was something I would remember for a long time. I looked at him expectantly and asked, "Yes?"

He leaned over and said, "Pull up your fly."

I pulled up my fly and walked onstage. "My name is Vincent 'Buddy' Cianci," I began, "mayor of the great city of Providence, Rhode Island. I am not an 'Eye-talian' (as President Carter had recently pronounced it) but an Italo-American and proud of my ethnic background.... It shall be from the cities and neighborhoods of the East and West that Republicans, Independents, and even Democrats with names that end in 'o' and 'i' or 'z' or 'ski,' they're the ones who will help us with the big win, because if we win the neighborhoods, we'll win in November." Standing there on that podium watching the arena burst into cheers, less than three years removed from the anonymity of a quiet Providence courtroom, was indescribable. I was in control. I was on my way.

Throughout the 1976 presidential race I campaigned enthusiastically for Gerry Ford. In addition to believing he was the best man for the job, I was also making my bones in the national party. I was asked to join the president's campaign steering committee, which basically determined the campaign strategy. Every few weeks we would meet in the Cabinet Room of the White House. But in October, I believe, they convened an emergency meeting. In his debate against Jimmy Carter, Ford had made the mistake of declaring, "There is no Soviet domination of Eastern Europe," and that Poland was "independent, autonomous, it has its own territorial integrity." That was a disaster. The media had jumped all over him, and an emergency meeting of the steering committee had been convened.

During that meeting I was sitting next to Melvin Laird, who, while serving as Nixon's secretary of defense, had run the Vietnam War. Ford sat comfortably in the center of the table, smoking his pipe. There was considerable debate about how we should deal with this problem. Finally, New York senator Jacob Javits stood up—nobody ever stood up at those meetings, but Javits stood up—and he said, "Mr. President, winning this election is not the most important thing. What is important is that you tell the American people the truth."

With that, Mel Laird kicked me hard under the table, then leaned over and whispered, "I always knew that guy was an asshole."

As the youngest and least politically experienced person on the committee, I spoke very rarely. But I was a quick learner. I kept looking at the polls and noticed that in several states we were trailing by only a few percentage points, but in those states we were losing the big cities by huge numbers. I figured if we could cut that margin in the cities we could win at least one or two of those states, and that could be enough to win the election. When I was told that Jimmy Carter belonged to a church in Georgia that did not allow black membership, I thought we had an issue that could help us in those cities. So at one of our meetings I finally spoke up. "Let me tell you something that I find hard to fathom. Here we are losing the black cities, the black neighborhoods, and that's killing us in certain states, but we have an opponent, Mr. President, who worships at a church that does not allow blacks." I looked around the room. "Does that have any currency to anybody here?" No one said a word. They were all scared of bringing race into the election. I disagreed. "I think that's got to be told. Whether or not we win the election, we should be exposing that to the American people. That's a disgrace, blacks can't worship in the same church as a candidate for the presidency of the United States."

There was a lot of debate about it. Someone suggested we check into it. Another person thought we should conduct a poll. It was finally agreed not to make a decision. We were good at that.

While I admired Gerald Ford, as president he made some decisions with which I strongly disagreed. For example, he had vetoed a bill that would have been very helpful to urban areas. My memory is that it was a jobs training bill, which was vitally important to a city like Providence. That created a real political problem for me. I couldn't support his veto, but I couldn't leave the campaign, either. I wasn't getting on Jimmy Carter's train.

I campaigned in cities throughout the Northeast. One day I was scheduled to speak at the University of Rochester and afterward attend a fund-raising dinner. As I got off the private campaign plane in the morning, a black reporter stopped me and asked, "How could you support a Republican president who vetoed jobs legislation?"

It was a fair question, and politically the best way to answer it was to change the subject. A basic rule of politics is that no matter how bad my guy is, your guy is always worse. "You know what really gets me aggravated," I said. "I'm here supporting the president because he worships at a church that doesn't discriminate. Say anything you want

about vetoes, but the basic American value is that you don't discriminate against people who want to worship at your church. I could never
support a presidential candidate who doesn't allow blacks to worship
at his church."

"How do you know that?" he asked.

"It's a fact," I said, hopefully. When I walked into my house the
next day, my wife had left a note for me. In large letters, she'd written,
Call the White House immediately! My statement was all over the
news. Ford's chief of staff, Dick Cheney, was deeply concerned. "What
did you do!" he demanded.

In those days Dick Cheney was considered a very reasonable man. I
liked him, but it's fair to say he was upset. "There's nothing I can do
about it now," I replied. "I said what I said." Fortunately for me, within
a few days it was forgotten as the next problem erupted. None of it made
a difference. The scent of Nixon was too strong, and Americans wanted
the Republicans out of the White House.

Several months later, as the Ford administration was ending, I was
sitting in Dick Cheney's office when his assistant, Jim Field asked me,
"You want to see the boss?"

Of course. As I walked into the Oval Office, President Ford was
cleaning his desk. Behind him I could see snow falling on Washington.
He put his arms around me and thanked me, and then he said somewhat wistfully, "You know, Buddy, I did so poorly in the black areas.
We just couldn't get any support there."

I have been called many things in my life, but shy is not one of
them. "You weren't supposed to," I said. "I'll tell you what, though, if we
had done what I suggested, we probably wouldn't be sitting here having this conversation."

It's almost impossible to believe that less than two years later, only
two years after speaking in front of the convention on national television and playing an important role in the campaign, I was actually
fighting for my political life.

By the time I started running for reelection as mayor I had suffered
several substantial setbacks, including the great blizzard of February
1978, during which the city had been buried beneath a massive

snowstorm for more than a week; a tragic fire at Providence College in which seven female students had died; the suicide of my chief of police and the accusation that I had driven him to it; a $7.5 million budget deficit that had forced me to raise property taxes by revaluing homes; and finally there was that terrible rape accusation.

The Democrats had been preparing for the 1978 election—when they expected the world would right itself and put their candidate back in office—since the day I'd won. For three and a half years the Democratic majority on the city council had fought every effort that I'd made. If I had nominated Horace Mann to run the school board, they would have voted him down. I remember telling a reporter, "We could send them the cure for cancer and the vote would be sixteen to ten, against." This election was going to be their payoff. They fully expected to put a Democrat back in office.

Except for that string of disasters, I had a strong record on which to run. During my first term we'd begun restoring the city. Downtown, the Biltmore Hotel and Union Station were being renovated, and we'd issued low-interest loans and grants to numerous store owners and landlords to upgrade their properties. Rather than tearing down buildings, we'd used historic preservation to create a new business district and were in various stages of recycling thirty buildings. On our waterfront we'd dredged the harbor, repaired warehouses, and started construction of a new marine terminal. In residential neighborhoods we'd painted houses, rebuilt streets and sidewalks, planted hundreds of trees, and provided more than fifteen hundred low-interest loans for homeowners to allow them to remodel their homes. We'd cleaned and opened up parks and senior citizens' centers and community centers. We'd reduced crime by 27 percent and added new cruisers and trucks to the police and fire departments, bought ten new garbage trucks, and began major repairs and modifications to our outdated sewage plant. But most important, we'd begun changing the image of Providence as a decaying city. We'd made it clear we were not going to let it die, and people had noticed. There was no great influx of jobs and people yet, but there was a feeling in the air that something big was stirring. That somebody cared. Me.

My opponent was the chairman of the Democratic Party, Francis Darigan Jr. He was a strong opponent, but because he was in charge of the Democratic caucus, I was able to pin everything that the council had done, or failed to do, on him. Usually the challenger has an advantage because he can attack the incumbent's record, but Darigan was forced to defend the record of the city council. So rather than being completely vulnerable to serious problems like our massive budget deficit, I was able to deflect at least some of the blame onto him for the city council's refusal to work with me. I reminded voters that the council had refused to pass the budget for several months, and then finally did so at the last minute almost without any changes.

At every opportunity I saddled Darigan with the decisions of the city council. One of the issues I raised against him, for example, was the fight I'd had with the council over funding for the police department's mounted patrol. The mounted patrol was completely my idea. The city council saw it only as a budget item, but I saw it as much as a quality-of-life issue. I'd seen how effective mounted cops were at crowd control and traffic duty in other cities, but I also noticed that when these beautiful horses clomped down the street, people stopped to watch them—and they smiled. The equestrian unit had a legitimate police function, but they also added ambiance and humanity to the police department. As I liked to point out, you can't pet a police car. The horses were just part of my vision. At about the same time we began installing old-fashioned gas lamps and sidewalks on Federal Hill to help create an historic atmosphere.

The city council had pencils and erasers rather than a vision of what Providence could become. I fought for my horses and I won—although admittedly we did have a minor scandal. About a year after the 1974 election, two zoo employees who were transferred to the police department to care for these horses were accused of being responsible for the death of a duck, whose body was found in a bison's water trough at the zoo! Actually, this story was more about filling open jobs at the zoo than the mystery of the dead duck. But in response one of the two men insisted, "That duck died of a heart attack!"

This was an actual headline in the *Journal*, DUCK DIED OF HEART

FAILURE. I don't remember the outcome of that case and I never saw the duck coroner's report, although I am quite certain none of our horses ever died of a heart attack.

But with all that we had accomplished, still the most important factor I had going in the election was that people liked me. Voting is more often an emotional choice than an intellectual choice. A voter just feels more comfortable with one candidate than the other one. People knew I was honest, I certainly was entertaining, they liked my family story, and they believed I was doing an acceptable job. If nothing had changed, I would have easily won that election.

But my positive image was almost destroyed and my entire political career was threatened five months before the election when a decade-old rape charge suddenly was published in a national magazine.

This was an old story. In 1966, while I was studying at Marquette University Law School in Milwaukee, Wisconsin, I'd met a woman and she voluntarily came back to my house. We were both single, we had a few drinks, and we eventually had consensual sex. That's what happened. Two or three days later she filed rape charges against me. According to the story she told police, I had lured her to my house under the pretext of giving her a part-time job typing papers, spiked her drink, and then raped her. She claimed that when she had started screaming, I took a gun out of a drawer and threatened to kill her. And when she warned me that she was going to call the police, I had laughed at her. Finally, she managed to get away from me long enough to call a cab, and when it arrived, she'd run outside. I supposedly had followed her and said loud enough for the driver to hear me, "We had a wonderful time and I'll call you. . . . We'll go out to dinner some time."

I was absolutely stunned. None of it was true. I had cooperated completely with the police. I had immediately given them permission to search my house—I hadn't cleaned up my place, so the glasses that had supposedly contained the spiked drink were still sitting on a table—and take with them whatever potential evidence they wanted to examine. And when I was asked to take a lie-detector test, I agreed. If I had been guilty of anything beyond bad judgment, I certainly would have made an effort to get rid of the evidence in my house, and I wouldn't have agreed to take a lie-detector test. Police chemists found nothing unusual in the drink that supposedly had been spiked, certainly nothing that would have made her groggy.

Being accused of a serious crime you didn't commit is frightening and infuriating. But there wasn't much I could do to prove my innocence; she was there and we had sex. At that time of my life, though, I still had faith in the legal system to reach the truth.

Three days after this incident the woman took an overdose of sleeping pills. She did it, she explained years later, because she was under tremendous stress, no one seemed to believe her, and she felt guilty for coming to my house.

Several weeks later we both took lie-detector tests. Much later, the media quoted the person who conducted the tests as saying that she had passed and I had "failed completely on three separate testings." That is not the way I remember the results being reported to me at the time, but obviously I can't prove that. I was very fortunate; I had had a lot of support behind me, including my friends and students at the law school. People who knew me knew I couldn't have committed a terrible crime like that. I didn't tell my parents, though; I just couldn't. Eventually, the district attorney decided that "due to a lack of evidence, prosecution was impossible." No charges were ever filed against me.

When the DA refused to prosecute, the woman's attorney threatened to file a civil suit against me. I decided to settle with this woman for three thousand dollars, much of which went to pay her legal fees. To me, this made perfect sense. I was graduating from law school and about to start my career. I just wanted to put this whole thing behind me as quickly as possible. If I had fought the civil case my legal fees would have been substantially more than three thousand dollars, so I felt the best thing to do was pay the money and go on with my life.

A candidate for the Senate once said that the worst thing that could happen to a politician was to be found in bed with a dead woman or a live man. It is also true that in politics your past is always part of your future. This was the kind of incident that easily could have destroyed my career—and I knew my political opponents would value it.

I did not learn until many years later that during the 1974 campaign, one of my opponents in the Republican primary had received an anonymous telephone call at her home informing her that I had been accused of rape while I was in college and that it looked as though I'd paid my way out of it. Nobody thought that information was particularly valuable; at that time so few people believed I had a chance to win that it didn't seem worth the effort to investigate it. But the election of 1978 was different. I've never seen any evidence that the publication of this story during this campaign was politically motivated, but I have no doubt that it was. I don't believe it was a coincidence that the media was tipped off about this case several months before the election.

I first learned that *The Providence Journal* was investigating this story when a young man doing some landscaping at the home of a *Journal* editor overheard a conversation about this and called a close friend of mine. I never knew how they found out originally, but I learned later that information about the story and documents also had been sent to several local and national television stations, magazines, and newspapers. Only the *Journal* pursued it. Clearly this was an attempt to destroy my campaign, but I understood that the *Journal* had an obligation to go after it. I guess I shouldn't have been surprised—politics is a contact sport—but I wasn't terribly upset because I knew there was nothing to it. The case had gone nowhere: I hadn't been arrested, charged, or indicted; I hadn't even been in a formal courtroom. The story was that there was no story. Except that it would damage my reputation and could have cost me the election.

The *Journal* sent two reporters to Milwaukee, one of them a woman who usually wrote lifestyle features for the women's page. I asked Herb DeSimone to go to Milwaukee to protect my interests. What he learned when he got there was chilling. While interviewing Dean Robert Boden, who had been the dean of the law school while I was attending school there, the female reporter had told him incredible, disgusting, and malicious lies about me in an attempt to get him to respond. Apparently, she also claimed to have information that an assistant law school dean had been involved and had protected me. This reporter was totally incompetent. In her quest for a sensational story she didn't let the truth get in her way. Her accusation was completely false; that administrator hadn't even been at the school at the time this incident took place.

In addition, the woman who had filed the charges refused to be interviewed.

When I learned on Saturday morning that the *Journal* intended to publish a story in its Sunday edition—based primarily on reporting done by this woman—I was furious. I met with two of the *Journal*'s editors and two of their lawyers in my office. I told them flatly that if they printed the story, I would sue them for libel. I pointed out that all the elements necessary to prove it in court existed. The reporter had lied to a source who would testify for me. I was serious; I felt I was fighting for my reputation, as well as my political life.

As I usually did, I got the paper that Saturday night and sat down in a restaurant to read it. And on the front page of that paper, in the middle of the winter, in the space obviously set aside for the story, the paper had printed a large photograph of a sailboat. And later I learned that the female reporter had been briefly suspended.

That wasn't the end of that story. There were lawsuits still to come. Somehow, a muckraking magazine named *New Times* had learned about the incident. It's my belief that the editors of that magazine had been given the story by the *Journal*, because once it was published elsewhere the *Journal* would be free to print it. *New Times* interviewed the woman who accused me, and she reiterated the basics of her story although she did change some of the minor details. In this article the writer inferred that I had made a $3,000 payoff to her to withdraw her criminal charges against me, which absolutely was not true.

The publication of the story in a national magazine was itself a news story, which allowed the *Journal* to report it. The *Journal*'s article included the details of its own investigation and the reasons it had not published the story. The primary Providence distributor of *New Times* normally received four hundred copies of the magazine, but he refused to accept any copies of this issue. Any doubt that the story had political implications was erased when Skip Chernov, who was challenging me for the Republican nomination, bought fourteen hundred copies and sold them in the city for twice the cover price. "The story is devastating," he said, "and I wanted to get it out." Later he added, "He's defeated."

It was imperative that I hit back as hard as possible. I issued a statement in which I pointed out, "The *New Times* article . . . is malicious and scandalous and the very worst example of what a public official must face from those in the media that thrive on scurrilous rumor, caring not what havoc they wreak upon people's lives in the name of profit, and also their political ends as well as the political fortunes of my opponents, who this article was obviously designed to help."

I also released a recording of a statement given by the Milwaukee deputy district attorney, a man I did not know, who had handled the case. "There was no prosecutorial merit to it," he said. "It would have been unfair to prosecute, you don't ruin people's lives by going into the judicial system just for the sake of going into the judicial system. There was no evidence."

As I had promised I would, I quickly filed a libel lawsuit against *New Times*. Many people believed my lawsuit against the magazine was done to provide political cover, that it was more of a strategic move to convince voters that the story wasn't true rather than a real effort to punish *New Times* for libeling me, and those people predicted confidently that after the election—win or lose—I would drop it. Those people didn't know me at all. In fact, I pursued this case for three years. *New Times* went out of business during that period, but I refused to drop the case. My reputation was at stake. We lost the case in the federal district court in New York, but I appealed and that decision was reversed. *New Times* decided to settle. They agreed to pay me a reasonable amount of money (the settlement prohibited disclosing the exact amount) and they signed a letter of apology—that I had written for them. I framed that letter, in which they apologized for the "discomfort" they had caused me, and hung it on my office wall. It hung there for the rest of my years as mayor.

But when this story was published, it was impossible to guess what impact it was going to have on the election. It was a front-page story, and if a bigger story hadn't suddenly appeared to knock it off, it would have remained the major story in the city for several weeks. The *Journal* and all the local TV stations would have continued to search desperately for new angles. But I got very lucky. Three days after the *New Times* story was published I managed to create a story big enough to get that one off the newspaper front pages.

I staged a constitutional coup against the city council and finally gained control of the city government in what has become known in city lore as the Wednesday Night Massacre. The "Gong Show" had scheduled its regular meeting on the night of July 12, 1978. Nobody anticipated anything unusual taking place, since the agenda called for the usual city business to be done. But they didn't properly appreciate that because we had forced the city council to remove two members who had been convicted of felonies, the Democrats held only a one-vote majority. I was sitting in my second-floor office in city hall that night with Ron Glantz as the council began its meeting on the third floor. What absolutely no one outside my office realized was that for the first time in memory, the Democrats were not going to have a majority on the floor. In addition to those two convicted Democrats, a third Democrat was in jail on an income-tax charge, and three more of them were in the hospital. It was an extraordinary opportunity. If we moved very quickly, for the first time since I'd been elected we would have control of the city council.

Many people don't believe this, but politicians are human beings, too! No matter how mature we have to act, every once in a while there is a gleeful moment to which you respond like a little kid. This was one of those moments, a combination of political sophistication as we understood the possibilities and adolescent glee as we anticipated the Democratic reaction. But first we had to pull it off. We sent an aide upstairs to the meeting with a stack of more than thirty nominations to city offices and boards that the council had routinely refused to consider for three years. Among the nominations was Ron Glantz for city solicitor.

As is usually the case in these meetings, no one was paying too much attention. It was all very casual. Basically, all the decisions already had been made by the Democratic leadership, and the meeting was simply going to formalize them. So no one objected at the beginning of the meeting when a Republican councilman proposed that there would be no adjournments or recesses without a roll-call vote. That meant the Democrats couldn't simply end the meeting the moment they realized what was happening. After that proposal was approved, the same councilman stood up and said quite distinctly, "I'd like to put the name of Ronald Glantz before the council to be city solicitor."

I think it took a few seconds for the Democrats to realize what was happening. They probably looked around the room and counted votes. They had nine votes—and we had eleven. And then the room erupted. People started screaming that this was illegal, that we couldn't do this. They asked for an adjournment, they asked for a recess, they complained we didn't have a quorum; they could have asked for the dark side of the moon, it wouldn't have made any difference. There was nothing they could do to stop us. We had eleven votes. This was pure politics. To get to eleven I had made deals with two black city council members who usually voted against me—one of them Lloyd Griffin—to appoint seven black and one Hispanic city workers to leadership positions. These were all qualified people who never would have gotten this opportunity under Democratic leadership.

Lloyd Griffin was a community activist who could deliver votes. I mean that literally: He would hand-deliver absentee ballots. It was well known in Providence that Lloyd had a bit of trouble differentiating between an absentee voter and a fictitious vote. Before he was elected to the city council I had given him a job as a housing inspector, but then I'd had to fire him. Some time later he was arrested for carrying a gun, and I testified in his behalf. When the prosecutor asked me why I fired him, I admitted, "I fired him because he was too honest."

That was not the answer the prosecutor wanted to hear. The judge asked me what I was talking about.

"He was in the newspaper saying that the city of Providence needed to do certain things, and I knew we couldn't do them. I told him that he couldn't get people all riled up expecting us to do things that we couldn't deliver. So I fired him for being honest, Your Honor. If you don't stop it that stuff can spread."

That was Lloyd Griffin, always looking for a deal. I got his vote and in return he got more minority members on city boards than ever before in history.

The nine Democrats stormed angrily out of the room. One of them stood in a hall just off the floor; another stood behind a rail in the gallery, trying to deny us a quorum to proceed; and the rest of them left the building and adjourned to a local pub. The city clerk and her two assistants walked out with them.

We passed thirty appointments that night. In addition to Glantz, we placed our people on the Zoning Board, the Building Board of Review, the Tax Assessment Board, the Civic Center Authority, the Board of Licenses, the Board of Contract and Supply, the Park Commissioners, and the School Board. We put our people on fifteen different city boards. We called them that night and brought them down to city hall and swore them in. Within a few hours we had taken control of the city.

By then I think the first lawsuits had already been filed. My Democratic opponent in the upcoming election, Francis Darigan, was shocked—shocked!—that I "was playing power games at the expense of all Providence citizens." The whole thing was a mess. A few days later both the old and the new license boards met at city hall and actually conducted separate meetings at different ends of the same conference table. One of the applications they fought over came from my primary opponent, Skip Chernov, who was requesting a vendor's permit to sell fourteen hundred copies of *New Times* magazine on the streets. The dueling boards couldn't reach a decision, so he decided to go ahead and sell them.

A week after this coup the city council met again. Before that meeting Ron Glantz traded insults with the Democrats, describing one of them as less than bright: "He thinks a caucus is what's left behind after you shoot a moose." For this meeting one Democrat had even checked himself out of the hospital, rolled onto the floor in a wheelchair, and with the agreement of the two black council members voted to rescind just about all but the minority appointments. The court cases continued into the following January. Eventually it seemed to come down to whether or not standing in the hallway or in the gallery could be considered part of the quorum. The superior court upheld all my appointments. But upon appeal, the Rhode Island Supreme Court overturned that decision, ruling that there had not been a quorum present. In January they finally issued an official decision, but it made no difference. By that time the rape story had become old news.

The Democrats tried to unite for the 1978 campaign, believing it was the only way to beat me. At a fund-raising dinner the secretary of state had proclaimed passionately that this election was about "the survival of the Democratic party in the city of Providence." The issue they focused on was the fact that I had raised taxes three times—once after we revalued property to 100 percent assessment—had run up a large deficit, and had caused the city to come close to losing its AA credit rating. It was all true. In response, I remembered the classic story about the honest young politician whose predecessor in office had handed him three envelopes on inauguration day, telling him to open them only in the worst situations. In the midst of the first crisis the young politician opened the first envelope and read, *Blame your predecessor.* He did that and it worked, he got through that crisis. A year later things were even worse and he opened the second envelope, which read, *Appoint a committee.* Once again he did that and it worked. And finally, another year later he was in a desperate situation and opened the third envelope. He took a deep breath and read, *Prepare three envelopes . . .*

I took that advice. The Democrats did it! The Democrats did it! I blamed the need to raise revenue on the Democrats. The Democrats ran the city council, the Democrats got us into this situation. It was the Democrats, every problem was caused by the Democrats. And then I gave my word that there would not be another tax increase the following year.

I also had the advantage of incumbency. There is no bigger advantage in politics than being the incumbent. I loved the campaign debates because they gave me the opportunity to rattle off statistics that I had memorized, statistics no challenger would know. Once during a debate, for example, my opponent claimed that after being elected he intended to reduce class size in Providence schools. Oh really, I responded, "that's wonderful. We'd like to do that, too. But do you know what it costs to reduce class size by three students?" Of course he didn't. "Three and a half million dollars. You said you weren't going to raise taxes, so where is that money going to come from?"

There are always ways to attack a challenger. When Patrick Kennedy was running for the state House of Representatives for the first time, in the mid-1980s for example, I had him on the radio show I was hosting during my first mayoralty interlude. "You want to represent this district?" I asked him. "Can you name four or five streets in your district?" He couldn't do that. He wasn't prepared to run for the state House, but he still had a huge advantage: His last name. After the election I asked the losing candidate, "When did you know you were going to lose?"

He responded, "When my campaign manager took a picture with Ted Kennedy and John-John on election day."

My last name never gave me any kind of advantage. I had to make up for that by knowing every fact about my city, and I did. During my debate against Darigan, I used every fact I could remember, and he countered with the facts he had learned. It was a typical campaign debate; my people thought I won, his people thought he won.

The week before election day the campaign started to get really nasty. Someone stuck bumper stickers reading GET THE GARLIC OUT OF CITY HALL—VOTE DARIGAN MAYOR on my campaign posters. I truly had no idea where they came from; I knew I didn't have them printed. Darigan was upset about them, too, although he claimed the stickers were distributed with the intent "to destroy the credibility I have earned with the Italo-American community." In other words, reverse bumper-sticker psychology. His campaign hadn't done it, therefore my campaign must have done it in an attempt to fool the Italian North End into thinking that Darigan had done it.

Years later Darigan told a gullible reporter that very early one Sunday morning he happened to be driving past my campaign headquarters in the Fourth Ward and saw Fourth Ward leader Tony Bucci and councilman Charlie Mansolillo walking out of the building carrying a stack of those stickers. He didn't say anything, he claimed, because he wanted to campaign on the issues and assumed that the voters would see through this deception.

I've known Charlie for more than three decades. There is more chance of me cooking pasta on a space shuttle than there is of Charlie participating in something like this. Fortunately, the Italians in that ward did not take the superdouble fake. We never discovered who printed and distributed those posters and, like the occasional graffiti painted on walls that read, DON'T VOTE FOR THE RAPIST it didn't seem to have an effect on the election.

There was also the problem of the questionable absentee ballots. In October, two weeks before the election, a ninety-six-year-old woman reported that she hadn't received the absentee ballot she had requested for the September primary. She didn't bother requesting a ballot for the election, she said, "Because they steal it from me anyway." The post office reported that it refused to deliver one hundred primary ballots to a particular house because the postman knew one hundred people didn't live there. The Democrats had built this political system and nobody really knew if it still existed. I certainly had to be wary of it.

Days before the election *The Providence Journal*, which had reported extensively on the rape charges, announced its support for my reelection. "Mayor Cianci has accomplished things of enduring value to the city of Providence," its editorial read. "He has gone a long way toward bringing the dying downtown back to life, seeing and seizing opportunities where others saw only despair. By taking advantage of every federal dollar, he has started to change not only the face but the economic future of the downtown area."

On election day the polls had the election just about even, "too close to call." I had a good feeling about it, but I always had a good feeling about it. An hour after the polls closed, the city's Fifth Ward, which was considered a Democratic stronghold, reported that I'd won that ward by about one hundred votes. As far as I was concerned, that was a landslide. If Darigan couldn't win that ward, it was over. As soon as those results were posted, he conceded. I won with 56 percent of the vote. A real landslide.

My election four years earlier had been possible because of a split in the Democratic party. But this time both Republicans and Democrats had voted for me. This was no fluke. The Democrats had to accept the fact that they would have to deal with me. Councilman Vincent Cirelli told reporters, "I think the Democratic majority is going to have to bend a little. We'll probably have to give him the appointments he wants."

In private, Cirelli was a little more candid. Charlie Mansolillo remembers that as he walked into the first city council meeting after the election, Cirelli came up to him, hugged him, and paid him what Cirelli obviously considered a great compliment, "Congratulations, Charlie," he said. "Now it's your guys's turn. Now you can steal all you want."

Amazing. Now you can steal all you want? Vinny Cirelli was quite a character. He said whatever was on his mind. Nothing was too outrageous. At one time I had recruited businessman Bruce Sundlun, who was later to become governor but at that time was simply a walking ego, to offer some financial expertise to the city. One day he had a meeting in Washington and was very late leaving for the airport. He told me, "I've been working on this project for you all day. Do me a favor, call the airport and tell them to hold the plane until I get there." Call the airport? I didn't know how to do that, but I figured I would try. While I was on the phone, Cirelli wandered into my office and asked what I was doing.

I told him, "Sundlun's gonna miss his flight back to Washington. He wants me to get them to hold the plane for five minutes."

Cirelli sighed and shook his head. "That's the problem, you're trying to do it the Republican way. That's not gonna work, you have to do it the Democratic way."

I didn't know there was a difference. "What's that?" I asked.

"Call the airport and tell them there's a bomb on the plane."

No thank you, Vinny.

My landslide victory in the election confirmed my reputation as a

Republican to be taken seriously. Governor Ronald Reagan intended to run for the presidency in 1980, and in 1979 he invited me out to California to ask for my support. I had no great passion for Reagan at that time, but I agreed to go out and meet him. What I really intended to do was to try to convince Ford to run again. After my conversation with Reagan I drove down to Palm Springs to see Gerry Ford. He had a house on the Thunderbird Golf Course. It was an absolutely gorgeous day. I walked around to the back of the house and he was completely relaxed, hitting golf balls. "I just went up north," I said. "I saw the actor. He told me he's serious about running."

Ford knew exactly what I meant. He said, "Well, Buddy, I know I have a responsibility, but truthfully, I just don't think I want to slosh around the snow in New Hampshire."

"What are you telling me?"

He swung again. "Well, we've just got to see. I'm not going to shirk any responsibilities . . ." We watched as his ball went flying down the beautiful green fairway on a perfect day for golf, and suddenly, walking through the snow before dawn on a cold New Hampshire morning didn't seem so appealing to me either. I was supposed to fly back to Providence the next morning, but the airlines were on strike. Ford added, "I'm going to Detroit tomorrow. I can give you a lift."

I said, "Mr. President, in all deference, if I want to get stuck anywhere by an airline strike, it ain't going to be downtown Detroit. It's going to be Palm Springs."

My accountant had asked me to call his cousin just to say hello when I was in Palm Springs. This cousin had been a prominent Providence doctor who had known my father. I'd made a million calls just like it. A quick hello, how are you, nice to meet you, good-bye. So I made the call from a phone in the hotel bar. "Your cousin asked me to call you."

The cousin was very polite, and after a few words he asked, "What are you doing for dinner tonight?"

Perhaps the last thing I wanted to do while I was in Palm Springs was have dinner with a gentleman I'd never met. Telling white lies, small lies, is part of the politician's handbook. "Gee, I'd really enjoy that," I said. "But I'm kind of busy tonight."

The cousin sighed. "That's too bad," he replied. "I wanted you to have dinner with me at Frank Sinatra's house tonight."

"Let me see if I can change my plans."

Sinatra's wife, Barbara, answered the door. The day before I'd spent time with the former governor of California, who was likely to be the Republican nominee for president, then I'd visited my friend the former president. But meeting Frank Sinatra was really special. I sat at his bar waiting for the rest of the guests to arrive. I asked the bartender for a martini and as he mixed it for me he said casually, "So you're really the mayor from Providence?"

He seemed impressed by that, and admittedly that surprised me. We were talking about Providence, not New York or San Francisco. "I am," I said proudly.

And he asked, "So do you know Raymond?"

Raymond Patriarca was the head of organized crime in New England. "Know him," I said, "I prosecuted him!" The bartender laughed. I ended up sitting in the kitchen with Sinatra that night, as he cooked Brazilian chicken. We talked about politics. He loved Jack Kennedy, he said, and hated Bobby. For an Italian kid, sitting with Sinatra as he cooked for you in his kitchen was a dream come true.

I had my own campaign decision to make. I was being pressured by the Republican party to run for governor in 1980. The two-term Democratic incumbent, Joe Garrahy, seemed to be vulnerable. Garrahy was a good guy, very affable, he didn't have any real enemies, but he wasn't very exciting, either. Party leaders believed I could get swept into office riding on the winds of change.

During this trip to California I'd met with two of Reagan's top aides: John Sears, who was running Reagan's presidential campaign at that point, and Michael Deaver. Both men wanted me to run, believing I could bring out Republican voters in the Northeast, which obviously would help Reagan. We sat in an office on Wilshire Boulevard and discussed our political differences. Reagan was much too conservative for me or Rhode Island. "You got to understand," I said, "it's tough to take a conservative point of view where I come from." Basically, I was telling him that I was in the church, but I was sitting in a different pew.

I knew that making the run for governor was politically risky for me. People liked Garrahy; he would be favored. And for me, a loss would badly damage my reputation. If I ran, I felt I would be sacrificing my ass for Reagan, and I wanted some protection if I did it. After that meeting I met privately with Sears at the Polo Lounge at the Beverly Hills Hotel. As I sat there I asked, very carefully, "So, John, let's say a guy like me, not me necessarily, but a guy like me runs for governor and loses and wants to get something in consideration for his run. What could a guy like me, not me, though, get, do you think?"

"That's easy," he said. "A guy like that could probably get to be head of the General Services Administration (GSA), or maybe an ambassadorship or a high-level position in the cabinet. Maybe assistant secretary of HUD, those would certainly be some of the options."

That was impressive. "You mean this person could have all that available?"

"Absolutely," Sears said. "That's the range that person would be considered for."

I asked, "Does the governor know this?"

And he responded with the best description of Ronald Reagan that I've ever heard: "That's the greatest part of working for Ronald Reagan. He doesn't have to know."

I knew Garrahy's people were getting very nervous when his chief of staff asked for a private meeting. This meeting was so private we met outside the state, at the Brook Manor Pub in Massachusetts. Attending this meeting were Bill Dugan, the governor's chief of staff, state senate majority leader Rocco Quattrocchi, and my friend Joe DiSanto, then my director of public works and the head of the Republican Party in Providence. Dugan laid it out clearly: "Mayor, you don't want to be governor."

That came as news to me. "Oh? I thought I did. What do you have in mind?"

"We'd like to talk to you about making you a superior court judge. It's a lifetime appointment."

"Can you do that?" They could. Now I was in the fascinating position of weighing political bribes. This for running, that for not running. It appeared that I could be a governor, an ambassador, a judge, or simply remain mayor of the city. None of those options were bad. I gave it a lot of thought. Finally, I met again with Garrahy's people. I told them, "I think we have a deal here." I could see the excitement on their faces. I was the only potential challenger who posed any danger to them. I continued. "I do want to become a judge, but not superior court. Make it Supreme Court and I'm out."

That excitement disappeared. "We don't have the power to do that," they said. Which I knew, of course.

"Then you don't have the power to get me out of the race." Obviously, I had no real interest in being a Supreme Court judge. I would have been bored to death being out of the action.

A career politician is always running, even when he or she is sitting in an office. The life of a politician is always about the next campaign, the next election. And when you look back on a life spent in politics, you remember it as a series of very different campaigns, and you remember each campaign with clarity. When I finally made the decision to run for governor, I believed I could win. And it did occur to me that both presidential candidates in 1980 had been governors, not senators. I would never have made the run simply to help Reagan. Besides, the promise of a job in the Reagan administration only had value if Reagan beat Jimmy Carter, and I certainly couldn't depend on that.

I had purchased a helicopter and I used it to campaign relentlessly throughout the entire state. For a time it seemed to be effective. Every poll showed me quickly closing the gap between me and Garrahy. But gradually things started going very wrong for me. It started during the winter, when I lost support from younger voters by canceling a Who concert at the civic center. This was one of the most popular bands in the world and it was sold out. But at a Who concert in Cincinnati about two weeks before they were scheduled to be in Providence, eleven people had been crushed to death in a riot. That's not going to happen in Providence, I decided, and pressured the Civil Center Authority to cancel it. I wasn't sure we could provide the security that was necessary. The promoter was outraged, pointing out that the band had performed in Buffalo the night following the riot without any problem. "They performed in Cincinnati with eleven deaths and Buffalo with no deaths," I responded. "That means when they perform their average is five and a half deaths." No thank you. The band sued us, but we won. Actually, the band forgot to claim the revenue from the advance ticket sales. Even after we had returned the money to everyone who requested it, we still ended up with about sixty thousand dollars. Canceling this show was a difficult decision for me, because the band was very popular with young people, but it was the right thing to do. And it was just the beginning of all the events that turned sour for me.

This turned out to be the worst campaign of my career. Basically, my running mate was Ronald Reagan, who was very unpopular in Rhode Island, and the Democrats could hardly wait to turn out to vote against him—and while they were in the booth, to vote for the Democratic candidate for governor. Carter won the state by more than ten percentage points.

In the campaign we were completely outmaneuvered by Garrahy. I don't know that I fully appreciated the power of the state until seven members of the city's Department of Public Works were indicted by the attorney general in May for a scam involving no-show jobs. Behind the indictments was the claim that several people involved were connected to the mob, the inference being that I was doing business with them. I didn't know anything about these jobs, although I certainly wasn't surprised. This is the kind of inbred corruption that went on in every major city in America, and there was very little any mayor could do to stop it. But for Garrahy, the timing was beautiful. Two months later two members of the police department were indicted for trying to scare a witness who was going to testify against one of them for passing bad checks. Again, a known member of organized crime was involved. I didn't know any of these people, but I got painted with that brush.

In addition to that, we had a fiscal crisis. Every politician tries desperately to hide any budget deficit before an election, and Ron Glantz assured me we would be able to hide the massive deficit we were facing.

But it leaked. Eventually we had to raise taxes, while at the same time Garrahy was able to return a small amount of money to every resident of the state because the state was running a surplus. Of course they were running a surplus: We sent money from our sales tax and the income taxes Providence residents paid to the state, and rather than returning a percentage of it to the cities, which they should have done, they sent it directly to individuals.

There is no better campaign literature than a check.

The Garrahy campaign was very successful in putting gum on my shoes. And as I later found out, they had some help. My chief of staff, Ron Glantz, had double-crossed me. I have no idea if he had made a deal with the Garrahy campaign, but he provided fiscal information to them that proved devastating to my campaign. In addition to that, just to put my campaign in cement, four days before the election he admitted to a reporter that we would likely have to raise taxes in Providence to close the deficit. Four days before the election. I later learned that after making that comment he went to Yonkers, New York, in Westchester, to apply for the city manager job. It wasn't far enough.

Glantz had no idea I'd found out that he had betrayed me. A night later we were in the helicopter, on our way to a place called Rocky Point, where I was scheduled to speak. I was sitting on one side of him, the pilot was on his other side, when suddenly I grabbed the stick and aimed us straight toward the ground. "Who told the reporters," I screamed at him. "I know it was you, Ronnie. Tell me it was you, you prick."

The pilot was screaming at me. Glantz denied it most of the way down. When we were maybe thirty feet from the water he suddenly felt the need to confess his sins. "Yeah, it was me. I did it." I pulled the chopper up and started cursing at him, telling him what I was going to do to him. He knew me well enough to know he really didn't know what I was capable of doing. My anger overwhelmed my fear, but he was terrified. That may have been the last time I ever spoke with him.

Six years later Glantz was convicted of extortion and perjury and sentenced to eight years in prison. After spending a few months behind bars, he suddenly remembered that I had solicited and been paid several bribes; apparently, he claimed he had received more than $350,000 from contractors doing business with the city and handed it over to me, and he wanted to talk about it in the interest of justice—and perhaps in exchange for a possible reduction in his sentence. The state interviewed him several times, and U.S. Attorney Lincoln Almond made the very unusual announcement that I was going to be indicted. Almond knew he needed other people to corroborate a story told by a man who had already been convicted of extortion and lying on the stand, and I suspect he was very upset when not one other person came forward. There was a good reason for that: There was no other person. I don't know what business Glantz was running from city hall, but it didn't involve me. Almond eventually dropped his investigation of me without an indictment.

For the first time in my life I knew a few weeks before an election that I was going to lose. The polls were devastating. It's difficult to describe my feelings, but it certainly was a mix of confusion, depression, and frustration. I have always been confident, always believed that no matter how difficult the problem, I can find the answer, I can turn things around, but in this situation there was no answer. I could feel it in the crowds. Here's how much I knew I was going to lose. Lloyd Griffin had been collecting absentee ballots for the election. His people would go to hospitals and the homes of elderly people to help them apply for an absentee ballot. Obtaining an absentee ballot required a notary, and Lloyd was simply helping out people. In fact, he was helping them out so much that he had the ballots mailed directly to his headquarters. When the ballots arrived, he might have taken them to the people who requested them. It's possible. I was told that his people were so nice they would actually help people fill out their ballots. And if, for example, they didn't want to vote for Mayor Cianci, they would happily put an "X" right next to his name.

A few weeks prior to the election Lloyd came to see me. I was sitting in my office in a crewneck sweater, he was in a combat jacket. He asked, "Mayor, have you ever seen thirty-two hundred absentee ballots in one place?"

My love of public service may have come from my mother, Esther, shown here holding me when I was one. Her great-grandfather was the Mayor of Benevento, Italy. My four-year-old sister, Carol, later earned two masters degrees.

My father, Vincent, was the first member of our family to graduate from college; he became a doctor. From him I learned to respect everyone—until they gave you a reason not to.

Top Left: I've been performing my entire life. By the time I was eight years old I was singing and telling jokes weekly on WJAR's Kiddie Review.

Top Right: In high school at Moses Brown I played football and wrestled. In the 1958 Rhode Island state wrestling championships I finished second in the heavyweight division.

Bottom: I was drafted in 1966 and reported to Ft. Gordon, Georgia. Eventually I received a direct commission, becoming a First Lieutenant in a Civil Affairs unit.

You know this is the formal swearing-in by my tuxedo. This was on the steps of City Hall. That's my wife, Sheila, behind our daughter, Nicole, holding the family Bible. On my left are Senator Claiborne Pell and Governor Joseph Garrahy.

Above: On January 1, 1975, I was sworn in as Mayor of Providence. We held the ceremony in my home at midnight because I didn't want to give my opposition another second in office. The ceremonial, public swearing-in took place the next morning.

Left: As every politician should do, we celebrated each inauguration as if it was the last one. Here, after being reelected for a third term in 1982, I am dancing the night away with the prettiest girl in the room, my daughter Nicole.

No politician ever walked in more parades or planted more trees or filled more potholes than I did. Here I am with my very popular girlfriend, Wendy Materna, walking in the Columbus Day parade, in the early nineties. That's Colonel Gannon behind us.

For a politician everything is a potential photo op. This is election morning, 1994, with my Cambodian houseman and friend Sovan Chhouk.

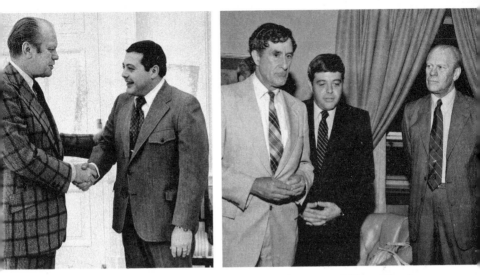

Left: As the young ethnic mayor of a great Northeastern city I was quickly annointed a new face of the Republican party. In early 1975 I was invited to the White House to meet President Gerald Ford, a great man whom I admired, although obviously not for his sartorial splendor.

Right: Two years after being defeated by Jimmy Carter, Gerald Ford returned the favor by coming to Providence to campaign for my reelection. Here we are with Senator John Chafee, who was the recipient of my biggest political mistake—not running for the Senate myself.

Within two years of my election I was a member of the National Steering Committee for President Gerald Ford's reelection campaign. Joining me at the White House *(from left)* Michigan Governor William Millikan, House Minority Leader John Rhodes, myself, campaign manager Rogers Morton, the President, the female head of the committee Patricia Hutar, future Attorney General William French Smith, and Texas Senator John Tower.

During my years in office I was privileged to greet many world leaders. In 1976 I joined Warwick Mayor Gene McAffrey and Rhode Island Governor Phillip Noel to welcome Queen Elizabeth. Two decades later I gave President Bill Clinton the key to the city.

Providence attracts many of the world's most popular journalists, actors, and government officials, including *(top left)* Supreme Court Justice Antonin Scalia *(top right)* James Earl Jones *(left)* Italian President Oscar Scalfaro and *(below)* Walter Cronkite—who came mostly to sample my world famous marinara sauce!

Top: I never lost an election for mayor, but I left office twice. After being convicted of assaulting my ex-wife's lover I resigned from office in 1984. *Left:* I was replaced by my now close friend Joe Paolino Jr., with whom I'm pictured about six years before this happened. *Right:* In 2002 I was indicted on twenty-eight counts and convicted of only one. Here I am leaving the courtroom during my controversial trial.

"Can't say that I have, Lloyd."

"Would you like to see them?"

"Yes, I would, but I'm not going to touch them. The last thing I want is my fingerprints on them."

At that moment one of Lloyd's associates walked into my office carrying a box on each shoulder and put them down on my desk. Lloyd showed them to me, like a poker player displaying a winning hand. Not one of them had a vote for governor filled in. "They can all be yours," he offered.

"Sorry, Lloyd," I said. "It's definitely not a seller's market here." Those votes were not going to make a difference in my campaign; I would have needed a lot more boxes. "But just to show you I'm not a hard-hearted bastard, I'm going to tell you where you can get rid of those ballots." I sent him to see two very white Republican candidates—both of whom beat their Democratic challengers in large measure due to an unusually heavy absentee turnout for them from black and elderly voters.

During another mayoralty election Lloyd was once again collecting ballots. My opponent knew that he bagged ballots. Lloyd called me in a panic telling me he had been tipped off—apparently by a city police officer—that the state police were about to raid his headquarters. He managed to get rid of the ballots, sending them across the state border to Massachusetts, where the state police had no jurisdiction. The police picked up a woman who worked for Lloyd named Carolyn Keys, whom I had appointed to the Civic Center Authority board. She was the best legal absentee ballot woman in the state. The police apparently claimed to have good information that she knew what had happened to these ballots. They took her to the state police barracks and gave her a total body search—outside and in—looking for those ballots. As a result she sued the state and won a very large judgment.

Even knowing I was going to lose this election, I still campaigned hard every single day and night. I didn't know how to do it any differently. The night before the election I was in the helicopter, flying back to Providence after my last campaign appearance. It was dark and cold. As we flew over the city I turned on the radio to listen to the news.

They were predicting a landslide for Garrahy, but they said about me, "He fought right to the end." I was very proud of that.

Garrahy got his landslide. I lost every city and town in the state, I lost every ward in Providence with the exception of Silver Lake, where I'd grown up. It was so bad that years later I suggested we hold a reunion of all the people who voted for me in this election, pointing out, "We can hold it in the telephone booth on Atwells Avenue." When I conceded on election night, I quoted Abraham Lincoln, who had also had been defeated in his political career, and then I said that I wanted to thank the people of Rhode Island for having so much confidence in me that they returned me by such an overwhelming majority to the job as mayor of the city of Providence.

Actually, I wasn't certain I wanted to go back. The thought of representing the United States of America as an ambassador was very intriguing. Not because I intended to solve the world's problems, but rather because I knew Providence had serious financial problems and I wanted to get out of there before everything collapsed. I knew that if I got out in time, if I left for what publicly looked like a promotion—"I took this job reluctantly because my president told me my nation needed me"—I would be able to claim I'd left the city in good shape. So it was time to call in the chips I'd earned. I also knew I couldn't wait, the new Reagan administration was already handing out goodies and the line was going to get very long. Less than two weeks after Reagan's inauguration I went to Washington to see his director of political operations, Lyn Nofziger. Rather than being in the White House, Nofziger's office was in the Old Executive Office Building.

Lynn was in his office with a kid named Lee Atwater, who was lying on a couch with his shoes off. Nofziger didn't have a desk in his office, I remember, just a round table with chairs and couches around it. His office walls were covered with pictures of Richard Nixon. The message was quite clear: If you aren't a Nixon man, don't expect to get anything.

We sat down at the table. He knew why I was there. Instead of wasting time saying hello and chatting a few minutes, he asked me directly, "Why do you want to be an ambassador?"

I told him honestly, "Because I want to learn a second language." Politics was Nofziger's life. He knew the answer to that question better than I did. But eventually we began talking about a range of subjects. I remember Lee Atwater told me, "We're going to give this president something that no president has had since Franklin Roosevelt."

"What's that?"

There was almost a gleam in his eye as he told me, "Control of the federal government."

"Okay, good," I said. "Well, I can be controlled." That's when we got down to the business of politics. He asked me what I wanted and I gave him my list. I wanted jobs for several people and I wanted federal grants for Providence. Specifically, I asked for a federal park, which led to the designation of Roger Williams Park as a national park. At that point a governmental organization called the Heritage Conservation and Recreation Service was still in existence, although it was one of those big government agencies Reagan intended to shut down. Nofziger picked up the phone and said to someone, "How much money is left in there?" It was about $20 million. "Give out whatever is committed then close it down."

That's how Providence got America's smallest national park. Senator Claiborne Pell was instrumental in pushing it through Congress, but it was in Nofziger's office that the funding became a reality. It's only a few square acres in the middle of the city, but we've got our own park ranger in his Smokey the Bear hat. It's also a historic site: The founder of our state, Roger Williams, is buried there.

Eventually, we began talking about my future as an ambassador. Nofziger sent me upstairs, where a fashionably dressed woman and I had a brief discussion about my credentials. My credentials consisted of a law degree, a master's degree, my experience running a city for six years, and the fact that I'd taken a hit for Reagan's campaign. Then she brought me into a small room and pulled down a map of the world. On this map every country was colored either red, yellow, or green. She explained, "Those countries in red go to career ambassadors; they belong to the foreign service and nobody can get them. The countries in yellow are already taken, but all the greens are available." She sighed and looked over the map, frowning occasionally as if she were in a supermarket picking out fruit. Finally, she said, "Costa Rica might be interesting for you."

Costa Rica? I have no idea why she picked it. But why not?

"Okay," she decided. "You'd do fine in Costa Rica."

I went back downstairs and reported this conversation to Nofziger. "She's talking about Costa Rica," I said.

He nodded. Obviously, he liked that idea. What harm could I do to our relations with Costa Rica? "What are you doing this Saturday?" I had no plans, I told him. "Good. Be at Andrews Air Force Base by noon."

That Saturday I flew to Costa Rica on Air Force Two for the inauguration of that country's new president, Luis Alberto Monge Álvarez. It was a wonderful trip. I went through the receiving line and met the new president, his wife, and his teenage daughter. But perhaps the highlight of the trip for me was the fact that I was among the tallest people in the country. I felt like John Wayne; it was the first time in my life I'd been one of the tallest people in the room. But after spending a few days there, I decided that the country wasn't a good fit for me.

That turned out to be a fortuitous decision, as the ambassador who was eventually appointed ended up going to jail for lying to Congress about the existence of military airfields in Nicaragua.

When I got back to city hall, Nofziger's office called to ask me how I liked Costa Rica. "Yeah, it's nice," I said. "But what other countries are available?"

Nofziger turned me over to an aide to Vice President George Bush. This was someone I happened to know because he was friendly with one of the secretaries in my office. This aide suggested I take the Dominican Republic. Two weeks later I was on Air Force Two again, flying to the Dominican Republic for the inauguration of its new president. Traveling with me were Ellsworth Bunker, who had been our ambassador to Vietnam during that war; his wife, Carol Laise, who was the head of the Foreign Service; and Jeb Bush, who I believe was representing the administration.

During the flight Ellsworth Bunker, who had spent his entire career in the State Department, provided tremendous insight for me about diplomacy. He had not wanted to be the ambassador to Vietnam, he told me. The only reason he had accepted the job was because he was in love with Carol, who was the ambassador to Nepal, and our government promised him an airplane so he could fly over the Himalayas to visit her.

I became friends with both of them on that trip, and every Christmas thereafter received a gift of Vermont maple syrup from them. Ellsworth Bunker seemed to know everyone in the Dominican Republic, having served there just after the assassination of the dictator Rafael Trujillo. He introduced me to the popular mayor of Santo Domingo, who eventually ran for president. During his presidential campaign he came to Providence because we had a sizeable Dominican population that was entitled to vote in the election. I also became friendly with him, which turned out to be very fortunate when I went to prison, where I met a number of Dominicans.

Finally, I was offered the job as ambassador to the Dominican Republic. I was already buying suntan lotion by the case when I was told by Nofziger that the nomination had to be approved by the Republican Senator, John Chafee. I didn't believe that would be a problem, but just to make sure I called Chafee's cousin, Frederick Lippitt, whose relatives owned *The Providence Journal* and who had long wanted to run for mayor. I told him that I intended to resign and he should get his oar in the water to replace me. I would support him, I promised, and I wouldn't tell anyone else about my decision. Of course, I had an ulterior motive. John Chafee was his cousin, and naturally I assumed cousin John would want to see Frederick become mayor.

Senator Claiborne Pell, the chairman of the Foreign Relations Committee which would have to vote on my appointment, agreed to support me. He said, "I understand your name might come over here for Senate approval. I want you to know I'll be your advocate."

The only thing standing between me and the beautiful beaches of the Dominican Republic was the esteemed John Chafee. I contacted

Senator Chafee and he asked me to meet at the train station. He was on his way back to Washington.

We sat in the backseat of my limo. I told the driver to get out of the car and then I explained, "I've spoken to the president and Nofziger and they want to give me this appointment. I've heard from Senator Pell and he'll support it. And now I need your support."

This was a very different man from the person who had sat in my dining room four years earlier with tears in his eyes, begging me not to run against him. "I don't know if I can go along with it," he said. "I don't think you're qualified."

You motherfucker, I thought. But I said, "What are you talking about? I stepped aside for you. You probably wouldn't be a senator if I hadn't done that."

"Well, you still have a lot of work to do here in Providence," he said, then added, "You'll be hearing from me."

I couldn't believe this, but there was nothing I could do about it. Two days later John Holmes, the chairman of the Republican Party in Rhode Island, and Richard Richards, the chairman of the national Republican Party, walked into my office. Holmes began, "You've been proposed to be the ambassador to the Dominican Republic, but there are other considerations. Do you have any money?"

Just like that; maybe not those exact words, but certainly that bluntly. I explained that I'd just run an expensive campaign for governor and I still owed about three hundred thousand dollars. That's like a million bucks today.

They got right to the point. "We'd like a hundred-thousand-dollar donation."

I laughed. This was absurd. There was no way I was going to give them money. "Let me ask you, do you want this in cash or will you take a check?" Either way, one of them said, it didn't matter. They were simply asking for a legal donation to the party. "I have to think about this," I finally said. "I've never been extorted before." I let Richards use my helicopter to fly to Newport. The more I thought about this demand, the angrier I became.

By the time Richards returned, I'd made up my mind. "You know what," I told him. "I don't think I'm interested anymore." My appointment disappeared. I certainly never heard from Chafee about this incident again. And just to show how angry I was, I resigned from the Republican Party.

Six

People believe that the last thing a mayor should ever do is raise taxes. That's completely wrong. The first thing a new mayor should do when he takes office is raise taxes. And then blame it on the previous administration.

I inherited a massive deficit from the Doorley administration. The Democratic city council had done a good job hiding it, but I had almost no money to work with. Nearly all of our revenue was committed to salaries, pensions, and other financial obligations.

The state certainly wasn't going to offer any assistance. The Democrats in power did not want to see a Republican mayor succeed. And the financial condition of the state was no better than that of the city. In fact, at one time a state representative named Bernie Gladstone actually introduced a bill to tax sex. His rationale was that we were taxing everything else, so why not pass a law that every time you had sex you had to pay a tax?

It's possible to be creative with issuing bonds and tax credits—for example, we gave tax incentives to the redevelopers of the Biltmore to make that project feasible—but what really requires innovation is dealing with the general operating budget. You have to make real-life, agonizing decisions. For instance, how much salt are you going to buy in preparation for the winter's snowstorms? You can be a hero and not raise taxes because you hope the city is going to get only four inches of snow the following winter, while in reality you know it's more likely it's going to get forty inches of snow—so rather than sufficient salt, you need a good excuse when you can't clear the streets. Or which programs are you going to cut?

The primary sources of revenue for a city are taxes, fees, bonds, and federal and state aid. Under state law at that time we could collect only property taxes. I've always believed a property tax is a regressive tax, and it was never intended to be used for the purposes for which we were forced to use it. No politician wants to raise taxes, but sometimes it's necessary. Certainly the most important thing to do when you have to raise taxes is find another entity to blame it on. After the first year it's tough to blame it on your predecessor, though, so what many mayors do is submit their budget before the state legislature allocates its money. I would submit my very carefully prepared budget to the city council in May, a couple of months before the state legislative session ended. Of course, that budget was basically a work of fiction, and if I needed another $50 million to balance it I would just write in $50 million in state aid. Voilá! I had a balanced budget. I would announce loudly that it would not be necessary to raise taxes.

And then when the state refused to come across with the imaginary money I'd put into my budget, I could blame the state for forcing me to raise taxes.

I got very good at raising taxes, but only because I had a lot of practice. Providence was in desperate financial shape. Several times during my years in office I had to cut the budget, put a freeze on hiring, lay off workers, and reduce services. A mayor can't win the battle of dollars. Trying to satisfy everyone is like being the mayor of Wonderland. I had union members in Providence threatening to strike because I wouldn't give them a substantial raise, and then these same people were turning around and screaming at me for raising their property taxes to pay for their raises. It seemed as if we were always desperate for revenue. When the city council cut the $102 million budget I submitted in 1976 by $6 million, I was forced to announce layoffs—unless the money was restored. As a result we had two thousand people in the streets threatening the city council if they didn't *hike* taxes. When I asked the city council to raise property taxes to meet our obligations in 1991, a bare majority of the city council decided to stop me, offering legislation to freeze taxes. I met with this group and asked them for their help; I wanted them to tell me what services they would cut to balance the budget. I wanted them to identify the fire stations they would close and the number of police officers they would lay off; I asked them how many kids they would add to each class to reduce the number of teachers. Did they want me to cut the heating oil allowance to the elderly or the preschool meals for children? After meeting with this group in my office, we all went upstairs to the council chambers, where we were confronted by one of the most amazing sights I'd ever seen: More than five hundred people had packed the council chambers to demand we raise taxes.

The council voted to freeze taxes. In response, I cut several programs that directly affected several of those council members who voted for it. What better way to make them understand the consequences of their actions? Among those programs I cut was the Downtown Providence Improvement Association, which was run by a council member's husband. He got laid off because she insisted on cutting the budget.

These financial decisions were always complicated. Every mayor at some time is in this same position, and decisions have to be made. I remember being really criticized for paying for books for students in private schools. People complained that they didn't want their tax dollars paying for books for religious schools, pointing out that the Constitution mandates separation of church and state. The argument seems compelling: Why should the city buy books for students who choose to go to private schools? As I responded in a speech, "You don't realize the big picture. If you want the Catholic schools to empty out because they don't have enough money to survive, then those ten thousand kids are going right into the public school system. You know how much your taxes will go up if that happens? We'll have to hire more teachers, buy more books, and build new schools. Paying for those books is the best possible deal for the city."

In addition to taxes, cities can raise revenue by issuing municipal bonds. A municipal bond is simply a long-term loan offering a guaranteed return to investors. What makes them particularly appealing investments is that the interest paid by the issuer is tax exempt. There are basically two types of municipal bonds: general obligation bonds, which are paid for from city funds; and revenue bonds, which are linked to a specific project and paid for by revenue from that project. All the revenue from the project goes into a specific fund that is used to pay off those bonds. For example, to raise the funds we needed to create a new world-class zoo, we issued revenue bonds. Those bonds were paid off by the receipts from the admission price to the zoo. Initially, though, we needed collateral—something of substantial value—to find an underwriter willing to back those bonds. The zoo structures were falling apart, but we did have the animals. Just imagine having to put up our elephants as collateral.

The zoo eventually became the most popular tourist attraction in Providence. But secretly, I've always wondered what would have happened if we were unable to pay off those bonds. How would you like to be the repo man sent by the bank to repossess our elephants? "Step away from that elephant, sir!" I don't think so.

Mayors use the threat of bankruptcy to convince residents to accept higher taxes, but in actuality a city the size of Providence can't go bankrupt. It may have an operational deficit, but its assets will always be substantially more than its liabilities. Providence owns land and property worth billions of dollars, including Roger Williams Park Zoo, buildings, and acres of land; and, most important, the city has the legal right to levy taxes.

The challenge facing me was to find means of raising revenue for the city other than the traditional methods. This was a constant fight in which I won many small battles, but I knew it was a war I could never win. No matter how much money a city raises, it always needs just a little more to operate.

We used a lot of clever financing to provide incentives for people to invest in the city. The federal and state governments want historic properties to be preserved, so they offer tax incentives—as much as 25 percent of the total cost of rehabilitation—to the developer. Fortunately,

Providence is the only major city in America whose entire downtown area is listed on the National Register of Historic Places. So for every dollar invested in renovating, developers were able to get back as much as twenty-five cents in a tax credit. The city is tax exempt—it doesn't pay taxes—so it can't use those tax benefits. Thus, there is no financial reason any municipality should own historic properties if it can be avoided. If a historic building needed to be repaired or renovated, the developer would pay for it. In those days a developer could take an accelerated depreciation on the building, or if the developer couldn't use the tax credits, he could sell them for cash at a discount. The law also allowed owners to donate the facade of a building to the state historic preservation commission. The commission would assess the value and allow the owner to depreciate it and take it as a deduction. For example, if you owned a building in a historic district, say city hall, and it had a beautiful facade, you could apply for a historic easement. That meant you promised the state historic commission that you wouldn't change the facade, which you had no intention of doing anyway, and in return you would get a deduction just as if you'd made a donation to a charity.

We tried to get as many facilities as possible named historic sites. In 1901, for example, the city opened the Providence Sewage Treatment System, at that time the largest chemical precipitation plant ever built, at Fields Point. In the 1980s we tried to get it listed on the National Register of Historic Places as one of the earliest chemical-treated sewage facilities in America.

I sold all the historic street lights in Providence. Now this was a beautiful deal for the city. Providence had replaced its oil lamps on the streets with gas lamps a hundred years earlier, in 1874. At that time the city employed seventy-five lamplighters and paid them a penny and a half per lamp they lit. Eventually, the city was electrified and those gas lamps disappeared. As part of our historical preservation program we installed brick and paving-stone sidewalks and more than 125 aesthetically pleasing replica gas lamps. A local landscape architect, Albert Veri, designed those gas lamps to be accurate down to the position of the screws. As with everything else we tried to do, there were people who objected to our efforts, claiming the streetlights weren't bright enough or there was no reason to replace a "real sidewalk that had been evolving for two hundred years," meaning it was broken and cracked, with a safe brick sidewalk that was described by those same people as "uniform—hokey, folky fake." They forgot safe, well lit, and charming.

It cost us almost nothing to do it. Basically, I used seventy five thousand dollars in federal community development funds, which were supplemented by substantial private donations. The lights eventually cost about twelve hundred dollars each, most of it paid from those private funds. Once they were in place, I sold them and others around the city to Johnson Controls for several million dollars paid upfront. That company got whatever the tax credits were worth, while we leased the lights back and paid rent on them and not one person cared who actually owned the lights. It was nothing more than a paper transaction, but it benefited everyone. A lot of the historic preservation we did was financed through deals just like this one.

We even sold air. The greatest thing any politician can do is get something for nothing. As I learned, it was once believed that the rights of a landowner stretched into the earth and up into the sky. But after World War II a farmer sued the government for trespassing because low-flying planes had scared his chickens, causing them to fly into a wall, killing themselves. The Supreme Court ruled that while air rights had limits, land owners basically controlled as much of the airspace above their property as they could actually use. That decision put a price on air and since then it has become a very valuable commodity. And one thing the city of Providence had was air. I sold the air rights connecting the civic center to the convention center for a couple of million dollars, but the fight I remember most was with Rhode Island Hospital.

Rhode Island Hospital is a tax-exempt facility that erected a large building right across the street from its main unit and connected the two buildings with a skyway. They had plans and permits to do it, but they neglected to make a deal with the city for the air rights between the two buildings. It's nothing, they told me; it's just a way for the staff to move from one building to another. Okay—I called our building inspector and asked to see the plans.

As soon as I looked at the plans, I realized this was considerably more than a passage between buildings. "Those sons of bitches," I said. "They're lying to me." The new building did not have its own power plant. All of its mechanicals—its heating system, electric system, everything—were powered from the original building. All those connections were hidden in the skyway. That skyway was the new building's lifeline.

They had offered twenty-five thousand dollars for the air rights. When I finished laughing, I suggested they start adding zeros to their offer. They actually thought I was kidding. The president of the hospital said, "Mayor, all we want is the air."

I replied—somewhat huffily, I admit—"That air belongs to the people of Providence!"

I refused to give them the permits to connect their buildings until they paid the city a fair price for those now very valuable air rights. There wasn't much they could do; and I had them over a city street. The administrators barraged me with phone calls, and came to see me to plead their case. In the media I was the Scrooge depriving the city of a lifesaving medical facility. Finally, the hospital agreed to pay for those rights, but we had to find a way to appraise its value. The hospital very graciously volunteered to tell me what it was worth.

No thanks, I told them. I hired an appraiser from New York and told the president of the hospital, "I'm going to look at this like General Patton has just landed at the Port of Providence and he is charging right up the street with his tanks and his big trucks, and they can't get through unless they knock down the bridge you built. How much would you charge them if they knocked it down? That's what it's worth."

Eventually they paid us six hundred thousand dollars for those air rights, which in the early 1990s was a considerable amount of money. Later we sold the hospital additional air rights as they connected more buildings in their growing complex.

While other cities were profiting from selling naming rights, I was reluctant to do that. Though we certainly needed the revenue, I believed it was more important for the city to reinforce its image. I insisted that everything we put city monies into bear the name of the city. It had to be named the Providence Something or we weren't going to support it. When developers rebuilt the performing arts center in 1979, for example, they retained its original name, the Ocean State Theatre. I was on the board of directors and I fought against that. I reminded them that the city had put several million dollars into the project while the state hadn't given them a dime. Finally, they submitted a request to the city for an additional three hundred thousand dollars for the seats. I told them I would not give them that money unless the building was renamed the Providence Performing Arts Center. The largest mall in Rhode Island was going to be called the Capital City Mall until I reminded them that the city had provided enormous support to get it built, and it became the Providence Place Mall.

I wanted the city's name on as many facilities as possible. When we began discussing selling the naming rights to the Providence Civic Center, admittedly I was against it—until it was pointed out to me that those rights conceivably were worth several million dollars.

A company would pay millions of dollars to put its name on a building? I wondered how much we could get for the naming rights to our beautiful Providence Sewage Treatment System?

I hadn't realized how much the naming rights were worth in promotional value or as a personal tribute until we were building the ice-skating rink in front of city hall. In 1991 the Providence Foundation had sponsored a five-day program to discuss the revitalization of downtown, or "downcity," as we refer to it in Providence. Among the speakers was an urban architect named Andrés Duany, who had been responsible for several successful projects, among them the development of the planned community of Seaside, Florida. One of the biggest problems we had to overcome was fear. After dark downcity was pretty much deserted; people thought it was dangerous and stayed away. One of Duany's proposals was to build a skating rink that would bring people into the area. The cost was estimated to be somewhere north of $2 million. But it was an essential part of the redevelopment plan.

This was probably the only skating rink I was ever going to build, so I wanted it to be big. Very big. As designed, it was almost fourteen thousand square feet, more than twice the size of the rink at Rockefeller Center. Ice-skating in the winter, an event center in the summer. Our city architects decided it should go right across the street from the Providence Place Mall, which made sense to me. But one night I was in the Old Canteen restaurant on Federal Hill, sitting with Joe Marzilli, who'd founded the place, and I was telling him all about it. "So where's it gonna be?" he asked me.

I said, "I'm gonna put it right across from where the mall is."

He shook his head. "No, it shouldn't be there. Nobody's going to come you put it there." This was a man who lived his whole life in the city. He knew how its heart beat. He began drawing a diagram on the tablecloth. He put the rink right in front of the Biltmore Hotel. "Here," he said flatly. "That's where it goes." It would replace an ugly, sunken bus turnaround.

I looked at his drawing. It made sense. "You know what," I said. "You're right." The next day I called the designer and told him, "Scrap the plans, we're moving the rink."

His answer was direct; "Are you nuts?" He reminded me that several study groups had taken everything into consideration and decided it belonged by the mall.

"It doesn't. It belongs right downtown."

Now all we had to do was raise the money to pay for it. I approached the big banks in the city. Fleet Bank agreed to give us almost eight hundred thousand dollars for the naming rights. I spent ten minutes with the chairman of Nortek, Rick Bready, one of the largest manufacturers and distributors of materials for building and rebuilding homes and businesses, and he wrote a check for $250,000. I approached the Wassermans, a family that had been important contributors to Providence projects for a long time. We were involved in several land-exchange deals with this family, so I introduced them to the concept of "linkage," meaning if you want something from the city, you'd better give something to the city. The result was the Wasserman Family Pavilion at the skating rink. I worked at the budget and no matter what I did, we were still about $150,000 short. I then approached Alan

Shawn Feinstein, a benefactor who had made substantial donations to so many different institutions that his name was on more than a dozen university buildings and elementary schools. I had once told him for enough money, we'd change the name of the city if he wanted to do it.

Alan resisted every attempt I made to get him to contribute to the ice rink. "It isn't really our thing," he insisted. Finally, on the day we were dedicating the rink I called him one final time. The president of Fleet Bank was waiting downstairs on the Zamboni we'd bought; we were going to ride over to the skating rink together. "Alan, this is your last shot," I said. "I'm going over there and I'm going to announce it and your name isn't going to be on it. It's your last chance." He still resisted, so I made the ultimate argument. "Look, I can't name the skating rink after you, but when I look out the window of my office, I see a little park across the street from the Biltmore. How would you like that park named after your mother?" I was desperate. It was the ultimate naming attempt. How could he resist? That's when he made his commitment.

In its first season the Fleet Skating Center attracted more than 150,000 people and became an important part of the downcity revitalization effort. And when Fleet was purchased by the Bank of America, the skating rink officially became the Bank of America City Center.

The largest fee we got for naming rights came from the civic center. Since this fourteen-thousand-seat arena opened in 1972 it had been, simply, the Providence Civic Center. It had cost the city $13 million to build and attracted about a million people a year to a variety of events. Providence College played Big East basketball there; the American Hockey League Providence Bruins played there; major concerts, the circus, and Disney on Ice were held there; and we hosted the biggest World Wrestling Foundation matches in the country at the center. So when we announced that we were putting the naming rights up for sale, we had several serious bidders. In 2001 we reached a ten-year $7 million agreement with Dunkin' Donuts. For that money they bought the right to call the arena the Dunkin' Donuts Center—or, as it has became known all over the country, the Dunk—as well as to put up their signage and sell their products inside and outside.

There were instances when revenue came from very unexpected sources. In the mid-1990s our superintendent of parks, a nice lady named Nancy Derrig, told me our Museum of Natural History owned a rare two-hundred-year-old Hawaiian spear rest, a carved fifteen-and-a-half-inch icon on which whalers would rest their spears, that was actually very valuable. "We have no use for it," she said, then mentioned we could get as much as $250,000 for it. Apparently, a whaling captain had brought it back to Providence almost a century earlier and donated it to the Franklin Society, which eventually gave it to our museum.

A quarter of a million bucks for a spear rest? Are you kidding me? "Go ahead and sell it," I told her.

We consigned it to Sotheby's in New York. Sotheby's put it on the cover of its magazine. Newspapers picked up the story. And a Hawaiian student at Brown called his mother and told her about it. Next thing I knew we got a call from Hawaii informing us that this spear rest was an important part of that state's cultural history, that it was used at funerals, and that therefore we couldn't sell it.

Nancy Derrig told me not to worry about it, that the secretary of the interior had a committee that ruled on this type of dispute and it happened to be meeting the following weekend in Myrtle Beach, South Carolina. I told her to take a lawyer from the city and go down there. "I'll handle it," she said.

Okay, fine, I told her, just call me when you're on your way back.

She called me the following Saturday afternoon. "We took a beating," she said. "It turned out a majority of the committee were indigenous people."

"That's definitely an away game," I agreed. "What'd they do?"

She actually had been in the meeting—and she wasn't precisely sure what had happened. The way I understood it, she said, "When the Hawaiian representatives made their presentation, the took some sandalwood, lit it on fire, and threw it around. Then they started chanting. The next thing I knew the committee reached a unanimous decision against us."

"Well, this requires action!" As far as I was concerned, they were scamming us out of a quarter of a million bucks. I hired Rhode Island's former governor Philip Noel to represent us. A judge he had appointed years earlier issued a restraining order against Sotheby's, prohibiting them from handing our beautiful icon to anyone else. I called Sotheby's to inform them of the court order, and told them I was sending the curator of our Museum of Natural History and two Providence police officers to New York to bring back the spear rest.

Sotheby's representative claimed that he had no right to return it to us. "Is that so?" I said. "Let me explain this to you. I have a court order here ordering you to turn it over to me. Either that icon is coming back with them or you're coming back for disobeying a court order. You can tell the judge whatever you want to tell him. But just so you know, let me tell you what we serve in the Providence police station because you're going to be spending some time there waiting to appear before the judge."

Sotheby's gave us back our magnificent icon. Now the chase was on.

Within a few days two Hawaiians, their lawyer, and Chief Sachem Thomas of the Narragansett Indian tribe walked into my office. Sachem Thomas took me aside and whispered to me, "Mayor, I really don't know about this thing. I just want to talk to you about our effort to get a casino. I need you to give me some help."

Great, the head of a local tribe was looking to preserve a relationship. I told him I didn't know what I was going to do about the gambling issue. I don't think that made him want to help me.

Nancy Derrig was in my office for this meeting. They ignored her, instead asking. "Can we see the icon?" They wanted to pray over it they explained. Why not? It was locked in a safe-deposit box in the bank. Nancy could not go with them, they said, explaining that they were not permitted to pray over the icon while any woman who has a menstrual cycle was in the room.

That was enough for me. I told our attorneys to negotiate the best deal they could get for us. This dispute had chilled the icon's value, so nobody was going to pay $250,000 for it. And besides, if it actually was a religious icon, they did have a legitimate claim on it. Eventually, they returned to my office to conclude the negotiations. We finally agreed that they would pay us $125,000 for it. Okay, it wasn't my quarter of a million, but it was still a nice payday for a spear rest we hadn't even known we owned.

I decided to try to make something positive out of it. "We'll have a Pacific Rim exhibit in the museum," I suggested. "And when we hand it over to you, we'll have a big ceremony to open the exhibit." Finally, we reached our agreement. As they got ready to leave, one of my lawyers asked, "Is that it?"

I said, "Not exactly. There's one more thing I want."

"What's that?"

I paused for effect. "I want Don Ho to come to my next fund-raiser."

Absolutely no one laughed.

I arranged a nice ceremony in the park in front of the museum to hand over the icon and open the Pacific Rim exhibit, with a luncheon to follow. This turned out to be a big deal; there was a lot of media coverage. Admittedly, negotiations hadn't gone exactly as we'd planned, but it was still going to turn out to be a good thing. Suddenly a van pulled up and the Hawaiians piled out. They were dressed in their native costumes, which looked to me like elaborate diapers, and they were carrying spears. I gave a nice speech. They didn't speak. Instead, they lay down on the ground and starting chanting in a language I didn't understand. Then they took the icon, got back in the van, and left. They didn't even stay for lunch.

After they'd left, reporters asked me if I knew what they had been chanting. "I can't be sure," I said. "But I think I might have a good case of slander against these people. I didn't understand what they were saying, but it sounded like they were saying something nasty about me."

Fortunately, though, they did leave a check.

Certainly one means of raising revenue for the city was to bring tourism, conventions, and events into the city. I tried to put Providence back on the destination map. I wanted people to come to my city to shop at the mall, see the exhibits at the museum, visit our world-class zoo, enjoy our parks and recreational facilities, buy tickets to sports events and concerts, and eat in our restaurants. I wanted to change the perception of the city.

Initially, that was almost impossible. The only organization that might have had a reason to come to Providence was the demolition industry. But we lacked the attractions necessary to lure other groups. I remember that when we were trying to convince the citizens of Providence that building the mall was essential for the rehabilitation of the city, we had a particularly raucous meeting. People were passionate about this issue. At one point, the president of a major construction company that certainly would benefit if we built it asked the crowd to consider whether groups would prefer to hold their conventions in Providence or in a city such as Syracuse that offered shopping and events.

Before he could really explain what he was talking about, a man standing nearby interrupted and said, "That depends. How are the hookers in Syracuse?"

After the Fraternal Order of Police came to Providence in 1975, we began to attract a few other small groups. I would always welcome them to the city. There was one group—I don't remember who it was— that was meeting at the Marriott. I was still a kid, and they didn't know me. I came into the ballroom and walked up to the head table. There was a riser next to it and I rested my foot on it—and when I did, the table collapsed. All the wine and glasses, several large bowls, a candelabra, everything went onto the floor. Under the circumstances I did the only thing possible. I walked over to the microphone and told them, "The mayor apologizes for being a little late. He asked me to tell you he'll be here in fifteen minutes." Then I got out of there.

The first significant event we attracted to the city after beginning our rehabilitation program was the U.S. National Figure Skating Championships in 1995. This was particularly important to us because it was broadcast nationally, which allowed us to show off the progress we were making and to begin changing opinions about the city. I had flown to Anchorage, Alaska, four years earlier to convince U.S. Figure Skating to come to Providence. Several of the cities we were competing with had put together flashy presentations. They had laser shows, giveaways, high-tech demonstrations to sell their cities. We had a two-minute video. The only real advantage we had to offer was our location: Providence is close enough to both the New York and Boston metro areas to draw from both of them. Each city had ten minutes to make its proposal to the committee, and it was supposed to be very private. No one was supposed to know what the competition was offering. I handed a bellman twenty dollars and sent him into that room; he returned with a complete report.

When my turn came, I took a long look at the audience and realized these weren't the type of people who were going to be impressed by a laser show. This was a khaki pants, blue blazer crowd, the type of parents who got up at 4 A.M. every morning to drive their kids to skating practice. The legendary comedian George Burns once said that the most important thing for any entertainer—and this certainly is true for any public speaker—is sincerity. And if you can fake that you can get away with anything.

I didn't exactly fake it as much as milk it. I said to them, "I don't know what anyone else has said to you, but I'm here to celebrate America, and Americans like you, who know what it means to sacrifice for your children." I told them how much it would mean to the city of Providence for them to come there and set an example for our kids.

I almost made myself cry, I was so sincere. I didn't bring Lloyd Griffin with me, so I didn't know how the voting was going to go. But as I walked out of the room I noticed a lot of people smiling at me. Finally, their expressions said, someone had recognized and thanked them for what they did all those cold mornings when they got up in the dark and for all that money they spent on skating lessons for their eight-year-old rather than on a newer used car.

And that is how the 1995 National Figure Skating Championships came to Providence. Admittedly, I liked to portray myself as the city's most persuasive ambassador, but there were a lot of people who made these things possible. Generally, to attract an event a city has to put together a competing offer, a package of benefits and services that will lure the convention or event and the dollars it brings to a city. In 1999 we teamed with our Italian partner city to stage the Splendor of Florence in Providence, an exhibition that included artists and restaurants and an exhibit of Renaissance paintings we had borrowed from the

Uffizi Gallery. A Providence native named Joyce Acciaioli, who had spent considerable time in Florence, came to me with the concept of bringing the artisans, craftsmen, art, music, and food from that city to Rhode Island. I thought it was a wonderful idea, and eventually people came from across the country to buy, eat, and spend. We had a home-and-away best restaurant competition with Boston—that we won. We hosted Taste of the Nation, a major food convention. But maybe the most unexpected events we hosted were ESPN's original X Games and NBC's Gravity Games.

Basically, to bring NBC's alternative-sports Gravity Games to Providence for three years, we had to transform our downtown into a dirt-bike racecourse and permit events to take place on our streets that we normally arrested people for doing in public. The revenue and the national TV exposure was very important. The Gravity Games were a made-for-TV event aimed at attracting a young audience that consisted of daredevil sports such as dirt-bike racing, skateboarding, bungee jumping, street luge—sleds on wheels going down our streets—and wakeboarding on our river. Although we'd built skate parks for our kids, skateboarding was prohibited on our streets and sidewalks. Usually, we issued fines to skateboarders and confiscated their boards, but during these Games we handed over the city to them. I didn't consider it selling out, rather buying in. When I was proudly announcing that the Gravity Games were coming to Providence, I held up a beautifully painted skateboard, which until that moment I had always despised, and admitted, "I shouldn't be holding this. It's like . . ." I couldn't think of anything to say, which was a very unusual position for me, but suddenly I added, ". . . marijuana."

From 1999 to 2002, for one week every year the city became a festival for young people. We had the Games, a Festival Village where visitors could try some of these events and get freebies ranging from Corn Nuts to deodorants, and a lot of alternative music. It wasn't really my type of music; for example, Smash Mouth canceled one year but the Sound of Urchin performed. I figured it was called alternative music because it was an alternative to real music.

There were some problems. We literally dug a big hole right in front of the statehouse for the dirt-bike course. On the Friday when the events were scheduled to begin in 1999, we got five inches of rain, turning the course into a huge mud box and putting us in the unusual position of having to dry our mud.

Hosting the Gravity Games turned out to be a great event for Providence. The first year we attracted two hundred thousand people, and each of NBC's five telecasts were watched by more than 2 million viewers. Tell me what that is worth to a city rebuilding its reputation. The second year more than 350,000 people came from seventeen countries, and the final year about 400,000 people made an estimated $28 million impact on the city.

We certainly didn't get every event we bid for, nor did we bid for every event. For example, Donald Trump wanted Providence to host his Miss Teen America pageant. I'd met him at the Vinny Paz–Roberto Duran fight in Atlantic City, and again at Liza Minnelli's wedding. It's probably accurate to describe him as an alternative businessman, because the way he did business was an alternative to anything I'd experienced. To host the pageant, he told me, it would cost Providence $1 million. "Okay," I said. "How many people is it going to bring in? What are we going to get out of it?"

"You're going to get a lot of publicity," he said. "We'll give you ten minutes on national television to talk about the city."

For a million dollars we could buy a million dollars' worth of publicity. We didn't need Trump for that. "Let me ask you this, how much do you get for commercials on the broadcast?"

He equivocated, but said it was somewhere between two hundred thousand and three hundred thousand dollars a minute.

"Okay," I said. "We'll take the ten minutes." I figured I'd go out and sell that time. At two hundred thousand dollars a minute, that was enough for us to make a big profit.

Trump did not think that was a good deal for him, which is why the pageant didn't come to Providence.

We also refused to introduce casino gambling in Providence, although that was a much more complicated decision. There is always the temptation to raise revenue by licensing different forms of gambling. Legalized gambling is that place where money, religion, morality, politics, and practicality collide. Rhode Island established a lottery in 1974 and even that was controversial. Connecticut's Foxwoods casino was less than an hour's drive from Providence. From the day it opened for gaming in the early 1990s, there was a steady stream of traffic going there over our border. Foxwoods had become the largest-grossing casino in the world, and a lot of that money came from Providence. It was a great deal for Connecticut, which was getting tens of millions of dollars a year from the Indians running the place, but a terrible deal for us. We were looking at it, no question about it, and maybe we were even a little envious. Though I personally don't gamble, if allowing casino gambling into Providence would benefit the city, it was my responsibility to at least listen to offers.

Early in 1993 an attorney made an appointment to see me about an "important matter that could greatly benefit the city of Providence." Okay. He sat in my office like the king of the world and said, "I represent one client."

"Oh really? Who's that?"

He said, "He's in the gaming industry."

I didn't know many people in that business. "What's his name?"

"Mr. Steve Wynn."

Mister Steve Wynn. Obviously, I was supposed to be impressed. "I never heard of him," I said, somewhat disingenuously.

He told me Wynn owned this and he owned that and he wanted to talk to me about opening a gambling operation in Providence. "Okay, well, before I agree to that, who can I talk to to check him out? Should I call the bishop? Can I call the president of Brown University? I mean, who can I check with to see what kind of reputation this man has?"

The issue of gambling in Providence had always been associated with organized crime, and we'd been very careful to stay far away from it. So I didn't intend to meet with anyone who was even rumored to be connected to the mob. He suggested I call the president of Brown, Vartan Gregorian. Gregorian was highly complimentary, telling me, "[Wynn is] one of the finest Americans you'll ever meet."

Two weeks later Steve Wynn came to my house for dinner. The

arrangements were made very quietly; we didn't want anyone to know this meeting was taking place. He flew in on his private plane and I had two policemen pick him up at the airport. I didn't know Steve Wynn was legally blind; he walks with a stick. He is an instantly likable person. We had a small group at my house and we talked about his plans. He painted a very beautiful picture of the future. Not just a casino but a resort, a destination. A place for kids. It would bring countless thousands of people to Providence.

By the end of this dinner I loved Steve Wynn. But as I explained to him, "I'm not gonna put my balls on the line for this unless I know it has a reasonable chance of being supported." I proposed that we hire a polling organization to test the waters. He agreed that I'd pick the pollster and he'd pay for it.

The poll turned out all right. About half of the respondents were against it, but compared to other polls I'd seen, I knew that wasn't insurmountable. There are ways of selling anything. That's when I began thinking seriously about the possibility. This is one of the most difficult decisions any mayor has to face. It seems so easy. We already had some forms of gambling: We had a state lottery, we had jai alai, I certainly could make the argument that this was just an extension of those games. And the potential reward was enticing. I was always trying to fill big gaps in our budget, and this seemed like a cure-all. The conversations began to get serious. Wynn sent George Lucas, *Star Wars* George Lucas, to Providence to scout locations. Apparently, Lucas was going to participate in designing this operation. Wynn was serious about building a resort destination, a place for families, but it was all going to be financed by gambling. Lucas finally decided it should be built right where we intended to put the Providence Place Mall. I knew Wynn's casino wasn't going to be located there, but I didn't want to tell him that yet.

Wynn returned to Providence. Instead of having a secret dinner at my house, I reserved a private room at the Blue Grotto Restaurant. Completely coincidentally, the owners of the Newport Grand, a jai alai fronton, as it's called, also happened to be dining there that night. Jai alai is a popular Spanish betting game in which players use lacrosse-type baskets worn over their hands to catch and fling a hard ball against a wall, and spectators bet on the outcome. The owners of the Grand had been trying to get into casino gambling for a long time. When they saw me in the restaurant with Steve Wynn, they immediately called the *Journal*. They knew that if Providence got a casino, they would be out of business, so they had to stop it. Once the media found out I was meeting with Wynn the whole project was in trouble.

After the *Journal* reported this meeting, a "Committee of 22" was formed to prevent casino gambling from coming to Providence. Never mind that people were taking bets on whether or not they would be able to stop it. This was a group of twenty-two community leaders, led by a young councilman named Joshua Fenton, firmly against allowing casino gambling in Providence. It consisted of bank presidents, college presidents, several successful businesspeople, and clergy members. This group issued a scathing statement warning that gambling would exploit "our city's poorest and most vulnerable citizens" and that we would end up "giving our economy over to crime bosses and broken dreams." I didn't necessarily disagree with them, but I wanted to see how it played out. After this publicity, though, it became too controversial. I wasn't about to fight for something I didn't believe in.

So I knew we weren't going to permit a gambling casino to open in Providence, but more important, I also knew that at that moment I was the only person who knew it. I figured maybe I could make something out of that. One Friday night a few weeks later I met secretly with representatives of the tribal council that owned the Foxwoods casino in Connecticut. I explained to them, "Let me be candid with you. We're considering getting into gambling. The way I see it, we're right off Interstate 95, so if we build a casino on the water, we're going to capture all that Massachusetts and Providence business that right now is going to you. Right now you guys are doing what, eight hundred million dollars a year, nine hundred million? Even if we do it wrong we're going to take three hundred million away from you. So I have an idea that can solve everybody's problem. We can be happy and you can be happy. Why don't you pay us not to build a casino in Providence?"

I had their attention. They asked me for a specific proposal. "How long can you keep gambling out of Providence?" That was a compli-cated question. I did not have the ultimate power. Changing the laws to permit casino gambling required state approval. I was a loud voice, but the state legislature was the choir. I certainly could lead the move-ment to stop it, if necessary, but I couldn't guarantee I would be suc-cessful. Of course, I didn't think it was necessary to get into all those details.

Instead, I replied, "It's simple. Every Friday or Saturday you take one of those ponies out there. You put a million dollars in the saddle-bags and that horse runs up to city hall maybe fifty or sixty times a year. That's how long it'll be before we get gambling in Providence."

I didn't think there was anything wrong with this. I still don't. I used to watch the buses leaving Providence to go to Foxwoods, every one of them carrying cash out of the city that we needed desperately. I felt this was a fair compromise. Eventually, the tribal council voted on my proposition—and we lost by a single vote.

That certainly did not end the debate about the virtues of casino gambling. We were also solicited by the chairman and CEO of the Sands Corporation, Sheldon Adelson, at one time the third-richest man in America. I had dinner with him one night at Capriccio restau-rant, during which I explained all the possible benefits and problems in bringing casino gambling to Providence. The CEO of Bally's, Arthur Goldberg, came to the city to try to do a deal. But it was tough; Provi-dence is a conservative city.

Eventually, I had to make a decision about it. The city council de-cided they wanted to put the question to a vote: Should casino gam-bling be allowed in Providence? The same resolution had to be approved by both the city and the state. If it passed, then gambling would be le-gal. But the city council put the question in the form of a resolution, which by law gave me the power to sign it or veto it. I think I had ten days to make a decision, and otherwise it was approved. Truthfully, I had very mixed feelings. I saw all the advantages; money. But I also believed the long-range impact it had on a city was questionable. The city was finally doing well. It was alive, beautiful, serene. We were re-building our city, and the thought of lighting it with flashing neon didn't really appeal to me. It was exactly the opposite of the city I envisioned. I also didn't think it was particularly good for our kids. But still, all that money.

Finally, early on Father's Day morning I set up a table on my front lawn and invited the media to a press conference to announce my decision. Until the night before I really hadn't known what I was going to do. That night had been a perfect Providence evening. The weather was perfect, thousands of people had come into the city for WaterFire, the restaurants were packed, there was music everywhere in the city, and I knew I didn't want to do anything that would upset what we had accomplished.

I actually had written two messages; one if I vetoed it, the other if I signed it. I spent considerable time trying to convince myself to sign it. But I couldn't, I didn't. Instead, I released the veto message: "While the landscape of America, and New England, is increasingly filled with gambling establishments, the increasingly shining reputation that sets Providence aside from other urban centers will not be tarnished by gambling, by taking money out of the pockets of our hardworking residents. . . . Providence has too much promise, is too precious, for us to entertain the idea of letting the chips fall where they may."

I once commented that Rhode Island would get into gambling when it lost money. That's exactly what happened. Eventually, the Newport Grand put in slot machines—and suffered greatly when the economy collapsed. Years later, by the way, Josh Fenton, who had led the fight against Wynn and me, opened a public relations and business consulting firm in Providence—and among his clients is Harrah's Entertainment, which bills itself as "the largest gaming company in the world." Harrah's was vying to build a casino in Rhode Island—and Fenton was their paid consultant.

Another major deal that I wrestled with was bringing the National Football League's New England Patriots to Providence. This was another one of those deals that was supposed to bring millions of dollars in revenue and prestige to the city. When Boston refused to commit to building a new stadium for the Patriots—according to rumors, it was because Massachusetts' pro-life Speaker of the House was feuding with

Patriots owner Bob Kraft's pro-choice wife—Kraft began searching for a new home for the team. Among the cities he approached were Providence and Hartford. It seemed like a good idea at the time. I thought it would be great to have an NFL team in Providence. It would have identified us as a major-league city. Providence would regularly be on display on national television. As I said, "You can have the greatest tool-and-die plant in the world, but it's not going to be written up as news." I really fell for the whole concept—just as Mike Bloomberg in New York and so many other mayors did. In fact, the condominium in which I now live is located right where the forty-yard line would have been. We hired an architectural firm renowned for building stadiums and had an impressive film done. Our plans called for a sixty-nine-thousand-seat stadium. All we had to do was figure out where we would get the several hundred million dollars it would cost to build it. I spent considerable time trying to figure out how to finance it. Eventually, we decided we could issue bonds to pay our share of the costs. This was a serious effort on my part. In January 1997 I flew to New Orleans to meet with Bob Kraft during the Super Bowl.

Though Governor Lincoln Almond also supported the concept, he wasn't as enthusiastic about it as I was. The fact that we disagreed wasn't unusual; what was unusual was the fact that he probably was right. I've never forgotten that at a national mayors' meeting I was sitting next to Chicago's Richard Daley, who had become a good friend, and we were talking about this issue. He said, "Believe me, Buddy, I'd much rather have a season of Monet than a season of the Chicago Bears." It took me a while to understand what he meant, and to agree with him.

If you've ever been to an Italian wedding, you know that at the end of the evening the band starts playing as the people sitting at each table pass a quarter. When the music stops, the person holding the quarter gets to take the floral centerpiece home. As I learned, when you go to an NFL meeting about building a new stadium, sitting around the table will be the commissioner of football, the owner of the team, a representative of the Players Association, the governor of the state, and you.

In that situation you don't want to be holding the quarter when the music stops—because then you get to build a stadium. You don't want that. That's a very dangerous table at which to be sitting, because those people have forgotten more about stadium finances than you or I will ever know. Here's a good rule of thumb: If building a stadium were a profitable venture, the owners of the team wouldn't be begging for someone else to do it.

During that meeting we discussed seating, luxury boxes, personal seat license commitments, parking revenue, every possible avenue of generating income from this stadium. And they all had one thing in common: The city of Providence would get the smallest piece. In addition, the Patriots wanted several more acres of property to build hotels, restaurants, and retail space.

The economic argument against building a stadium is strong. The state would have to establish a public stadium authority to build and own the ballpark. The state would issue about $140 million in bonds, which would be paid back from stadium revenues. Almond insisted on that. But there simply was no serious public support for the stadium. Basically, a football team plays sixteen games a season, half of them at home. And those eight Sundays when the team is playing are wonderful. People are streaming to the stadium, they're tailgating in the parking lot, they're buying team souvenirs. But they're also stopping the city dead. The traffic is so bad that people who are not going to the game stay out of the city. The shops and the restaurants are deserted. When the game is over, you've got to clean the mountain of trash left behind.

And that stadium sits there for 357 additional days. Right in the middle of town. Empty. Occasionally, Pavarotti will come to town and fill it, but figure another twenty events a year; okay, thirty. And for those events the stadium is competing against the performing arts center, the civic center, and our other arts and recreation venues. As I learned, in almost all situations, there is no economic argument that supports building a new stadium. I like Bob Kraft and I respect him. He was always completely honest and honorable in our negotiations. And after it was clear that we weren't going to give him the land he wanted or to pay for his stadium, he told me, "If I just dealt with you and I didn't have to deal with the governor, we would have built that stadium in Providence."

I believe he meant that as a compliment. But as Richard Daley pointed out, it isn't expensive to stage an exhibition of Monet paintings, and it draws tens of thousands of people to the city and generates tremendous revenue, while for most of every year, a stadium sits empty.

Lincoln Almond and I fought publicly about it. I told reporters, "I like to get things done. I like to set a goal and put my team on the field. . . . The governor is more reflective and deliberative than I might be. I like to show results for the people who pay my salary."

I didn't think that was a particularly nasty thing to say about him. But when he responded, "Cianci's plan at the outset didn't even pass the laugh test," I really let loose.

I didn't hold back. "Almond is an indecisive leader and a prisoner of the suburbs, a man ignorant of urban problems and someone who doesn't dream big or take risks to attract projects to the state." As it turned out, though, Almond was right about the stadium, but for the wrong reasons.

Eventually, Bob Kraft built his stadium in the town of Foxborough, Massachusetts, and to his credit he paid for much of it himself. Ironically, this stadium is only a few miles from Providence; it's much closer to us than it is to Boston. It's so close, in fact, that visiting teams and the media normally stay in Providence hotels—and tens of thousands of their fans spend the weekend, and their dollars, in our city.

Rather than build a stadium or a casino, we went for retail. There is nothing that brings people to a location more than a large shopping center with abundant and easily accessible parking. In fact, Providence had been built on retail. The Arcade, the first indoor shopping mall in America, had opened in Providence in 1828. It was three stories tall and looked like a Greek temple, and it attracted people from a wide area. In 1976 the deteriorating shell was designated a National Historic Landmark and we began a substantial renovation program, which was completed in 1980. In its past, downtown Providence had been well served by converging train and streetcar tracks that carried shoppers into the city. But while Providence had a long history as a shopping center, we didn't have much of a present. The nearest major shopping mall was in Warwick. Providence residents typically went to Boston or New York to shop. In the mid-1980s, during my hiatus, Mayor Joe Paolino began laying the groundwork for a major regional mall. Developers wanted to build a modern office building downtown, but after conducting a detailed study, they realized there was no market for an office building but great need for retail shopping. In 1987 Paolino announced plans for what would become the Providence Place shopping mall. When his term ended in 1990, he ran for governor against my friend Bruce Sundlun. I ran for mayor. When Sundlun won, he offered Paolino the position as Director of economic development.

The downturn in the real estate market basically killed the mall. When I resumed office, it wasn't much more than an overly expensive dream. But the concept always made great sense to me. In addition to being a magnet to bring people into the city, it would capture that substantial sales tax revenue that was going to Boston, New York, and Warwick. A report financed by Governor Bruce Sundlun, who supported the project, claimed it would recapture more than $2 billion in purchasing power then going to out-of-state stores, create almost three thousand construction jobs and twenty-eight hundred permanent jobs, and generate as much as $5 million annually in tax receipts for the city.

There was tremendous opposition to it, much of it led by Aram Garabedian, the principal owner of the Warwick Mall. The *Boston Globe* won a Pulitzer Prize for its editorials criticizing the proposal. It was pretty obvious why Boston and Warwick didn't want the competition: A substantial percentage of the revenue a Providence mall generated would come right out of their cash registers. The state had given the Warwick Mall a beautiful property-tax deal. In fact, at one of the countless hearings to discuss this, I wanted to make the point that the Warwick Mall was paying almost nothing in property taxes. I found a business in Providence that was being taxed at the same property-tax rate as the mall. At this meeting State Representative Steven Smith held a photograph of Garabedian's mall, and then held up a photograph of a hairdresser's shop in a depressed neighborhood and said, "You'd think the Warwick Mall would be paying a higher tax rate than a hairdresser's shop on Broad Street."

Financing this mall was probably the most complex development deal I was involved in. At one point Governor Sundlun and I flew to Syracuse to meet with Robert Congel, who had been a partner in the successful development of nineteen malls with the Pyramid Companies of Syracuse, New York. We were there to conduct due diligence, to find out if this guy really had the clout to make this thing happen. When Congel's corporate jet picked us up in Providence, and after landing in Syracuse taxied directly into the hangar, I began to figure, well, maybe he did. We met in Congel's office, which basically overlooked the entire universe. He pressed some buttons and shades covered the floor-to-ceiling windows. He pressed other buttons and screens came down. Congel narrated a slide show that basically showed us how many zillions of dollars the company was worth. If their object was to impress us, they definitely were doing a good job of it.

The slide show ended, the screens retracted into the ceiling, the shades rolled up, and we began discussing the project. As we did, several young executives walked in and out of the room, among them Congel's son and daughter. Finally, Sundlun asked him bluntly, "You've got a nice operation here, and we've met your son and your daughter, but we're talking about substantial investments from both the state and the city, so who takes over if you die?"

Congel didn't even hesitate. He looked Sundlun right in the eyes and said, "We practice dying here once a month." Then he turned to me and asked, "How 'bout you, Mayor, you have any questions?"

"Oh yeah," I said. "How do I meet your daughter and take her out for dinner?"

The Pyramid Companies had agreed to use private financing to construct the mall, but in exchange, both the state and the city had to forfeit more than $200 million in property-tax and sales-tax incentives over a thirty-year period. It wasn't as outrageous as it sounds: This was all new money coming into the city. If the mall wasn't built, we wouldn't see most of it anyway. In addition, the state and the city had to build a four-thousand-car parking garage, at a cost of almost $100

million. We agreed to raise our $47 million with a bond issue. It seemed
as though every time the phone rang or I attended a meeting, the city
ended up receiving less money. But we needed this mall. We agreed to
let the owners of the mall collect about $4.5 million in annual property
taxes from their tenants that otherwise would have gone to the city,
and to use that to pay off some of their debt. I had to continually remind myself what a good deal this was going to be for the city.

This was a very fragile deal that could have fallen apart numerous
times. For example, to satisfy banks that this mall was viable, the developers needed to attract at least one anchor tenant, a store whose presence would draw shoppers from the entire region. The state and city
urged the developers to bring in the recognized "Rolls Royce of retail-
ers," Nordstrom department store. Nordstrom, which is known for its
quality products and service that attract a very upscale clientele, had
done more than $4.5 billion in sales in 1996. By this time, a man named
Daniel Lugosch III had bought out Congel and become the developer
of the mall. He approached Nordstrom and couldn't nail down a commitment. Finally, Governor Sundlun, Joe Paolino, Lugosch, and I met
with Nordstrom executives in Seattle to try to convince them to change
their minds.

The meeting seemed to be going very well until Sundlun began discussing his plan to raise tax revenues. "I suspect you have heard some
troubling things about the state budget, but I want you to know we're
making substantial changes. For example, we're going to be broadening
and expanding our sales tax to include clothing and shoes."

Nordstrom's largest-selling items are clothing and shoes.

It felt as though the room had been struck by an ice age. Sales taxes
raise prices; higher prices hurt sales. I kicked Sundlun under the table
and immediately interjected, "Ah, doesn't the governor have a great
sense of humor? There's no way we would ever put a sales tax on that."

My friend Bruce Sundlun was defeated in the 1994 Democratic primary, and Republican Lincoln Almond, who had campaigned against
the mall, was elected governor. But when Almond took office, he
changed his mind and rather than killing the deal, he insisted we rene-
gotiate it. Eventually, the amount of sales taxes the developer got to

keep was reduced by more than a third. In October 1996 the legislature and the city council finally approved the tax plan. This was the biggest real estate deal in Providence history. Throughout the entire process, each time it looked as if we had a deal I quoted the newly popular cliché "It's not over till the fat lady sings." So to celebrate the deal I actually hired a very robust soprano, dressed as a Wagnerian character, to sing an ode to the success of the mall on the steps of city hall. "The debate is over," I announced. "We're building the mall. The fat lady has sung!"

The $450 million, seven-story Providence Place Mall, which opened in 1999, was the largest development project in Rhode Island history. The mall contains 1.4 million square feet and 160 stores and restaurants. In fact, the mall is so large that a group of eight artists constructed a 750-square foot apartment in an area above the parking garage and nobody noticed them. They brought in more than two tons of construction materials and furnishings and lived in this secret apartment on and off for more than four years. The mall has been a substantial success. Polls taken before it was built reported that a substantial majority was against building it if we had to use public financing, but polls taken after it opened have consistently shown that the public strongly supports it.

The mall has proved to be an important piece in the renovation of Providence. And it really was built on tax policy. The cost to the city was reasonable. We were able to provide incentives for the developers by using the tax revenues the mall would generate, and the city has profited from the additional tax revenue directly attributable to the mall.

There are few things more important for the prosperity of the city, or more difficult for a mayor, than new construction. The days when a builder could simply decide to erect a new building, then do it, are long gone. New construction requires the cooperation of numerous public and private agencies and organizations and it can take years to move an idea from paper to the moment when the first shovel hits the ground. As mayor, I tried to nudge the process as much as possible. For example, in order to convince the Textron Corporation to participate in the renovation of the Biltmore Hotel I agreed to lease them an empty lot next to the hotel for about five grand a year, in case they ever wanted to expand. While the renovated hotel was doing well, there was no interest in expanding. Eventually Nortek, a Fortune 500 company, moved to Providence and wanted to put a building on that lot. When their attorney came to see me I told him, "That shouldn't be a problem."

The phrase, "that shouldn't be a problem," is the definition of optimism—as opposed to reality. I spoke with a top executive at Textron and said, "You've got a lease on the land and you're not using it. I'd like to take it back because we've got a company that wants to develop it."

"That shouldn't be a problem," he said.

We scheduled a meeting between attorneys for Textron and Nortek for the following Saturday. That afternoon the head of Nortek called, "What's going on?" he asked. "I had my lawyers waiting there and they never showed up."

On Monday I spoke with the Textron executive. "You know," he said, "we've made a moral commitment to our law firm that if we ever gave up the land we would give it to them."

Oh really? "Let me explain something," I began. "You're not the redevelopment agency for the city. The only reason you got that land was to expand the hotel." The law firm had decided to build a three-story building on the land.

I invited them to my office to discuss the situation. It was a friendly invitation that they would not dare turn down. Two executives showed up and began telling me about their moral commitment to their law firm. I interrupted, shaking my head. "I told you that you could have the land if you intended to expand the hotel. You're not going to expand the hotel so the city is going to take it back."

When they mentioned their moral obligation one more time I stopped them. "What are you talking about, a moral obligation? You promised something to a law firm that isn't yours to promise. And what do you know about moral obligations? The rumor is you guys own Bell helicopter and have been bribing Iranians to buy them. Moral obligations, come on."

The meeting did not end well. As they stood up one of the executives threatened, "We're walking out this door and never coming back."

"Good luck. And don't come back." As soon as they were gone I called our redevelopment agency and told them to condemn the land, end that lease. Nortek was a tremendous opportunity for the city; it translated into millions of dollars in economic activity, the creation of hundreds of jobs and a beautiful new building. I wasn't about to trade it for a three-story building.

Our redevelopment agency condemned the property. I had to get approval from the city council, and I didn't expect any problem with that. This was too good a deal. But to my surprise the council turned me down, primarily because certain council members believed money was changing hands and none of it was going to end up supporting their projects. I didn't lose these types of deals that often and I was furious. Just livid. As I set at my desk fuming I glanced at the window—and right in front of me was a large vacant lot. It was owned by Fleet Bank and they had told me that if I could find an anchor tenant for that land they would put up a building. And I had the tenant.

It was a beautiful deal. Fleet Bank, Nortek, and Gilbane Properties (a construction company) became partners. I was able to get a federal government grant which allowed the city to loan them the money to build a large parking garage, which was the financial key to making the building economically viable. It gets even better. Coincidently, Textron's law firm also handled Fleet Bank's legal work, and apparently Fleet Bank was a substantially larger client. A Fleet Bank executive called that law firm from my office. "What's this I'm hearing about you building a new building downtown?" he asked. "How about you forget about that and become our partner and take space in our building." The law firm really had no choice; if they wanted to keep the bank as a client they had to agree. The deal was made.

When we were preparing to announce it I received a phone call from a senior vice president at Textron, who wanted me to arrange a meeting with him and the Nortek executive heading this project. "Oh," I said sadly, "I'd be delighted to give you his number but it won't do you any good. He doesn't believe you; you stood him up at the beginning of this deal." The building was originally called the Fleet Center, but after the bank merged with the Bank of America, it became BOA's headquarters in the city.

There was one other tourist attraction we did purchase for the city: the sailing sloop *Providence*. This was a replica of the original *Providence*, which was the first ship commissioned during the Revolutionary War, and eventually was commanded by John Paul Jones. This 110-foot ship was built in 1976 and was forced into dry dock in 1995. I don't quite remember why I felt the city needed a navy, but we organized the Providence Maritime Heritage Foundation to purchase it. It was available for charters, served as a sailing school for teenagers, and even played a leading role in *Pirates of the Caribbean: Dead Man's Chest*. But I will never forget the celebration when it arrived. It was a beautiful day and a large crowd had gathered to welcome the ship. Everything was done very nautically. I was piped aboard, and as we formally took possession of the ship, we fired its cannon.

And instantly every single car alarm within a two-mile radius began blaring.

Seven

A Providence superintendent of parks named James Diamond said once, "Buddy Cianci is at his best when he is in trouble and at his worst when he is at the top." If he was right about that, the election of 1982 showed me at my very best, because it would have been very difficult to be in more trouble.

By the end of my second term I could not accurately be called a lame duck. Instead, I was, as a former Providence politician once said, "Dead, D-e-d, dead." My effort to rebuild the city had cost a lot of money, money the city didn't have, so we went into substantial debt. To deal with that debt we had to raise taxes and cut jobs, which happen to be the two worst things a politician can do.

Not counting assaulting his estranged wife's lover, but that would come later, when I was at the top.

My union problems had begun in 1977 when, as part of an austerity budget, I'd been forced to lay off 182 city workers. Laying off workers may be the most difficult decision a mayor has to make. Not just politically, but as a human being. It isn't numbers, it's people. As the laid-off workers shouted at me, "You're taking the food out of my baby's mouth." Well, I understood that, but sometimes there is no alternative. If you can't meet the payroll, you can't keep people employed. I can't imagine any politician goes home at night feeling he or she has accomplished something when employees have been laid off.

In response to those layoffs, the union ordered a slowdown and then went out on strike. Eventually five hundred tons of garbage were piled up in the streets. That wasn't particularly bad for me politically. It proved I was being tough with the unions to try to save the taxpayers' dollars. The strike lasted sixteen hours, then a top executive of the International Laborers' Union, Arthur Coia, agreed with me to allow an arbitrator to decide if the city could lay off workers. After a hearing, with certain restrictions, the arbitrator found we had a contractual right to do so.

When we renegotiated their contract two years later, we managed to include a seemingly innocuous clause that allowed us to use a private contractor to collect the garbage.

After a $12 million budget deficit had forced me to lay off an additional four hundred city workers in late 1980, we struggled through another eight-week dispute that ended in a general strike by two thousand public service employees, a strike which eventually left the city with mountains of garbage and shut our schools. Strikes are political chess games: Each move makes a big difference in the outcome. But most important is the support of the public. The more a strike inconveniences people, the angrier they become at the strikers. They're not interested in arguing about a raise; they want their garbage picked up, mass transit to be on time, and their kids to go to school. This strike took place soon after I'd lost the gubernatorial election, and it would be fair to say I was not particularly popular in Providence. But when the teachers refused to cross a picket line, seventeen thousand students were forced to stay home, and their parents were furious—at the unions. Eventually, the unions conceded that I had the power to lay off city employees but claimed I had to lay off the most recently hired people. To settle this I agreed to take back eighty employees with seniority and lay off the same number of junior employees, while the union agreed to allow me to lay off about 250 people of my choosing.

In early 1981 the city was faced with the largest budget deficit in its history. I was candid about it; though I placed some of the blame on the Democratic city council for the budget games it had been playing for years, I also admitted, "I've learned from the job every day. And

I've made mistakes over the years. Like everyone makes mistakes." I'd tried to do too much too quickly. To keep the city solvent I had to ask the city council for another significant property-tax increase, which resulted in large demonstrations against me and even the occasional death threat. I wasn't even thinking about running for reelection. I was coming off an election in which I had lost almost every ward in the city, I had the unions strongly allied against me for breaking their strike, and I had taxpayers furious because I'd raised their taxes. I had done a lot of good things for the city, but many of them were still works in progress. Politically, most people believed I was d-e-d.

There was a lot of speculation I wouldn't march in the St. Patrick's Day parade that year. I didn't think I had any choice. If I didn't march, people would believe I was afraid of the reception I would receive. I marched and the reception, at best, was mixed. Usually, I walked about half the parade route and then sat in the reviewing stand, but if I had done that this year the media would have written that I didn't have any guts. I walked every foot of that route and heard all the boos. I do remember marching down Weybosset Street and watching a really angry man cup his hands around his mouth and boo loudly—and then watched happily as his wife slapped him.

As I discovered, there was a significant advantage to being so unpopular: It was very difficult for me to alienate anyone else. While I hadn't made a decision about running for reelection in 1982, I certainly could read the polls, which made it obvious I had very little public support. Joe Paolino, who was then the president of the city council, claims that I told him during an argument over the budget, "I'm out of here. I'm not getting reelected and I'm probably not even going to run." I don't remember saying it that clearly, but it certainly was the way I felt. I wasn't concerned about earning a living; I had my law license, I was well known, I knew I could do well as an attorney. So for the first time in my career I was free to do whatever needed to be done without worrying about the political consequences. As one of many steps I took to reduce expenses, I decided to cut the number of public works employees on sanitation trucks from four per truck to three. Three was plenty. As I reasoned, if you put three men on a spaceship and they could fly it to the moon, why did you need four men on a garbage truck? I believe we were the only city in Rhode Island that hadn't reduced the number of men per truck. And in return for cutting one man, I said, "To show I'm not a hard-hearted bastard, we'll have the citizens bring their garbage out front so you won't have to go around back, and we'll reduce pickups from twice weekly to once a week."

Basically, it started a war.

The head of Local 1033, Joe Virgilio, came to my office and warned, "You can't do this. We're a big union; in fact, there's only one union bigger than us."

I wondered, "Which one is that?"

"The Soviet Union," he said flatly.

Of course I could do it. The number of men on a truck was not mandated by contract, so I had the right to make that change. The department responded over the next few weeks by vandalizing garbage trucks and private vehicles, failing to pick up the garbage, or dumping it in the street; we even caught four men drinking in a bar when they supposedly were working. Finally, I'd really had it. One night I met with Public Works director Joe DiSanto and about forty-five supervisors, foremen and workers from other public service departments. These people had been forced to collect garbage piling up because of the slowdown and they were furious. DiSanto asked me to get rid of the sanitation department. "All of them?" I asked.

He nodded. "All of them."

The next day I fired the entire department, all sixty-five city garbage collectors, and announced that I intended to privatize the department. Under the contract signed in 1979, I pointed out, this was completely legal. Maybe it was a harsh way of handling the situation, but I had the power to do it and I did it. It made national news. Eventually, I even got a phone call from President Reagan congratulating me. This was long before he fired all the air-traffic controllers. He told me it was a bold step to take and that he supported my decision.

But after a few hours even I began to feel that maybe I had been too tough. Early the next morning I went to the truck depot to meet with Virgilio. I wasn't afraid of these guys; I went there all by myself accompanied only by fifty police officers in full riot gear and thirty more officers in reserve. I didn't exactly walk into the lion's den; it was much more dangerous than that. A year earlier I'd faced an estimated three hundred hostile spectators at the city council meeting held to vote on my property-tax increase. "Resign," they had shouted, "resign!" I told Virgilio that his people had no options. Film taken by police the day before showed his men tossing garbage on the street. It had been aired on the news. I said to him, "No labor arbitrator in the world is ever going to rule for you. I've got the legal right to fire every one of your guys, and after seeing that film no one'll ever blame me for doing it." Then I made him the only offer he was going to get. After speaking to him, I went out into the garage and stood on a stage in front of the men I'd fired and I laid it out for them. If they ever make a movie of my life, this is going to be one great scene.

"Let me tell you people something," I began. "The taxpayers of this city have put up with an awful lot. And the job you're doing has left a lot to be desired. That's why I've taken the steps that I have. But that can change; it's up to you, if the work you do today and in the future improves." I offered them their jobs back, but only as temporary employees, subject to being fired at any time. "We're going to allow you to take the trucks out today. If your performance is up to what it should be, you can come back Monday. And the same goes for Tuesday.

"The judges of the performance will be the one hundred and fifty-six thousand people of the city of Providence. Are you going to do the job? Yes or no?"

They looked at me like I was nuts. Nobody said a word. Then Virgilio, who understood that I was throwing his people a lifeline, answered for them, "Yes. Of course they'll do the job." Virgilio put the best possible spin on it, but he knew I had them. For a politician I was in the strongest position possible. In all probability my political career was over. There was nothing they could do to hurt me. I walked out of that garage convinced I had settled a difficult situation. And that day they did pick up the trash. That day.

Naturally, I was feeling pretty good about the resolution of the sanitation strike. But then I had to deal with the workers at the sewer plant, who also had been on strike. The slowdown in the sewer plant had caused waste to back up into some basements. They had to pay something for that. These workers had been given six days a year of guaranteed overtime. That was a little bonus they got, six days extra pay whether or not they worked those days, and believe me, they never worked. "That can no longer happen," I told them. "From now on you get paid only those days you work."

Their representative told me, "Mayor, you get your lawyer and we'll get our lawyer."

"There are no lawyers," I said. "And no six-day guaranteed overtime."

In response, the sixty-seven sewage-plant workers walked off the job. The strike spread quickly through the city. Parks Department employees joined in, and we had to close our parks and the zoo. The sanitation workers struck and mountains of garbage began simmering in the July heat. Eventually eighteen hundred workers went on strike. I'd given the trash collectors an opportunity to keep their jobs and they'd gone on strike. They were finished. I took advantage of that clause in their contract that allowed me to hire private contracters. I made a deal with a Cranston company. They supplied the crews and several trucks, but they didn't have enough equipment. So we sent a group of people into the Public Works lot and they drove out with a dozen or so city-owned trucks. I met with the attorneys representing the Cranston firm. They wanted me to guarantee that their men and trucks would be safe if they picked up the garbage. I told them, "For as long as it's necessary there's going to be a fourth man on every truck. It's going to be a police officer with a shotgun."

With that, I became the first mayor in history to have police officers riding shotgun on garbage trucks.

There was no precedent for this, so there was no possible way of predicting what might happen when those trucks left the parking lot. When I'd first run for mayor, it had never occurred to me that I would be sending out a small army with shotguns to scare strikers. It would be accurate to say I was concerned. Unlike now, the people we were dealing with then were old-time head-breaking union members who saw their jobs disappearing. A lot of them felt they had nothing to lose. We had been getting reports that the union intended to use tractor trailers to block the main intersections, then crash into the trucks. I received a lot of death threats. I sent my wife and my daughter out of town, and armed guards were stationed in front of my house around the clock. I ordered police officers to accompany the trucks to prevent any problems, and I sent along my people to report on any issues.

Of course, very few people knew that the shotguns the cops were carrying weren't loaded. There was no way I was going to send men with loaded shotguns into a potentially explosive environment. The situation was already volatile; I didn't need to take the chance it would get worse.

There was a lot of shouting and cursing. One striking worker drove his pickup truck into a garbage truck, not exactly the brightest move, but the garbage got picked up that day. And the next day. And the day after that. On several occasions striking sanitation workers tried to interfere with pickups, but mostly failed to do so. In one situation two hundred strikers surrounded two trucks and tried to stop the private contractors from doing their job. Police broke up the confrontation before it got out of control.

As it turned out, standing up to the strikers was the best possible thing that could have happened for me. The people of Providence were irate—at the city workers. I told Virgilio, through the newspapers, "This is Waterloo. Either for him or for me, but it's Waterloo. Hopefully for him." For the first time in almost two years my popularity began rising. As the situation got worse, my poll numbers continued to improve. The city was standing up to the strikers, and the people liked it. Rather than succumbing to these people, the city developed a sense of camaraderie, of shared hardship. The strikers had hit the city with their hardest punch, and we took it and just kept going. We were Providence, we were tough Rhode Islanders, and these people were not going to stop us.

After five days Virgilio pleaded with me to take the armed guards off the trucks. In return, he agreed that the union would remove its picket lines from all collection points. In the interest of public safety, I said magnanimously that I'd put my shotguns away. Believe me, I was thrilled to do that.

But as long as people continued to support me I had no interest in negotiating a settlement with the union. I demanded capitulation. The fact that I had put guards on garbage trucks had gotten the attention of the national media. For me, politically it was getting better every day. But for the union this strike was a disaster. One afternoon I was in an office in the Public Works Department when Arthur Coia came in from Washington. There was no reason for me to meet with him, so DiSanto told him I was getting a haircut. DiSanto sat down and began negotiating with him, but I'd told him to give up nothing. As they talked, about one thousand union members were rallying just outside the gates.

A police officer interrupted the meeting to tell Coia that someone needed to speak with him. He came out in the hallway, coincidentally just outside the room in which I was waiting so I overheard their entire conversation.

Coia huddled in that hallway with his son, who was also a union official, Virgilio, and a man who I assumed ran the vending company that had been feeding the strikers gathered outside. The vendor wanted to be paid, so Coia told him to go over to the union hall and they would give him a check for about $1,800. When the vendor left, Coia exploded at his son and Virgilio. "This fucking mayor fucked all of you and you let him. You called this strike without me knowing about it. You didn't call me and now he's got you in a jam. You're losing. I had to pay eighteen hundred bucks for coffee and cigarettes and you guys got a Jew lawyer who's fucking you and you even buy him lunch . . ."

It was hard not to laugh. I could have kept the strike going, but after sixteen days I realized it had to end. The city had figured out how to get along without the strikers, which made the strikers furious. I was afraid somebody was going to get hurt if we didn't end it. Virgilio was desperate and pretty much accepted my terms. The private carter agreed to hire many of the garbage collectors I'd fired, which was a perfect solution. They were off the city payroll and got their jobs back. They were being paid by a private company, so we no longer had to contribute to their pension funds or health care. That company also owned and maintained the trucks, so over the years the city saved a fortune.

The sewage plant workers lost their guaranteed overtime, but I gave them a small hourly wage increase. "The city of Providence ran almost near to normal," I said in announcing the settlement. "I think that's what frustrated the union. I think we won; in fact, I know we won. It was either us or them, and there was no question it couldn't be them. Virgilio, Coia, and the rest of that crowd must understand that they don't run this city. They never will."

For his part, the best Virgilio could say was, "We preserved the dignity of every worker. I'm satisfied with the settlement. When a strike is over it doesn't do any good to say who got the upper hand. . . .

"We had some issues. The issues are resolved. You don't weigh them on a scale. You go into negotiations and see what happens."

Putting supposedly armed guards on garbage trucks attracted international attention. After the strike ended I got a letter and a follow-up phone call from the British embassy inviting me to London for a conference sponsored by private industry. There was a growing movement in England to privatize government services, and they wanted to hear about my experience. When they told me I would stay at Windsor Castle, I accepted the invitation.

I'd actually briefly met Queen Elizabeth several years earlier during her bicentennial visit to the United States. The British embassy had informed me the Queen would be landing in Providence and wanted to discuss security arrangements. When they realized she actually was landing in Warwick, they were too embarrassed to rescind my invitation. So I was standing on the tarmac with Rhode Island governor Phil Noel and the mayor of Warwick when she arrived. They gave us very strict instructions about greeting the Queen: We were not to touch her, but if she extended her hand we were permitted to shake it. If she spoke to us we were to respond to her as "Your Highness," and say "ma'am." "Do you understand?" I was asked. I understand, I said.

As the Queen got off her plane, Phil Noel grabbed her arm and said, "Queen, say hello to the mayor." As the city's welcoming gift to the Queen, Gorham Silver, which was located in Providence, had created a silver plate that was a replica of the silver service on the sailing sloop *Providence.* I didn't realize it at the time, but during the Revolutionary War *Providence* was the first ship to fire on the British navy. Unfortunately, the Queen did know it. And in return, the Queen sent me a picture of herself in a leather frame. She didn't even sign it.

After the ceremony at the airport we went to Newport for a reception. We were sitting on a platform erected in the town center with the mayor of Newport, Humphrey Donnelly III. When he was introduced to the Queen, he smiled and said to her, "You may be Queen Elizabeth II, but I got you beat. I'm Humphrey Donnelly III." The Queen never returned.

Of all the unexpected experiences I had as mayor, being invited to Windsor Castle was arguably the most unique. As I drove there, at least some small part of me refused to believe that Mrs. Cianci's son was staying at Windsor Castle. At the gate I told the guard, "I'm Mayor Cianci from Providence, Rhode Island."

He checked his list and replied, "Yes, Mayor. We've been expecting you!" My speech to the conference eventually was published.

The garbage strike resuscitated my political career. As the *Journal* reported later, after my loss in the 1980 gubernatorial election, "Many people thought the public humiliation was so great that Vincent Cianci, Jr. would have to quit as mayor. Even if he stuck it out it appeared he had almost no chance of winning another election."

The decision we made to privatize sanitation resulted in substantial savings for the city. With the tax increase and the cuts we made, our financial condition improved. By early 1982 we had a million-dollar budget surplus. I was also fortunate enough that almost $3 million in federal grants we had requested finally came through, allowing us to repave streets and sidewalks throughout the city. People could see that we were making progress.

But politically I was in a box. I had missed my opportunity to run for the Senate and I had been defeated in a run for governor. I had no interest in Congress. If I intended to continue in politics, the office of mayor was all that I had. The question was never whether or not I wanted to run, but rather, if I did run, could I win?

Few people gave me much of a chance. Certainly the Democrats weren't going to vote for me. They saw this as their opportunity to finally get rid of me. I spoke with Fred Lippitt, whom I had offered to support for mayor if I became an ambassador, and he made it clear that he intended to run as a Republican in 1982. And even if he had dropped out of the race, it was doubtful I could get anywhere near 50 percent of the vote. There wasn't a single poll that had me much above 42 percent. But it occurred to me that if there were three candidates in the race, I probably wouldn't need more than that. So there really was only one avenue open to me: Run as an Independent and hope that the Democrats and Republicans split their votes enough for me to squeak through with a lot less than a majority. That's what I decided to do.

"Independent" in this case meant running independently of support from the Democratic or Republican parties. It could have just as accurately been called the Buddy Party, because I was the entire party. Running as an Independent meant I had to build my own party from the newly paved streets and sidewalks to the top of the new and renovated buildings in the city. Steve Smith, who was working for Darigan, was friendly with Freddie Passarelli, who was a member of my advance team. They would speak often and Freddie would ask Steve, "What time'd you get home last night?"

The answer was always, "Nine o'clock. How 'bout you?"

Steve would sigh; it was always 2 A.M. or 3 A.M. or even 4 A.M. Every night.

Freddie remembers a night his phone rang at 4 A.M. "Where are you?" I yelled at him.

"I'm in bed," he said. "Why? Where are you?"

"Where do you think I am at four o'clock in the morning? I'm at the farmers' market, campaigning. By the choo-choo trains," meaning the railroad station. Freddie met me there within the hour.

If I was going to win reelection, I would have to do it without the support of the *Journal*. Although the newspaper had endorsed me in my two previous elections for mayor, those days were done. Our love affair was over. There were at least two reasons for that, and as far as I was concerned neither one had anything to do with the good of the city. The *Journal* wanted to buy a parking garage, but they wanted me to use the city's authority to issue $10 million in bonds from the Off Street Parking Authority, which would have allowed them to borrow the money they needed at about half the usual interest rate. I wasn't against it, but it obligated the city to pay off those bonds if the *Journal* failed to do so. I asked their attorney for a copy of their financial statement. He agreed, but instead of providing a financial statement, he gave me a letter telling me that *The Providence Journal* was worth more than $10 million. I knew that, but I wanted to see a legitimate financial statement.

Instead, the paper deposited $10 million in a bank and pledged it to the bond issue. That way they didn't have to disclose their financial condition. But my request infuriated the owners of the paper.

We had a second brawl over the issue of allowing workers at the renovated Biltmore Hotel to unionize. The *Journal* was one of the owners of the newly opened hotel and did not want to pay union wages. I felt the city had been instrumental in getting the hotel deal done and that we had the right to make sure employees had the right to make their own choices. On the radio station owned by the *Journal* I said I thought it was unconscionable that they wouldn't let these people unionize. In response, the *Journal*'s publisher, Mike Metcalf, came into my office waving a sheet of paper. His face was bright red as he said to me, "This is the most antibusiness statement I've ever seen." Then he turned around and walked out of my office.

So I knew I would not receive the support of the *Journal* in this election. I was getting more Independent every day. I knew I had a solid base of supporters to build on, but obviously I had to expand that. This is where the power of the incumbency becomes so important. I was able to make some moves that my opponents couldn't match. The Jewish vote on the East Side was very important, for example, so I did everything possible to appeal to that community. My campaign manager for that election, Bruce Melucci, tells the story that I called him at home one Saturday night to invite him to go the Philharmonic with me. He said, "Mayor, since when do you like classical music?"

"It's not my favorite," I told him.

"So what are you going to the Philharmonic for?"

"I want the Jewish people to see me there."

During this election I was more Jewish than Ben-Gurion—that is, when I wasn't being more Italian than Garibaldi, more Irish than Saint Patrick, or more Cambodian than . . . whoever. I campaigned at every synagogue and went to bar mitzvahs and other events. The city paid for the installation of an elevator for the disabled in the Jewish Community Center, and I personally donated money to the Holocaust Monument. Oy, was I Jewish. More important, at the suggestion of high-profile members of Providence's Jewish community, I invested $2 million from the city's pension fund in Israeli bonds. It was a legitimate investment. The interest rate these bonds were paying wasn't substantially different from what we were getting from traditional investments, and was well within the parameters tolerated by our investment advisers. And in return, I became the first New Englander to receive the Guardian of Peace Award from the State of Israel, and they named a forest after me. Or at least a few trees.

Even more important for me than our Jewish residents or any ethnic group in this election were the unions. In addition to votes, unions provide money and manpower; they do mailings, they get out the vote. The unions weren't strong enough to win an election standing alone, but it was almost impossible to win without their support. Since the strike I'd done as much as possible to heal the rift it had caused with the unions. As the financial crisis eased, in addition to giving raises to the maintenance workers I was able to do the same for the police officers, firefighters, and teachers. But I don't think anyone believed I could convince the city unions to endorse me in this election—except me. If there is a single word that sums up the basis of a successful career, not just in politics but in any business, it's "pragmatism." The essence of politics is not "What did you do to me yesterday?" but rather "What can you do for me today?" It's doing those things that make the most sense rather than allowing your feelings to get in the way. Certainly there was a lot of animosity toward me among union members, and some of them weren't exactly my favorite people. In this situation, though, I needed the unions' support a lot more than they needed to support me.

Several weeks before the election I spoke at the meeting of the Providence Central Labor Council at which it would decide whom to endorse. When I finished my speech, I received polite applause. There certainly was very little enthusiasm for my candidacy. But as I walked out, I ran into one of the union's lawyers. I said to him, "I got to tell you, not endorsing me is the dumbest thing you guys can do."

He smiled at me as if I was crazy and said something like, "Come on, Buddy. After what you did with the shotguns? You're kidding me."

I knew I had one opportunity to get the endorsement. At that time the union had a picket line around the Hospital Trust National Bank. It was a complicated situation. Members of that bank's board of directors were also on the board of the Brown & Sharpe Company. The unions had been on strike against Brown & Sharpe for more than eight years; at that time it was the longest strike in the country. They felt that by convincing people to take their money out of the bank they could force Brown & Sharpe to negotiate a settlement. "You know what kind of assholes you guys are," I continued. "I had to send the cops over to the Hospital Trust Bank this morning so people could get through your picket line. All you're doing is pissing off people. I'll bet you that more people end up putting money in that bank because of those picket lines than taking it out."

He hadn't even slowed down. "So what's your point?"

"I think I got a deal for you. You're trying to get people to take out a hundred thousand, two hundred thousand. How would you like to do a deal where you take three hundred million out of there?"

Now he slowed down. "I'm listening."

As mayor, I controlled the board that administered the city's pension fund. That gave me the power to determine in which bank those funds were deposited. At that time we had about $400 million on deposit at the Hospital Trust National Bank. "The retirement board meets every two weeks," I explained. "It's meeting again next Thursday. If I don't show up and the city finance director doesn't show up, you'll have enough votes to control the board. You got your people standing out there in the rain and the cold and they're not doing you any good. I'm telling you, with one stroke of a pen you could do more than you can with five thousand picket signs."

He stopped and looked right at me. "What do you mean, Mayor?"

"I mean exactly what I said. If I suddenly have another appointment Thursday night, you'll have control of all that money. In two seconds you can move hundreds of millions of dollars out of that bank and move it across the street to Fleet. But in order for someone to do that, you would have to give them the endorsement."

He didn't have the power to make that decision himself. "Give me ten minutes. Let me go talk to some people." He returned a few minutes later, nodding. "We want to do this," he said. "Thursday, we're going to move the money and then when the meeting is over, we'll endorse you."

"Fuck you," I said nicely. "If I walk out of this hotel without your endorsement, you will never get control of that money. I'll give you five more minutes to make a decision."

That night the council endorsed my candidacy.

The *Journal* never figured out what happened. They couldn't figure out how I had managed to get the endorsement of a union that I'd stood up to with shotguns only months earlier. After the union moved the money out of Hospital Trust, I called that bank's president. I was furious, I told him, but there was nothing I could do about it. Those bastards got control of the board from me.

That endorsement was extremely important to me. Even if individual members of the union wouldn't vote for me, at least the union wouldn't be stuffing envelopes for my opponents or driving their voters to the polls.

Once again Frank Darigan was my Democratic opponent, and this time he might well have beaten me if Fred Lippitt hadn't stayed in the race. The theme of my campaign was simply, "I've made mistakes along the way, but look at us now."

In order to minimize my chances, the Rhode Island Board of Elections listed my name at the bottom of the seventh column on the voting machines. It was so far over and down that we joked we should be handing out gift certificates to a chiropractor to the people who twisted their backs voting for me. It was an obvious attempt to destroy even the small chance I had. No one could recall when anyone listed only at the bottom of the last column won an election.

The seventh column had been used so rarely that we weren't even certain the levers would work. Prior to the election we got permission from the court to inspect the voting machines. We sent our mechanic over there and, as we suspected, those levers were very difficult to move. We had to lubricate every voting machine in the city of Providence. And once we knew they would work, we had to teach our voters how to find the Independent line. In 1964, while running for governor, John Chafee had done a television commercial teaching people how to split their vote. He literally showed them how to pull his lever and managed to win the election.

We desperately needed some kind of gimmick to remind people how to vote for me. Coincidently, the Rhode Island lottery had recently created a scratch-off ticket called Lucky 7's, which was being heavily advertised on television. We created a round sticker in which my name was associated with the Lucky 7's, and we pasted them all over the city. But even then I was still trailing in all the polls.

I had done everything possible, but on election day it appeared my political career was finished. Though it was still close, it looked as if Darigan was going to win. The first indication we got that I had a chance came from the East Side. The Jewish vote for me had been substantially stronger than we anticipated; in fact, in this election I got a higher percentage of Jewish votes than Italian votes. The election remained extremely close throughout the entire night, but vote by vote I pulled ahead. Lippitt wasn't really a factor, and it was debatable whether he took more votes from me or from Darigan. But people had reached across the machine and bent down and pushed my lever. When all the votes cast that day were counted, I was ahead by almost eight hundred votes and chiropractor's phones were ringing. That meant that the election would be determined by about six thousand absentee ballots—and that year I had the support of Lloyd Griffin. I'd actually gotten it by default. It was about two weeks before election day that state troopers had raided his campaign headquarters and strip-searched one of his volunteers, going so far as to look inside her vagina for ballots. Griffin believed the Democrats had ordered the raid, so he certainly wasn't going to support Darigan. He knew Lippitt had no chance, which left me. There have been many stories written that I made a deal with Griffin for those votes. It isn't true. I did not know where Griffin got his absentee ballots and I didn't make inquiries. I did not pay Griffin for them or in any other way offer him payment. If you read the stories about me, they often suggest that I was acting dishonestly—while my opponents always seem to be honest, upstanding men. Well, that's not the way politics works. Politics, as I have explained, is the art of making deals. I made my deals—the deal with the union for its votes, for example—and these were exactly the same types of deals made by many of my opponents. Does anyone believe it was simply a matter of bad luck that my name appeared on the bottom of the seventh column on the voting machines? My opponents were never subjected to the same relentless, intensive media coverage that I received.

The myth is that Griffin's absentee ballots enabled me to win this election. As the *Journal* later reported, "Cianci beats Darigan amid charges of mail-ballot abuse by Cianci supporters that are later documented by a three-month *Journal-Bulletin* investigation.... The outcome of the election could have been affected, the investigation shows." In fact, those six thousand absentee ballots were split almost evenly. After all those ballots were counted, I had gained about two hundred votes and won the election by slightly more than one thousand votes. To overcome the lead I had when the polls closed on election day, Darigan would have had to have won almost every single absentee ballot. He didn't.

There were a lot of surprised people in Providence after that election, admittedly including myself. During the campaign, I'd promised several of my supporters that win or lose I was going to meet them for a postelection lunch at Murphy's Delicatessen. When I walked in there the day after the election was certified, I saw a major real estate broker in the city who had supported Darigan sitting with some members of my staff. I shook his hand and said, "It's nice to see you here. I don't want any of my guys giving you a hard time, because we need every-body now, and maybe we can convince you to work with us. In fact, the reason I'm late getting here is that I just got a letter from the University of Tokyo. They want me to recommend a Providence citizen to go over there and teach kamikaze school. They wanted you but I turned them down. I said, 'He can't do it because he's going to be too busy trying to find renters for all those empty offices the city used to rent from him.' "

Another evening I attended some function at a church and as I walked in, I noticed several members of Darigan's campaign staff. I knew most of them. "I thought you guys would have your bags packed by now," I said. They all laughed and began introducing me to the people I didn't know. The brother of one of them was a state representative. I said to him, "Tell the mayor what you want to be when you grow up."

"You know, Mayor, I'd really like to be a Providence police officer."

"I have a much better deal for you than that. I'm going to show you how to make a million dollars." I paused and then added, "All you got to do is bet someone that you'll never be a Providence cop." Truthfully, though, within a few years he would have lost that bet as he ended up on the police force—and became a strong supporter of mine in later elections.

After the election I was unexpectedly invited to a caucus of the Democratic members of the city council. One of the council members said to me, "Mayor Cianci, a lot of people who work for the city did not support you in this election, but they're our people, and we want to make sure there is no retribution against them."

As a conciliatory gesture I stood up and agreed with him. "That's fine," I said. "Just give me their names and addresses and I'll take care of them." The response might actually have been the loudest laugh I ever got in a council gathering.

The toughest election of my career was over, but the toughest fight of my life was about to begin.

It's impossible to ever accurately describe the toll that a political career takes on your personal life. But for a long time my marriage had existed mostly in public. Neither Sheila nor I was particularly happy about our relationship or had any illusions about it. We argued too much, and when we weren't arguing, we barely spoke to each other. If it hadn't been for my political career, we probably would have divorced years earlier. But politics was the family business and Sheila understood the responsibilities of a political wife. Show up, smile, be charming. Whenever there was an event I wanted her to attend, my secretary would call her and tell her about it. Most of the time she was quite good about fulfilling her political obligations. I think we stayed together because we each gained from it. I had a nice family picture to put on my posters and an attractive woman to accompany me to events, and she had the prestige and power of being the mayor's wife. And she loved that and used it.

I have always accepted my responsibilities for the failure of our marriage. I made a lot of mistakes. But neither of us was an innocent party. Whatever I did—and I did do it—I was extremely discreet about it.

My political career had kept us together. We were barely married; in fact, we had almost divorced just before I ran for governor. When it appeared in 1982 that my career was going to end with a loss, I think we both realized that that would also be the end of our marriage. In fact, while we were still living together and attending events during the campaign, we were actually negotiating the terms of our divorce. There wasn't a lot of hostility or rancor—there was never that type of passion between us—but it was a difficult divorce. She kept demanding more and more, knowing that I was in no position to fight her in public. I assumed she was simply trying to protect our daughter. But eventually we reached a settlement: I paid her four hundred thousand dollars, which was a substantial portion of everything I had, and finalized our divorce. As my third term began, I moved into a rented carriage house.

One Saturday night less than two weeks after our divorce had been granted, my life changed completely. I was getting ready to go to an event when I received a completely unexpected phone call from a woman I had worked with years earlier in the attorney general's office. She was the niece of a very close friend of mine, a successful Providence contractor and sometime political adviser named Raymond DeLeo.

I'd met DeLeo several years earlier through my political mentor Herb DeSimone, and since then we'd spent considerable time together. He owned a hotel in Florida, and my wife and daughter had stayed there. I hadn't thought anything of it, have a good time. But what this woman told me absolutely stunned me. Apparently, my former wife and my close friend had been having an affair for several years.

This woman and I met for lunch the next day and she proceeded to tell me an incredible story. She was feuding with her uncle over some property, she explained, and had decided to get even with him by telling me about this open secret in her family. Gradually, the situation became clear. Throughout our entire divorce process DeLeo had been quietly advising my wife. And he didn't want her to get a divorce, because when she did it would be showtime for him. He would have to choose between his wife and his mistress—and if he left his wife, it would cost him millions of dollars. The longer it took for our divorce to be finalized, the more he could delay his decision. No wonder her demands kept growing.

I called my divorce lawyer, I called my campaign manager, I called several other people. Then I went out and cut the ribbon at the opening of a jewelry trade show. At some point I went by my old house, which was being emptied so we could sell it. I found a cardboard box of audiotapes in a cabinet. On several of the tapes Sheila was discussing our relationship—and her affair—with her psychic, and on one tape even mentioned "my assassination." But one seemed to be an audio sex tape made by my wife and DeLeo.

At the house I also found photographs of DeLeo at Disney World with my wife and daughter.

I have a temper, though I'm almost always able to control it. But the more this news sunk in, the angrier I became. It just continued to grow inside me, eventually growing beyond my ability to contain it. I had been lied to by my wife, betrayed by a friend, and ridiculed by both of them. They were laughing at me behind my back. I tried to call DeLeo several times but couldn't reach him. Finally, in the early evening he answered the phone and I asked him to come over to my house. I didn't have any plan, I didn't know what I was going to do, but I wanted him to look me in the eye and admit that he had been having an affair with my wife.

According to reports in the *Journal,* DeLeo claimed that when he arrived at my house my divorce lawyer, Bill McGair; my close friend and Public Works director Joe DiSanto; and a Providence police officer, James Hassett, were there with me and that I was "in a frenzy . . . Cianci was spitting and cursing, and . . . the mayor hurled liquor in his face and screamed death threats at him. DeLeo said the mayor wanted a $500,000 settlement for his affair with Cianci's wife." DeLeo also accused me of slapping him, punching him, and spitting on him; he claimed I tried to push a lit cigarette into his eye, threw an ashtray at him, and tried to hit him over the head with a fireplace log. He said I threatened that if he didn't agree to pay me half a million dollars I would "put a bullet in his head" and destroy his business and his standing in the community. Eventually, an assistant attorney general stated that DeLeo suffered "serious injuries" in an assault she described as "a planned vicious and sustained physical attack" in which I used my "hands and fists, punched him, hit him, slapped him and kicked him repeatedly."

Those claims made me look like Buddy the Ripper. I was a one-man crime wave; if I had done this in a smaller town, I would have personally raised the crime rate 10 percent in that one night.

Believe me, if there is one day in my life I could take back, this would be it. Those few hours changed my life. What actually happened was that I called DeLeo and asked him to come over. He claimed I told him DeSimone was going to be there and we had something to discuss. Maybe I did; I don't remember that. When he arrived, McGair, DiSanto, and Hassett were there. DeSimone came over almost two hours later.

It started as a loud, angry discussion. I accused him of having an affair with my wife and he denied it. That made it even worse. I was furious that he would look me in the eyes and lie to me about his betrayal. Maybe if he had been honest with me, if he had admitted it, had said, "You weren't paying any attention to her so we got together," anything like that, I might have understood it. Maybe.

DeLeo and I were in the living room by ourselves. As the argument got more heated, we both stood up. There was some pushing, shoving,

I made some threats. I really don't remember who threw the first punch. It certainly could have been me, but I just don't remember. It very quickly became a brawl. Eventually, Hassett came into the room and separated us.

We went at it just like that a few times that night. At one point I remember picking up a fireplace log and threatening him, "I should hit you with this thing," but then I threw it down. Admittedly, that was putting him in reasonable apprehension of bodily harm, which under the law is assault with a dangerous weapon. But I never hit him with it, I never swung it at him. I didn't try and burn him, either; instead, I took a half-smoked cigarette out of my mouth and flung it at him. I did throw an ashtray across the room, in his general direction, but I didn't throw it at him. Admittedly, I had a temper, and on occasion I threw things when I got angry. Joe Paolino remembers arguing with me during his first term on the city council. I needed his vote to confirm a director and he wouldn't give it to me. I cursed him out and he protested, "How can you talk to me like that? Someday I could be married to your daughter." I had a gold Dunhill lighter on my desk and when he said that, without thinking, I picked it up and whizzed it past his head. I missed; I always missed, I never intended to hurt anyone. And I missed when I threw the ashtray toward DeLeo.

DeLeo and I went back and forth. We were sitting on couches. I was drinking. "Why did you have an affair with my wife?"

"I didn't."

"Bullshit." What was obvious to me was that while he was sleeping with my soon-to-be ex-wife he also was advising her how to screw me out of almost half a million bucks. I told him I wanted that money back and if I didn't get it I was going to sue him for alienation, and his affair would go public. He was married and had kids, and I was pretty certain that that was the last thing he wanted to have happen. I'm sure I did threaten him if he didn't pay me, but it was more of a playground taunt—"If you don't give me back my lollipop, I'm gonna beat you up"—than anything real. It was the ravings of an angry man who had been betrayed by someone he trusted, and maybe with some alcohol sparking my rage.

We were there about three hours. While he was there I called Sheila and told her that her boyfriend was at my house. She immediately called Herb DeSimone, who rushed over and eventually managed to calm down the situation. DeLeo was never restrained and he never tried to leave. Maybe he was too scared to leave, as he claimed; that's possible. Several years later DeLeo told a *Providence Journal* reporter that I had threatened to shoot him if he hit me back or if he refused to sign an agreement to pay me five hundred thousand dollars, and that Patrolman Hassett was standing nearby with his hand near the gun on his hip.

A few days later I did call and then meet a wealthy friend of Sheila's who I believed had known all about the affair. When she denied it, I got angry. She later claimed that I had threatened her, which made a nice story to go with the whole package.

It took me several days to calm down. Finding out that this affair had been going on behind my back for years, and that people around me had known about it, was absolutely devastating to my ego. Maybe I didn't love my wife, but I despised this betrayal by a friend. And believing that DeLeo had orchestrated my very difficult divorce settlement, costing me a lot of money, added financial injury to insult. In most situations, though, this eventually would have been forgotten, two former friends fighting over a woman. It would not have become a legal case. But this was not most situations. I was the mayor of the city, and my irresponsible actions were a weapon that could be used against me politically.

DeLeo wanted the story to go away. There was no benefit for him to it becoming public; all it could do was destroy his marriage and his reputation. But it was impossible to keep it quiet. Sometime later I got a phone call from a reporter, Brian Rooney, Andy Rooney's son, asking me for a comment. My belief is that my ex-wife wanted it to escalate, that she was afraid something was going to happen to her. Obviously, I didn't say anything to Rooney. But the story had leaked and was becoming public.

I was confident I could handle it. I had always been able to handle any situation, and while I knew my actions were completely wrong, I believed that people would understand my anger. DeLeo and my ex-wife continued to deny their affair, so after I was indicted I hired a private detective to provide proof of their relationship. He watched as my ex-wife put on a wig and met DeLeo at restaurants in Boston and other places. He discovered that Sheila had taken a trip to California with him and they had registered at a hotel in Carmel. A voice specialist I hired confirmed the identity of the voices on the audiotapes I'd found.

Our confrontation had taken place on March 20, 1983. It was more than a month later before it became public. Apparently DeLeo was friendly with the U.S. attorney, the very politically ambitious Lincoln Almond. When Almond heard DeLeo's version of the story, he contacted the head of the state police, Colonel Walter Stone, with whom I had previously feuded. When I was running for governor, I had said publicly that one of my first actions would be to replace Colonel Stone. And now this situation had fallen into his lap. No way he would pass it up. He began an investigation. And that is how a stupid fight between two men escalated into the political version of Ali versus Frazier.

I've always believed that Almond, and the state attorney general Dennis Roberts II, saw this as the perfect crime—for the Democrats. Roberts was just as ambitious as Almond; in fact, his uncle had been the mayor of Providence and governor of Rhode Island. If I was convicted, the Democrats would be able to get rid of me, and it would generate major headlines in which Roberts would be featured as the noble protector of justice. I don't think it would be unfair to suggest that Dennis Roberts II had votes in his eyes when he convened a grand jury to determine if a crime had been committed. But before I was scheduled to testify in front of the grand jury, Ray DeLeo and I reached a settlement in which he agreed he would not press criminal charges and in return I would not sue him for alienation of affections. DeLeo told prosecutors he wouldn't sign a complaint, but Roberts wasn't going to let go of this opportunity so simply. Prosecutors told my lawyer that I didn't have the right to negotiate a private settlement to a criminal case. When DeLeo went before the grand jury, he refused to testify, claiming his Fifth Amendment right against self-incrimination. Only after a judge granted him immunity from prosecution did he reluctantly testify, and when he did, he told the grand jurors that he did not want to press criminal charges against me, that we'd "resolved our personal differences." Only later did I learn that the one significant question DeLeo was never asked in that hearing was whether or not he was having an affair with my ex-wife. According to a confidential memorandum from that hearing, the prosecutor was told not to ask that question of DeLeo. I testified in front of the grand jury in late April. While being questioned, I admitted, "I've been wrong in this marriage in many ways, many many ways, and I've put my personal political career in many ways apart from my family." I said that I didn't blame Sheila for what she did, but rather who she did it with, "a close personal friend. A person who I trusted. It wasn't as if she went off to California and met somebody."

There is a well-known cliché that a prosecutor has so much power that if he wanted to he could indict a ham sandwich. They wanted to indict me. So it wasn't difficult to convince a jury to indict me for two counts of extortion, kidnapping, conspiracy to kidnap, assault with a deadly weapon, and assault and battery. Officer Hassett was also indicted on the kidnapping charges, although how DeLeo who voluntarily came to my house and was free to leave at any time could be kidnapped, I didn't know.

Responding to the indictments, I told the media, "Well, I've had better Tuesdays." After an army of TV stations had set up their cameras in my office to record my statement, I said solemnly, "I've called you here today to announce a dedication date for the new Dudley pool." They all laughed, but when we went live at six o'clock, I said, "This is a personal, domestic matter and, in my opinion, probably should not have gone as far as it has." When possible, I tried to make a joke about it. Speaking at the graduation ceremony at the Rhode Island School of Design a few days after boxer Marvin Hagler had knocked out his opponent in two rounds at the Providence Civic Center I pointed out, "Unfortunately, I've had fights in my living room that lasted longer than that."

But it wasn't funny. It was terribly painful. We all have the capability of being many different people, and we pick and choose carefully which parts of us to expose to the world and which parts to keep deeply hidden. Now the worst part of me was on public display. Though it was obvious I was fighting for my political survival, the stakes were actually considerably higher. There was a real chance I was going to go to prison. Certainly I was guilty of losing my temper. I was guilty of bad judgment and stupidity and even arrogance—but I was not guilty of the serious felonies with which I had been charged.

I pled innocent and went back to work being the mayor of Providence. Among those things I accomplished while fighting these charges was the successful replacement of Parks Superintendent James Diamond, who had claimed I was running an "incompetent, immoral and corrupt" administration. Diamond responded by leading a political effort to hold a recall election, a vote on whether I should be removed from office. In order to force a special election, Diamond's group needed to gather 13,249 signatures within 120 days.

I didn't try to fight back. As I told a reporter, "What have we done wrong in the city? We've had three surpluses in a row. We're running with $1.6 million in increased revenues this year. . . . We're the leading city in America on new construction, 22.8 percent. . . . We've got construction, redevelopment, historic preservation. . . . I don't know what these recallers' complaints are other than political. No one accused me of stealing money from the city. No one accused me of doing my job badly or wrong. . . . I believe it's political."

Like me, many people saw this as a referendum on my fight with DeLeo and were vocal in their support. Eventually, Diamond's group filed more than enough signatures—until my people got a chance to examine their petitions. The sheets were filled with bogus names and signatures. Lists of names had obviously been taken right out of the voting registration book. In one ward everyone whose last name started with a "D" had signed the petition, and there were entire streets in which every single person seemed to have the same signature. By the time the Board of Canvassers had completed its count in April, the recall drive had failed by almost four thousand votes. Clearly, the citizens of Providence had not taken up pens against me. But by that time it didn't matter. I had made my decision.

Though legally this was a criminal case, it had all the elements of a political trial. It was going to generate a great deal of publicity, which certainly could help an ambitious attorney build a political career. In fact, in what was considered somewhat unusual for this type of case, Roberts and three other attorneys appeared personally in court—far more legal power than had been available to me when I was prosecuting mob boss Raymond Patriarca. Just to make sure the trial got enough publicity, Roberts actually invited the woman who had accused me of rape to testify against me—as a character witness.

I intended to go to trial, and I believed I had a strong chance of winning. There was no way I was guilty of the crimes for which I had been indicted. The only real evidence against me was DeLeo's reluctant testimony, and DeLeo did not want to testify. And, in fact, the three other people who had been in my house that night would testify that much of his story wasn't accurate. The wealthy friend of Sheila's living in Palm Beach did not want to return to Providence to testify about the second extortion charge, and signed a sworn statement that I had not threatened her; but even after she produced an affidavit from her doctor explaining she had Crohn's disease, a Florida judge ordered her to testify. The support I'd received the preceding weeks had proved I was still popular in Providence; even if I wasn't acquitted, I knew it would be very hard for a prosecutor to convince twelve residents of the city to unanimously find me guilty of these trumped-up charges.

The trial was eventually assigned to a very strict judge, who made several pretrial rulings against me. In probably the most disappointing ruling, he refused to allow my attorney to question DeLeo about his relationship with my ex-wife. Finally, the judge offered me a deal; if I went to trial and lost, he was going to sentence me to jail; but if I took a plea to some of the charges, I would not go to jail.

That was certainly one of the most difficult decisions I'd ever had to make. These were serious criminal charges; I was facing as long as seventy-one years in prison. If I went to trial, there was the chance I would be convicted and sentenced to prison. If I pled guilty, I would not go to jail, and, according to the way my attorney interpreted the city charter, under certain circumstances there was also a strong argument to be made that I could continue in office. For a few days I was determined to go to trial, but then I accepted the fact that the stakes were just too high and I had to plead guilty. I changed my mind from day to day, practically hour to hour. Most of my friends and aides were urging me to fight. My private investigator was adamant that the prosecutor's case had fallen apart and that we would win in court. I took my ten-year-old daughter, Nicole, to lunch and tried to explain the situation to her. She asked me to plead. Finally, I reached the only sensible decision. As much as I didn't want to turn a domestic fight into a felony, I agreed to plead no contest to assault, a misdemeanor, and assault with a dangerous weapon, a felony. This meant I was pleading guilty to punching, slapping, and kicking DeLeo (the misdemeanor) and jabbing him with a lit cigarette, hitting him with an ashtray, and attacking him with a fireplace log (the felony). That wasn't what had actually happened that night; nobody had burned anybody, nobody had hit anybody with a log or ashtray. But I had no options.

We didn't make a deal with the prosecutor; we took the judge at his word. There was no plea bargain, but after I pled nolo contendere Roberts dropped the four felony charges of kidnapping and extortion. Later the charges against Officer Hassett were also dismissed. Whether I would be able to remain in office was completely the decision of the judge. If he gave me a deferred sentence or placed me on probation, technically I would not have been convicted of a felony and would be able to stay in office. But if he gave me a suspended sentence, I would have to leave office. My future was in the hands of Judge John Bourcier.

Two weeks later I stood before the judge. I had been in many courtrooms in my life and participated in numerous trials, but I'd never stood in that spot before. It was not a comfortable place to be. Roberts had asked for a three-year sentence, in which I would actually serve four months in prison. My attorney asked for a deferred sentence. The sentencing was being televised live. The judge asked me if I had anything to say. Was he kidding? Me miss a chance to speak? I began, "If there is a day in my life I could live over again, it was March 20, 1983. I am sorry for that behavior. I have always been sorry for that behavior because I inflicted harm on a man" who was "my friend for fifteen years . . . I can assure this court from the bottom of my heart that I am sorry, that I made a mistake. I know this type of conduct will never be repeated and never will occur again in my life."

Judge Bourcier responded that he was "convinced the laws of this state have been broken" and while sentencing me to jail "would serve no useful purpose," he did not want me to "walk out of this courtroom without feeling the sting of judicial sanctions for . . . actions committed against another human being." He gave me a five-year suspended sentence on the felony charge and a one-year suspended sentence on the misdemeanor. I took a deep breath. As he had promised, I would not serve time, but at that moment my political career was over.

I walked out of that courtroom and into the rest of my life. At that moment I had nothing: no job, no family, nothing. But as I walked down the street, trailed by a mob of reporters, people kept encouraging me, trying to give me a lift. A young man came up to me and embraced me, thanking me for everything I'd done for the city. As I passed the Fleet Center, which was then under construction, the workers on the top floor stood and cheered.

Ironically, I was not the only one whose life was changed drastically by that confrontation with DeLeo. Many people had predicted a bright political future for Dennis Roberts, but in the next election for attorney general he was defeated by a woman named Arlene Violet, a nun who had left the Sisters of Mercy religious order to run for the job. She was a Republican who fought the Democratic machine and became the first female state attorney general in America. There were a lot of people who believed Robert's prosecution in my case cost him the election—apparently, including Roberts himself.

One evening many months later I was sitting by myself at an East Side restaurant, as I often did, having a quiet dinner. Usually, I'd take that time to catch up on my reading. On this night, though, who should walk into the place but Dennis Roberts. He was by himself, too. By this point Roberts's political career had ended, not only because he had lost the election but because he had been arrested for drunk driving the night before the governor was scheduled to announce his appointment as a judge to the state's superior court. Obviously, the governor couldn't make that appointment. To my surprise, Roberts came over and sat down with me. We were civil with each other. And then he said to me,

"You know, if I hadn't prosecuted you, I'd be a judge and you'd still be mayor."

"You're absolutely correct," I said. It was as close to an admission that he'd made a mistake as I'd ever heard.

Two days after being sentenced, I held what was universally believed to have been my final press conference as mayor. I'd gotten used to being in front of a battery of cameras, but this time it was different. I wasn't fighting my opponents, I wasn't trying to mold public opinion, I wasn't honoring anyone. I was saying good-bye. "I don't know what my plans are going to be," I said. "I don't know if I can practice law. I don't have an office. . . . I don't even have a car."

I couldn't resist. "So if anybody sees me hitchhiking. I wish you would do me the courtesy and pick me up." I added that I would have to be looking for a job, which might be difficult as "I don't think you can find in the want ads any jobs that say, 'Ex-mayors: Please apply here.' "

I hadn't made any notes, but I've never had difficulty finding the right words. "Ronald Reagan tells a story . . . after he completed two successful terms as governor of California . . . of walking outside, getting into the backseat of his car—and there was no one (in the front seat) to drive him. That may happen here."

I concluded by admitting, "I think I might have been a little more discreet over the years. But that's kind of an understatement. But I guess I am who I am and I guess I'll always be what I am." Of course I thanked everyone and reflected on the situation and wished my successor, Joe Paolino, well, saying I would assist him in any way that would be helpful.

It was such a strange day. I walked away from the podium, and the TV crews began breaking down their equipment, turning off their lights. The reporters shouted a few more questions, but I kept going, right out the door. And as I walked down the street, nine and a half years after my upset victory over Joe Doorley, I couldn't help but think about one of those last questions a reporter had shouted at me, "Will you run again?"

The city charter clearly stated that a mayor convicted of a felony while in office could not continue in office. But it was silent on whether that same person could run for a new term and serve if elected. And there was another election scheduled for that November.

Eight

’m no angel. I’ve stretched some boundaries and in the end I served four and a half years in a federal prison with a prison mate who, it was later revealed, disposed of the bodies of people killed by organized crime by dropping them into barrels of acid. Well, compared to him, I guess I was an angel.

Was there corruption in the city of Providence? Absolutely, just as there is corruption in Boston and Philadelphia and every other major city. There were people in the city selling just about anything that wasn’t nailed down, including manhole covers. Who knew there was a market for stolen manhole covers? But was I involved in this corruption? Until the day I go to my grave I will continue to insist that I was not. I admit that I used jobs as currency to get the support I needed, I admit I used campaign money for everything from a personal helicopter to get around the state to paying for dinners, and on occasion I even used my influence to do favors for people. I even admit that I rewarded my friends and supporters and punished my political enemies. But not one time did I put money in my own pocket. I never took a bribe, I never took a payment for a political decision, I never received a kickback. Not one cent, not once.

Were there problems in my administration? Obviously. I made mistakes; I admit it. But I had every agency in creation investigating me, and the most serious offense they could ever come up with was that people lower down in my administration were taking bribes and I should have known about it and stopped them. Here's how thoroughly I was investigated: During one of these wild searches, the postman happened to mention to my driver that the FBI was looking at my mail. They saw a bank statement from Credit Suisse and figured I had a Swiss bank account. Credit Suisse had branches in Providence, but when the FBI learned that my secretary, who handled my money, had a broken leg, they accused her of breaking it while skiing in Switzerland. That would have been accurate only if Switzerland were in New Hampshire, where she'd suffered her skiing accident, she told them.

The fact is that no political system can prevent corruption. People don't want to believe it, but it's ingrained in the system. When I became mayor, the Democrats had been in power so long that bribes were considered part of the cost of doing business. That was what Cirelli was referring to when he told Charlie Mansolillo after my reelection that it was now acceptable for us to steal. That was Rhode Island politics. There were opportunities every day; if I was on the take, it would have been easy. For example, I got a call one day from former Mayor Joe Doorley's cousin, Bobby Doorley, who asked me to meet him at the Brown University Faculty Club. It turned out that the Miller beer distributor in Providence was upset that only Budweiser was sold at events inside the civic center. I had nothing to do with that, but it wasn't hard to understand what was going on. The president of the city council was working for Anheuser-Busch, so what beer was going to be sold there? We met with the distributor, who asked me point blank, "How much is it going to cost me to get my beer in there?"

If I were looking for a payday, this is the type of offer I would have welcomed. "It's not going to cost you anything," I said. And we opened up the facility to his product. But, proving that no good turn gets appreciated, I saw the distributor a few months later and said, "I hope you're satisfied. You got your beer in there."

"Yeah, maybe," he said, "but they really gave me shitty locations."

Believe me, the money was there if I had wanted to take it. And some members of my administration did take it, and for that I was found responsible and went to prison. But after I was released from prison I was sitting at a restaurant talking to someone who told me he also had been in trouble. He had been indicted with mob boss Raymond Patriarca for scamming union contracts. "When I got indicted," he explained, "I had to go see the old man. I told him, 'We need a million dollars for the trial.' " 'A million dollars,' he said. 'What for?' I told him it was to pay the lawyer. He was furious, telling me, 'For a million dollars, we should have the lawyer, the judge, and the whole fucking jury.' "

The perception is that it's the officials running the departments who have the most opportunity for corruption. In fact, it's midlevel municipal employees who have the power to choose who gets contracts, jobs, licenses, and tax benefits that can be worth a lot of money, and there are people willing to pay them to make the right decision. I'm not defending it, I'm explaining it. Corruption exists on all levels of government, from commissioners to low-level employees. Everybody becomes king of his or her own fiefdom. And corruption doesn't always involve cash payoffs. Say, for example, a nice guy who owned a linen-supply business had donated to my campaign and worked in the election and, in gratitude, I appointed him to the licensing board. In that position he helped to decide who got a liquor license. From that moment on who do you think restaurants are going to buy their linen from? The Tax Assessment Board determines the taxable value of a property, giving members of that board the power to raise or lower taxes. Every city board has the power to affect lives, and there are people who are going to try to take advantage of that. It's human nature. It exists on every level; parking attendants will take a few bucks to put your car up front so you can get out quickly, and some commissioners will accept a sort of thank-you for getting your son a job. The banks would give sweetheart mortgages to government officials, who in turn would watch out for the banks.

I got in trouble because people believed I knew everything that was going on in the city. They got that idea because that was the impression I wanted them to have. I wanted voters to believe I was the ultimate hands-on mayor, but in fact, the city had as many as six thousand employees, and obviously no one could know everything that was going on. For example, when my friend Joe Paolino served as mayor during my hiatus, the police arrested a drug-dealing murderer named Peter

Gilbert, who immediately flipped and offered to provide information about the mafia. The police decided that the state prison wasn't safe enough for him, so they actually built an apartment inside the police station for him. The prosecutor arranged a ten-year plea deal for Gilbert that allowed him to serve his sentence in that apartment. A murderer was living inside the police station and Mayor Paolino knew nothing about it.

Gilbert got some great deal: In exchange for providing information, he was given free use of the apartment, was allowed to fly to Florida to visit his family eight different times, managed to get alcohol and drugs, had use of a car, and was even given permission to go skydiving. In 1988 he was driving up to Connecticut, supposedly to go skydiving, when he got into a minor traffic accident and had a fatal heart attack. Some skydiving trip—the police found nineteen bags of cocaine inside his parachute bag. Like me, Paolino was sitting at home on a lovely Sunday morning and opened the newspaper. It was a front-page story. He read it, and reread it, then called the police chief and asked, "What the hell is going on?"

He had known nothing about it. So if Mayor Paolino hadn't even known that an admitted Mafioso murdering drug dealer had an apartment in the Providence police station, how could I be expected to know when a low-level city employee was cheating on his overtime?

Even the man who succeeded me when I went to prison, David Cicilline, has encountered problems. Cicilline continually positioned himself as the anticorruption candidate, although his brother went to federal prison for his involvement in a courthouse corruption scheme, and his former driver, a policeman who is married to his longtime executive assistant, was arrested and charged with being a member of a cocaine-dealing ring that also involved other Providence cops. Absolutely no one is claiming that Cicilline knew anything about these crimes.

During my terms in office, the system made corruption easy. It wasn't as if I was hiring astronauts with Ph.D.'s to run programs; instead, I had people who had worked their way up in a system that accepted a certain amount of graft. I never sanctioned it, but to claim I didn't suspect some of it was going on would be silly. I didn't know specifics, but I knew enough about human nature to know there were people who would take advantage of their position. I had run as the anticorruption candidate and I tried to change the culture, but it was very difficult. In the first weeks I was in office I got several complaints that unionized housing inspectors were reporting for work in the morning and then disappearing. One complaint specifically identified the bar at which these employees were drinking while supposedly working. I asked the police department to check it out and see if these were no-show jobs. As a result of that investigation we ended up firing several people.

On another occasion, detectives investigating workplace theft inside the city's sewage plant asked each of the plant's forty-two employees to take a lie-detector test. All forty-two refused.

One night I was at a party when a man who owned an electrical contracting company came up to me and asked casually, "Did you get the thousand bucks?"

"What are you talking about?"

He told me he'd given one of my directors a thousand dollars that was supposed to get to me. I went right back to my office and called that director. He claimed he had no idea what this guy was talking about. Well, I intended to get to the bottom of it, so I made the mistake of bringing the two of them into my office. When I repeated what the contractor had told me, that man looked at me as if I was crazy. "I never told you that," he said.

"What the fuck? Of course you told me." He denied it completely. But that was the last day I ever spoke to that director. I tried to fire him, but I didn't have the votes in the city council. I had a crook working for me and I couldn't fire him. What kind of system is that? When I realized I couldn't fire him, I decided the law needed to be changed. That's when I began my long fight to change the City Charter. As I told a reporter, "I'm not saying anything illegal occurred, but let's face it, the buck stops here." I took as much power away from him as possible, requiring him to get sealed bids from five vendors on all routine purchases of less than fifteen hundred dollars, but there really wasn't much I could do to stop it. The director eventually pleaded guilty to making false statements on a totally unrelated charge after we changed the charter and I fired him. Eventually he was granted immunity to testify against my city solicitor, Ronnie Glantz, who also was running his own operation.

In 1979 the city owned a fleet of garbage trucks. Glantz and Tony Bucci, the city Democratic chairman, came up with an interesting scheme. Glantz had contacts in the state police department declare that our trucks violated certain codes, so on his own he made an emergency deal to sell those trucks and lease ten garbage trucks for more than two thousand dollars per truck per month from a dealer named James Notarantonio. Glantz and Notarantonio drove to Massachusetts and met with Bucci, who demanded a kickback for the deal. Notarantonio eventually agreed to the deal and paid them seventy-seven thousand dollars before he apparently stopped paying. I knew nothing about any of this; much of it took place when I was in California meeting Reagan and Ford.

When the FBI began an investigation, Notarantonio rolled over. He testified that he had stopped making these monthly payments because "Mr. Glantz was getting ready to retire from the City of Providence and therefore, it would be like feeding oats to a dead horse. I didn't need him, he wasn't there, he couldn't do me any good."

Eventually, the FBI interviewed me and an agent asked, "Where were you when this happened?"

I offered what might rank as the single strongest alibi in history: "I spent that time with former president Gerald Ford and California governor Ronald Reagan. So go ahead and indict me if you want. They're going to be my defense witnesses."

Glantz and Bucci were convicted and went to jail for their involvement in this scheme. I was never implicated, but Glantz had been my appointee, he was my guy, so even though he had left the city the stink pervaded my administration. People began to believe that because I was surrounded by these people, I must be guilty of something, anything.

There's no question that some people I hired were corrupt; people who worked for me went to jail, and I regret that—though of course not as much as I regret the fact that I went to jail for a crime I didn't commit and knew nothing about. My political enemies would like people to believe that not only did I know about every scheme, I directed many of them and profited from all of them. There were stories told about people handing me bundles of cash. None of those stories are true. Proving that, however, is extremely difficult. How can I prove I didn't take cash? The reality is that if I wanted to make money from the job, there were numerous opportunities to make a substantial amount, not just a hundred here or a thousand there.

It's completely accurate for me to state that few politicians have been investigated as thoroughly as I have been. At times it seemed as though every government agency was pawing through my life trying to find a single thread to pull that would unravel a life of crime and corruption. The FBI spent months—months—trying to find even a shred of evidence that I had committed a single crime. The IRS went through every bank account and investment I had, trying to find funds I hadn't earned and couldn't account for. It conducted a complete forensic audit, demanding every receipt for every expense I claimed, and I provided those receipts to them. In fact, at one point two restaurants I owned had suffered substantial losses, but my accountant advised me not to claim those deductions, telling me it would be a red flag that would result in an IRS audit. So I hadn't claimed the losses. But while gathering all my financial records for the IRS I finally decided to claim them. As a result, the IRS sent me a refund check for $235,000.

When the IRS agents told me about my refund, I asked, "Can you guys come back next year?"

The question for which I have no real answer is why they continued to come after me. But they came early in my career and they came often. The fact that they were unable to find any evidence that I had done anything wrong didn't dissuade them. Clearly, there was the perception that Providence was corrupt and that corruption must go all the way to the top. To me. I was the big prize; getting me was a career maker, and my political enemies had learned they couldn't get me at the ballot box. This was their only option.

All those investigations found absolutely nothing beyond the stories told by people looking for a better deal from a prosecutor. Either I was a criminal mastermind able to outsmart a legion of those investigators from a variety of federal agencies, or I hadn't committed the crimes I was accused of. There were thieves in my administration, but believe me, there were many more people who turned down these so-called personal growth opportunities every day. For example, the chairman of the Board of Licenses, Ray Dettore, Jr., constantly had to deal with people who believed they had to pay a bonus to get a city license. He likes to tell the story of the day he came into the office and saw three brand-new suits and an expensive coat and a top hat hanging on a coatrack. "What's that?" he asked one of the secretaries.

"It's for you," she said. It turned out that there was a hearing scheduled that day on a request to license an Hispanic social club. The owner of that club had left two of those suits for Dettore. When the police sergeant got there, he also asked about those suits. When the secretary told him the story, he started laughing. "What's so funny?" Dettore asked. "The coat and hat are for you."

In the places where these people came from, this was expected. In those countries, when you had a problem or needed something from the municipal government, you had to make an offering.

On another occasion Dettore showed up for work and found an envelope containing ten one-hundred dollars on his desk. A man no one recognized had dropped it off. This was the most interesting bribe offer he'd ever received—he didn't even know who was bribing him. He xeroxed the bills, then handed them over to the city's legal department. And he never found out where they'd come from.

Manny Vieira worked his way up from a technician in the Communications Department to its director. He worked for me from the day I took office. At one point he discovered that a supervisor was not only putting himself in for overtime, he would also approve overtime payments for employees who would give him a piece of what they were paid. Manny caught this guy when he claimed to be working overtime— while he was on vacation. Manny went directly to the attorney general and those people were fired.

Ray Dettore and Manny were typical of the vast majority of our employees. They were completely honest. I understand the way the media works: Corruption makes headlines; nobody writes about the people who show up every morning and simply do their jobs. When Manny was running his department, he had a substantial budget. As he told a reporter, "There were times when the mayor would suggest I speak to someone. But he always said, 'If he gives us a better price or a better product, then consider him.' But that was it."

I was accused by several people, in addition to Glantz, of accepting bribes, but these accusations always came from people who were in a jam and looking to make a deal with the authorities. These were usually people who were caught accepting bribes or facing other legal problems, who told the people offering those bribes that of course the mayor knew about the deal and approved it. What else were they going to say? That the mayor doesn't know anything about it, so they may not be able to do what the people were paying them for? Of course not. No one has ever produced the slightest evidence that I put a penny in my own pocket.

Anyone who worked for me knew how I felt about bribes; they all heard me say, "If I ever catch any one of you guys playing games when it comes to money or anything like that, I'll cut your balls off." I said it often and I meant it.

Actually, I had something better than money to offer people. I had jobs. I had a lot of them and I used them as currency. In addition to the regular city jobs that the mayor's office controlled, the federal government was providing large grants for development and new construction for all kinds of projects that resulted in jobs. Many of these were middle-management and lower-level jobs, and while that doesn't seem important, the people who filled these were actually the people who made the city work on a daily basis. They conducted the inspections, handed out the tickets for code violations, renewed the licenses, laid the asphalt, sent out the bills, and dealt face-to-face with the people of Providence. Giving someone a job gives them instant credibility and usually some degree of power. The use of that power is the problem. Does anyone think it's possible for a mayor to know about every piece of paper that goes across every desk in the city every day?

In politics, giving jobs is known as patronage, and, contrary to claims made by *The Providence Journal*, I neither invented patronage nor perfected it. Patronage was being used by the Chinese before Christ was born. In the Roman Empire the Praetorian Guard auctioned off the office of emperor. I never sold jobs; I bartered them. I used jobs to reward supporters and win the support of those who opposed me. As I've often said, you can't buy your enemies, but you can rent them. I remember a conversation I had with the state commissioner of education, who was lamenting the fact that Rhode Island was the only state without a state education formula, meaning there was no specific equation for determining how much money for education the state returned to local municipalities. I told him, "What you have to do is go up to the legislature and make your case, and the best possible case you can make is to hire the legislator's son."

Politics is simply the art of trade and barter, and I had jobs to work with.

There's nothing wrong with patronage. Remember, a political party is a group of people legally organized to accomplish a single purpose: to take over the government by nonviolent means. Taking over a government requires an army, and when that army has won the war, you don't put your soldiers in the brig, you reward them by making them part of the process. As I've written, please let me know the next time a victorious politician holds a press conference and announces, "I'd like to thank everyone who contributed to my campaign, worked for me or voted for me; however, I have three hundred jobs and I'd like all my enemies to come forward so I can give out these jobs."

There were two broad ways of using jobs to your advantage: directly hiring people or allowing loyal council members to use the patronage organization to build their own constituencies by handing out jobs. Like it or not, this is the reality of municipal politics. Long before we had computers, I used to keep a map in my office, similar to the White House ambassadors' map, except that my map had various colored pins stuck in it. Each pin represented a job, and each color represented the person who had filled it. For example, blue pins represented people I hired, red pins represented someone hired by councilman Ray

Cola, yellow pins someone hired by Vinny Cirelli. We wanted the most pins in those wards that were strongest for me. It had been a tradition in Providence that certain jobs belonged to certain neighborhoods almost by birthright; for example, if a job opened in sanitation it belonged to Fox Point. The Fifth Ward filled openings in the police and fire departments. Another neighborhood had Public Works. Council members would use those jobs just as I did, to deliver votes and reward loyalty. That's just the way the system worked.

Obviously, I needed the support of a majority of those council members. When I needed to pass my budget or legislation, I had to have their vote. And sometimes there was a price for that. This isn't a secret. These people weren't going to support me because I was a nice guy or simply because they believed in good government. Those votes had value. Councilman Ray Cola, for instance, was a great guy, but every time he needed something he would call me. Ray had more cousins who needed jobs than anyone in history. He had to deliver for his constituents, too. Once, I remember, I needed his vote for a bill that would have raised taxes. I invited him to my office to discuss it and he said, "You know I want to support you, Mayor, but I can't vote for any tax raise."

I pulled out the map, which showed his district filled with blue pins. "Ray, why the hell do you think we need the money. These are all your people."

Ray played the system as well as anyone. One day a young man showed up at my office without an appointment. He sat there for several hours and finally I asked him to come in. "What can I do for you?"

He didn't look at me; his head was bowed as he said, "Mayor, I've been working for the city now for about five weeks . . ."

That was interesting. I'd instituted a hiring freeze three months earlier and as far as I knew no one had been hired since then. How could he have been working for the city for five weeks? "You have?" I asked. "That's good. So what's the problem?"

He shook his head. "I haven't gotten paid yet."

This was getting really interesting. "What do you mean? You're supposed to get paid after two weeks. Maybe three when you're starting.

Let's find out what's going on." He told me his name and said he was working in the sanitation department. But when I called that agency, there was no record of him ever being hired. "What are you doing there?" "I'm on the truck, picking up garbage. I've been doing it for five weeks."

"All right, let's go through this. How did you get this job?"

"Well, Councilman Cola took me down to the sanitation depot at four thirty in the morning and he told me, 'Get on truck five and don't get off.' So that's what I did."

Knowing Ray, I have to admit this did not come as a complete surprise to me. Well, I thought, we have a choice here. We can all be embarrassed or we can handle this. I told this young man we would take care of it, and I called Ray and asked him to come down to city hall. About a half hour later I looked out my window and I could see that Ray had arrived. Ray had an oil company, and he had come down on one of his large trucks with his slogan COLA TODAY, WARMER TOMORROW on its side. As I watched, Ray took out a paper bag and put it on the hot hood of the truck and stood there waiting. I had no idea what he was doing.

Several minutes later he walked into my office carrying that paper bag and smiling. "Mayor," he said. "Look, I brought you some warm bread . . ."

Ray left the office promising me he would allow me the privilege of hiring and firing city employees. I could have blustered, I could have threatened him, I could have fired the kid, but I knew that at some point I would need Ray Cola's vote.

I reminded the Personnel Department that nobody got hired, absolutely nobody, unless I signed the paperwork. Me, nobody else. So naturally I was surprised when the head of the Water Supply Board informed me that he'd "taken care of that guy" I'd "wanted [him] to take care of."

Once again, I had no idea what he was talking about. "I didn't tell you to hire anybody. We've got a hiring freeze."

"I don't know about that, Mayor, I got these papers right here with your signature on them."

I asked him to send those papers right over to my office. It wasn't my signature. I looked to see where the new employee lived. Then I got on the phone. "Ray, would you come down right now, please."

When he got there, this time without warm bread, I asked, "How did you hire this guy, Raymond? You forged my name, didn't you?"

"Me? I can't even write, Mayor."

I asked him, "Ray, who do you think is running this city, you or me?" When he paused to think about that, I knew I had no chance with him. But there was nothing I could do about it. I needed his vote. I needed all their votes. We always had trouble passing our budgets. Even before Bruce Sundlun became governor, he wanted to be involved in the process. Once, when the council was about to vote on our budget, he called to ask, "You got the votes for tonight?"

I said, "The *Journal* endorses the budget, the Chamber of Commerce endorses it. I've spoken to the council members and we're close. We'll get there."

Fifteen minutes later he called me again. "You got a pen and some paper?" I did. "Okay, write this down. [This council member's] cousin has to be a battalion chief and [that council member's] son needs to be put on some commission . . ." He went on like that, telling me about other jobs council members needed in exchange for their votes. "This one has to get this . . ."

"Bruce," I said. "Stop it. I don't need you for this. I can do that all by myself."

Not everybody got everything they wanted every time. And competence mattered—believe me, competence mattered. The people who got the jobs had to be able to do them. There was a lot of trading involved.

One year we had to pass a supplementary tax bill to keep the city government funded. That was a tough vote for the council. Sundlun counted the votes for me and told me, "You're one vote short." We had to figure out where to get that vote. Sundlun returned and told me, "Xavier's girlfriend has to get a job with Blue Cross benefits."

Councilman Eddie Xavier was a teamster, a tough guy who didn't like me at all. But at the same time he was telling reporters that the city needed to be fiscally conservative, he was asking for a job for someone. He had me. "Tell him okay," I said to Sundlun.

Sundlun returned a few minutes later. He said, "He doesn't trust you. He wants it in writing."

This councilman wanted a job for his girlfriend in exchange for his vote and he didn't trust me? Okay. I wrote on a piece of paper: *I, Vincent Cianci, promise to appoint Xavier's girlfriend to a job with Blue Cross benefits.* Sundlun handed it to Xavier, who eventually showed it to Vinny Cirelli. Cirelli probably laughed at the fact that I'd folded so easily as he crumpled up my note and threw it on the floor, where it was later found by a *Journal* reporter who published it the following day.

Xavier explained it was a joke and blamed it on me, claiming that I'd initiated the whole thing.

We learned how to use these jobs. Once, for example, we had an opening for a part-time judgeship. Among the people who wanted it were our deputy city solicitor, the chairman of the Board of Licenses and the deputy director of the Department of Planning and Development. We couldn't afford to lose our deputy city solicitor, so we made her the director of administration, which paid more than the judge slot; moved the director of the Board of Licenses into the deputy city solicitor job, which quadrupled his pension; and moved up the deputy director of the Department of Planning and Development. The judgeship went to a woman. The people who did a good job always knew we were looking out for them and that there was opportunity, but they also knew their continued good fortune depended on me being reelected. That's how my family continued to grow.

We got really creative with the jobs we had. After we successfully changed the city charter, which reduced the size of the city council, one of my original supporters—a member of Democrats for Cianci, Philip Almagno—was going to have to run against a popular Democrat, Louis Stravato. Stravato did not support me as strongly as Almagno did. It was going to be a very competitive race that would bring a lot of passionate Democrats to the polls—and when they got there, a lot of them were going to vote against me. Almagno's opponent agreed that if Philip dropped out of the race, he wouldn't campaign against me.

Philip took a job we offered him in the Bureau of Weights and Measures and retired from the city council. It worked out perfectly: the Democrat didn't campaign against me, I won the election, and Phil Almagno stayed in Weights and Measures for more than twenty-five years.

In addition to using jobs, I learned how to use the power and influence of the office of the mayor of the City of Providence to help people and, admittedly at times, to do less than help people. It would not be precisely accurate to say that I drew a firm line in the sand that I never crossed. Sand shifts, the line moves. The system sometimes was flexible. I was always being asked to do favors for people, always. This person's son wants an interview with this department. A parking sign had been put in front of that person's house that took away his second parking spot. I once had an aide who took an adjustable mortgage from "that Yabba Dabba Do" bank, as he described it, and his payments skyrocketed beyond his means to pay them, so I called the president of the bank, who transformed it into an affordable fixed-rate loan. I admit it, I did favors for friends. If someone needed a passport on an emergency basis, I would get it for him; if he was having problems with a city agency, at times I would try to smooth it over. I would arrange for marriages to be conducted at city hall on New Year's Day for young couples who couldn't find another place—and I would buy the champagne. I always believed there was no crime in helping out people, unless of course doing so was a crime. When John F. Kennedy Jr. was graduating from Brown University, an aide who had been close to his father and the head of the Kennedy Library, Dave Powers, came to see me. It turned out that from his stay in Providence, John-John owed a substantial amount of money for parking tickets, somewhere between twenty-five hundred and a zillion dollars. Who knows exactly how much it was, but apparently the university wanted the tickets paid before he would be allowed to graduate. O'Donnell asked me, "Can you handle that?"

I couldn't believe it. "If I do that you know it's going to end up in the papers," I said. "You're asking me to take a hit for a few thousand dollars? You're kidding me, right? I'll pay for them out of my own pocket first." Believe me, I wasn't paying somebody else's parking tickets so fast. But it was the most politically appropriate way to turn down that request.

Eventually, the Kennedy family paid those tickets.

There were occasions when I did use my influence with the police department. In 1975 the leader of the effort to unionize migrant workers, César Chávez, came to Providence for a rally. Several of my liberal friends asked me to recognize him, which I did, even though it got me in hot water with the unions. After the rally a number of Brown students set up picket lines at supermarkets selling non-union-picked vegetables. Several students were arrested, among them a young man named Chip Cronkite. A few days later he came to my office and sat in the waiting room for several hours until I had time to see him. He was upset, and explained that he didn't think he should have been arrested, because he wasn't on private property. I think he was afraid having an arrest record might hurt him. I called the police department and got rid of the case. Honestly, I had no idea who this kid was until his father, Walter Cronkite, walked into my office several weeks later to thank me. Cronkite was in town for a speaking engagement. We spoke for a little while; Walter Cronkite was then arguably the most respected man in America and it was a pleasure to meet him. We met again a few weeks later, when he was broadcasting the Republican convention and I was a speaker. When I was announced as a speaker, he introduced me to his national audience as "a rising young star of the Republican party who'll knock down the walls of Kemper Arena." He did not mention that I was also the guy who'd gotten his son off the hook.

There are several major universities in Providence and I always considered them valuable resources. They brought young people, creativity, and dollars into the city, and in the future I believe they will become even more important to the city's economy. But I did have my problems with them, in particular with Brown. I used to go to Brown football games; in fact, on occasion I'd sit with the band and play the cymbals. Sometimes the university president would sit with me. He didn't play the cymbals; perhaps he lacked the training. In 1976, for the first time in years, the football team shared the Ivy League championship. After winning their last game the fans tore down the goalposts. I was in my car driving home when I got a call from the police department informing me that Brown security had arrested five or six students and wanted them prosecuted. "For what?" I asked.

"Destroying university property." They wanted us to arrest students for tearing down the goalposts. It was an amazing request.

"That's interesting," I responded. "You know, I looked on the tax rolls and found out the goalposts were assessed at zero." Maybe I was making this up, but it sounded official. "So how can you prosecute someone for destroying property worth nothing?" They had to let those kids go.

I knew the presidents of the universities, and admittedly there were times I called on them for a favor. Or two. Or more than two. And naturally, the fact that I was the mayor appeared to do me absolutely no good. I was in my office on the Friday afternoon of a Labor Day weekend when Frank Sinatra called me. Several months earlier he'd performed at our civic center and we'd been photographed together in his dressing room, me handing a fire department helmet to my pal Frank. "Mayor," Sinatra said, "I just saw your picture in *Town and Country* with the president of Brown. How good do you know him?"

I know him pretty well, I told him.

"Here's the problem. My mother's doctor's kid applied over there and got refused. Can you do anything for him?"

"That's a tough one. Maybe if I had known about it when he applied, but . . ."

"I'm in Atlantic City," Sinatra replied, obviously not hearing a word I said. "I got to go do a show. Can you get back to my secretary, Dorothy, and she'll find me between shows."

Five days before the semester was scheduled to begin he wanted me to convince the president of Brown University to admit Frank Sinatra's mother's doctor's son? I thought, Why now? Why didn't he wait until Wednesday, when school actually began? Under normal circumstances this would have been impossible, but *Time* magazine had recently published an article claiming that people who made a large donation to Brown got preferential treatment. The administration was upset about it, so what was normally impossible had become completely, 100 percent out of the question, no possible way, forget it.

But this was Frank Sinatra.

I found Howard Swearer, the president of the university, at work on a tennis court and made arrangements to meet him at his house. When we sat down, I explained, "This very distinguished thespian, this singer, dancer . . ." Howard didn't buy it for a minute.

"Let's get the director of admissions over here."

Jim Rogers, the director of admissions, was equally impressed. "Didn't I see your picture with him in the paper recently? I think you were giving him a gun to the city."

I asked the director of admissions, "What are you doing here? It's almost seven o'clock, aren't you usually walking your rat around the East Side by this time?" He wouldn't do anything to help, either. Finally, the president explained, "Tell him I can get him into another Ivy League school, but not Brown."

Eventually, the doctor and his son came to Providence and we met with Brown's president. The kid ended up graduating from Cornell, and I never heard from him again.

The reality is that I had so much influence at Brown that when my two nephews applied there, exactly 50 percent of them were accepted. I had a fine relationship with Howard Swearer. So when my nephews had applied, I called him and said, "Howard, whatever you can do I'd appreciate it." I'm sure every university president gets endless calls like that. Both of my nephews were excellent students and fully capable of succeeding at Brown. And I knew that Brown's acceptance policies had always been flexible enough to admit students who had a prominent last name or generous wealthy parents, or whose relative had made a contribution to the university. So I was surprised when Jim Rogers called and said, "I have good news. We've accepted one of your nephews."

Oh. "Excuse me, but how is that good news?" I replied. The conversation escalated from there both in tone and tenor until we ended up accusing each other of being parts of the human anatomy. I called Howard Swearer, who sympathized with me but explained that he didn't have the authority to overrule his admissions director. He did agree that the director should not have called the mayor a part of the human anatomy on the phone.

Ten minutes later the director called back and offered the most insincere apology in the entire history of human anatomical insults. Still, in a perfect world I would have accepted it graciously and acknowledged the fact that just because I was the elected mayor of this great city, who had dedicated his life to the welfare of its citizens twenty-four hours a day, seven days a week, I shouldn't really expect any favors from a great university such as Brown. But in this less-than-perfect world I was pretty angry. By the time this conversation ended we were screaming at each other, actually inventing new parts of the human anatomy to suggest.

Suddenly, I remembered that people had been complaining that the dorms at Brown were rat traps, and I realized we had been negligent not to have inspected them. Petulant? Me? I suggested to our building inspector, who happened to be my cousin, "Those buildings are rat traps. The students shouldn't be living there. I want you to go up there and violate every one of them." My cousin, incidentally, was qualified for the position and did an excellent job. He eventually became the vice president of Johnson & Wales University, which has several campuses around the country. Well, maybe there was a little nepotism there, but he was extremely well qualified. He probably was the best building inspector the city ever had; he was knowledgeable, competent, well-respected, and honest.

"I can do that," he said, "but you don't want me to. But I do have a real problem about that hyperbolic paraboloid they want to build."

Oh? Coincidentally, the university had filed an application with the city to build a multimillion-dollar hyperbolic paraboloid sports center. A hyperbolic paraboloid is a type of freestanding structure that has no intrusive supports. There was only one other building like it in the country, at Georgetown University. Brown had gone through the application process—they'd made peace with their neighbors—and all they needed was an approval from the city to begin construction. That's all they needed. I knew they eventually would have to be given that approval, but basically it was up to my zoning board to determine what "eventually" really meant.

I called the head of our zoning board, Rookie Viola, whom I had serving on a month-to-month tenancy because he'd completed his term. He was allowed to continue to serve until I appointed a successor. And I had no intention of ever naming a successor. "You know that hyperbolic paraboloid Brown wants?" He did. "Don't do anything with it for a while."

"Anything you want, Mayor."

Several weeks later Howard Swearer asked me to his house for a drink. His wonderful wife, Janet, was there. We had a drink, discussed the weather, and finally he asked me why I was holding up approval for the hyperbolic paraboloid. I sighed. "Howard, you know how frustrated I am," I told him. "But you know, you and I, we're just figureheads. We're like the Queen of England, we just wave at crowds. We laugh, we smile, we give out happy-birthday proclamations. You think I have control of the zoning board? I don't. Just like you don't have control of the admissions guy. I don't have any authority over the zoning board. They do whatever they want."

"Is that what it takes? Get the kid in?" he asked.

"It doesn't take anything, except maybe a little diplomatic courtesy. They could have at least put the kid on the waiting list, so I'm not embarrassed in front of my family." I finished my drink, we shook hands, and I left.

Three days later my nephew was informed he had been added to the waiting list. Ah, progress. I called Rookie and told him, "You know that hyperbolic paraboloid? I want you to put it on the agenda for the next meeting. Now, read my lips. When they ask you about the hyperbolic paraboloid, I want you to say, 'We like it, it looks good, it's one of the best hyperbolic paraboloids on our list. So we're putting it on our hyperbolic paraboloid waiting list. Soon as there's an opening for an hyperbolic paraboloid, we'll let you know.'"

Even Howard Swearer couldn't help laughing at that remark. As it turned out, Brown never had to make a decision. My nephew ended up attending Boston College. And years later he graduated from Brown's medical school, proving my point that he was qualified to go there. And Brown got its hyperbolic paraboloid, which they proudly did not name after me.

I did that; I used my public power for personal reasons. I admit it. It probably wasn't the right thing to do, but it certainly felt good. There have been other occasions when I was accused of using—or misusing—my power to get even with people, and in those cases it wasn't true. One night I went with my girlfriend Wendy Materna, my sister, and my brother-in-law to a popular restaurant named Amsterdam's. The kid monitoring the door told me there was a five-dollar per-person cover charge for those people who intended to go to the bar to hear the live music. We were there to have dinner. I didn't like that, but I wasn't going to make a big deal about it, particularly after I saw that the place was mobbed. I could see that people inside could barely move. It was much too crowded for us to be able to sit and talk. So we left and went someplace else.

We didn't go inside because the place was uncomfortably and dangerously overcrowded, not because the kid at the door wanted me to pay a cover charge. I also knew that they served alcohol to minors, which I knew because my daughter had been served there and she was still a minor. This was potentially a dangerous situation: a badly overcrowded bar-restaurant serving alcohol to minors. I called the fire department and suggested, "It looks like this place is so jammed you couldn't fit another person in there."

A fire marshal determined that they were almost 25 percent over the legal capacity and closed down the place. Amsterdam's entertainment license was briefly suspended. The owners of the place claimed that I had ordered it shut down because the bouncer, who was so new in town that he didn't know who I was, had tried to charge me five dollars.

If I hadn't been there, I might have believed that story, too. It just wasn't true. If the kid at the door didn't recognize me, I suspect the owners or other people inside did, as I was arguably the most recognizable person in the entire city. And if they had insisted on charging me twenty dollars for us to get in, I would have paid it. But I didn't think I should pay a cover charge to have dinner. And if we had gone in, we would have sat at a table and I would have leaned across that table and whispered to Wendy, "WOULD YOU LIKE SOMETHING TO DRINK?" to which she would have replied, "WHAT? I CAN'T HEAR YOU."

Days later the owner of the restaurant came to my office. He later told a reporter that in his "humble, low-key, and factual" manner he'd started explaining to me that his bouncer had counted the number of people in his place, but that I'd cut him off, warning him, "You don't want to get into a pissing match with me. Because you're a cup of water and I'm Niagara Falls."

Well, that does sound like me. In fact, he did claim that his restaurant hadn't been overcrowded and that he was careful to observe all the city's regulations. In response I asked him, if he was so concerned about following the laws, why did he serve alcohol to minors?

Gambling in Casablanca? *Mon Dieu!* "Oh, no," he insisted. "We don't do that."

"Don't give me that shit," I said angrily. "I know you do, because one of them is my daughter." The restaurant received a fine for overcrowding, and their entertainment license was briefly suspended. And the next time I went there for dinner, which I did many times, it was considerably less crowded.

The situation that caused me the most difficulty—publicly, financially, and finally legally—was a confrontation I had with the University Club. In the mid-1970s Judge Paolino, whose nephew eventually succeeded and preceded me as mayor, suggested I join that club for political reasons. "You should expand your horizons," he told me. The application process included finding two members to sponsor me. My sponsors were State Supreme Court Justice Powers and the former governor, John Chafee. Judge Paolino told me it would take a couple of years and, if I was still room temperature, I'd be asked to join. Then I forgot about it.

In 1978 my secretary was cleaning up my files and found the recommendation letters to the University Club, and asked me what I wanted to do about them. Good question: Paolino told me it would take two years, but four years had passed and I hadn't gotten a response. I called Judge Paolino, who said he didn't know what had happened. That was strange. I spoke with the president of the club, who admitted that I had been blackballed. "Oh, really?" I said. "By whom?" "Ed Mauro." Ed Mauro had been a strong supporter of my opponent in my first election. Mauro and his father had been part of the Democratic operation for years. Doorley had appointed his father to the Providence Redevelopment Agency. They just didn't like me, and I guess he was showing me how powerful he was by keeping me out of a club I didn't really want to belong to anyway.

Still, it was insulting, and nobody likes to be insulted. But I understood he had the right to blackball me. Somehow for the next two decades I managed to survive without being a member of this club. According to reporters, I spent much of that time fuming about it, which was absolutely untrue. I didn't need another place to go and I certainly didn't need to belong to that particular club to boost to my ego.

Still, at least a few members of the club seemed to take pride in the fact it had rejected me, which for them was apparently an accomplishment. They had successfully kept me out of their club. At one of their Christmas parties in the mid-1990s they hired a local comedian whom I knew and liked—he actually did a good imitation of me—to portray me, and he got a big laugh by coming onstage as if sneaking into the club. Now that, I felt, was unnecessary. Nobody likes to be ridiculed. That I didn't forget.

In life, there are always going to be people who think they are better than you. I learned that when I was in school, where because of my background I was not included in everything. At that point in my life it didn't bother me very much, and what I learned later was that when you finally get to know those people who didn't want to include you, you realize you didn't want to be part of those events anyway.

Literally two decades after I had been blackballed, the club was being remodeled and had applied to the city for approximately twenty-three variances. Most of them had been approved, but one of them had been turned down. I called the building inspector to find out about this problem. The club wanted to install a new elevator, he told me—without also putting in a new firewall. And without that firewall their plans didn't meet the fire code. It would be a stretch to claim that I didn't smile, but I had not interfered with the process. "Give them permits for the rest of the work," I said.

"We have."

"But not to put that fucking elevator in," I added. I probably smiled again. Club officials immediately decided this was my way of getting even with them for their insulting behavior two decades earlier, and for that comedian. Installing a firewall was very expensive and, they believed, unnecessary. They appealed to the Board of Review. I certainly wasn't going to do anything to help them. I knew of cases in which years after a variance was granted, people had been hurt in an accident, and their lawyers had showed up waving that variance. I just wanted to make sure these people met every single legal specification. Every. Single. Last. Specification. And I told my staff exactly the way I felt.

The club officials sent me a letter officially requesting a meeting. I responded exactly as they had responded. I did nothing. I didn't answer it. Maybe I was immature, but there are times arrogant people need to have their bad behavior thrown right back in their faces. The club thought it was amusing to ridicule the mayor of Providence at a Christmas party? That was their right. Turning down their application because it didn't meet the building code? That was my duty!

Finally, two club officials called and asked to meet with me, the city solicitor, and the building inspector. One of those officials walked into my office with a bumper sticker from my campaign stuck to the back of his suit. I assumed I was supposed to think that was funny, that suddenly we were all friends. I didn't laugh.

The club president asked me politely to "tell the building inspector what to do."

"I don't tell him what to do," I replied. I think he noticed I wasn't laughing when I said it.

"Look, we understand you're mad because you didn't get accepted to the club."

I raised my eyebrows in surprise. "Oh? I didn't know that because I didn't get a letter back."

They responded, "You didn't answer our letter, either."

"Let me ask you, what does Emily Post say about answering letters? How long should you wait to have a letter answered? Three weeks, four weeks maybe. I've been waiting twenty-two years for your letter." It may have been at about this time that I reminded them of an old proverb I'd made up, "Be careful of the toe you step on today because it may be connected to the ass you have to kiss tomorrow."

One thing led to another and one of them said, "By the way, you never got rejected."

"Oh, really, I didn't know that."

They saw an opening here. "Your application was withdrawn," one of them said hopefully, then added, "We would like to make you an honorary member of the club."

While I hadn't been waiting twenty-two years to respond to that invitation, it did feel good to tell them, "I don't want to belong to your club. But if I did want to join a club, why would I join yours? If I belonged to a club, I'd probably like to go there at night and have a drink, and I couldn't do that at your club."

Why not? they asked.

"Well, I don't know who your lawyers were, but it must have been Abbott and Costello because when you applied to expand the square footage of the club, you also needed to reapply for a liquor license. You didn't do that. So why would I belong to a club where you can't get a drink?" Obviously I was playing with them—and enjoying every minute of it. But everything I said was absolutely legal. The law was quite clear: If you expanded the square footage of any premises in which alcohol was served, you had to reapply for your liquor license.

Ray Dettore, the head of the licensing board, had inspected the club. "When I took a look at the place," he told me, "all that was being changed were the squash courts, which were being made regulation size, the restaurant, and the bar. After inspecting it I told them that they had to get clearance from health and fire to get their license reissued."

In political terms, this is known as "bustin' balls." They hoped I was kidding. Instead, I got Dettore on the phone. I asked him, "When we spoke earlier today, didn't you tell me that the University Club couldn't have a liquor license until they submitted a new floor plan approved by the board?"

"They never applied to us for it," he said. "The time period's over, so they can't have it."

I hung up the phone and suggested, "Make sure you tell that to Abbott and Costello."

A few days later the president of the club hand-delivered a letter praising my stewardship of the city and welcoming me to the club. I never used that membership. The Building Board of Review rejected their application to install an elevator without a firewall. Eventually, the club appealed our decision to the State Building Board which overturned our city board's decision. That was fine with me; the city was legally protected and I'd made my point. I still would not get in that elevator.

What I didn't expect was that a few years later the federal government would be so desperate to find charges against me that they would actually accuse me of extorting an honorary membership from the University Club by withholding a building permit. That's turning a feud into a legal case. The jury found me not guilty.

I used the power of the office to get things done that I wanted done. For example, when I looked out my window across the broad expanse of Kennedy Plaza, I saw the Industrial Bank building, and I noted that they flew the American flag only on holidays. I like the sight of flags flying, and I suggested nicely to the bank that they start flying the flag every day. They ignored that request, so I told reporters, "In the days ahead, I would like to be able to look out the windows of my office and see the flag proudly flying on the Industrial Bank building . . . and to point this out to all the visitors who come in my office to invest in this city's great future."

The bank president replied that in order to fly the flag, a worker had to climb out the window to reach the pole, and he didn't want to put employees in unnecessary danger.

So I was trying to kill workers. That must have been some conversation inside the bank: "Let's see, who is going to climb out the window to fly the flag today?"

I suggested that they were wrong: "To continue to offer these factors as excuses for not properly displaying the American flag seems to me incredible in light of your cooperation to solve the most complex and far-reaching monetary problems." In other words, fix the flagpole or move it.

They remained resistant until I pointed out that the city kept a substantial amount of money on deposit at the bank. That's when they announced the new policy—they would fly the flag every day and no one would have to die to do it.

I was always very careful about asking favors of the police department. The last thing I wanted to do was compromise people who had dedicated their lives to law enforcement—and I also knew that nothing would thrill *The Providence Journal* more than learning that the department had done something for me. I was so careful about it that when my dog Tucker got lost, I called Colonel Gannon and put it to him this way: "Let me ask you this hypothetical question. Suppose the mayor called you and told you that his dog was missing, what would you do about it?" That way, it was entirely his own decision.

Gannon hesitated. "Let me ask you, does this mayor still have a Southeast Asian houseboy?"

Yes, he does, I said.

"Then I would go and check the kitchen. And if there's a leash on the stove, eat out." Then he hung up on me.

There was one instance in which a police chief did try to do me a favor, unfortunately. The mother of a young man who had applied for the police department and failed the test had come to my office to complain. The kid failed the test; there wasn't anything I could do about it. But I wanted to be the good guy. I called the Colonel and put him on speakerphone so the woman could hear. This way she would know that I tried. I said, "Colonel, Mrs. So-and-So is in my office. Her son failed the test. What can we do about it?"

I expected that he would tell me that there was nothing he could do. That was the correct answer. But instead he responded, "Oh, Mayor, have him come right over. I'll have him take the test right here in my office."

Obviously, there were some favors I couldn't do. One night, for example, a friend of mine woke me up and said, "Mayor, I just got stopped for driving under the influence. The cop is giving me a lot of crap and I'm not really drunk. I was hoping you might talk to him."

This wasn't something I did very often; besides the fact that driving drunk is one of the most dangerous things you can do, an elected politician who gets caught helping a friend beat a DUI is done. But I figured I might be able to make it a little easier on him, depending on how bad it was. "Is there anybody there besides the cop?" I asked.

"No, not really," he said. "Just the Channel 12 News truck I hit."

I'll be going back to sleep now.

Admittedly, in my position I received perks that were not available to other people. You have to remember that when I was first elected we were living in a very different time, long before the existence of political correctness. I also think it's fair to point out that every job has extra benefits. But I was invited to every cultural event in the city and attended many of them, I had a chicken dinner at every charity fundraiser, when I had any type of problem I could find someone to fix it quickly, and I could even get zoo officials to open the zoo for me in the middle of the night to show off the city's giraffes.

There was one situation in which I truly did exercise my power to make a point. Late one summer night I was coming home after campaigning and when I got to my house, the entire street was dark. It was 2 A.M. and there wasn't a single light on in any house. I saw yellow lights flashing on the next block and told my driver to go there. It was a power company truck. There was a man working down in a manhole and I asked, "What's going on here?"

He recognized me. "We're changing some switches, Mayor," he said. "We sent out a notification that we were going to shut the electricity off."

"Oh, really?" I said. "Well, I never got one." I knew they'd never sent a letter.

"We sent it," he said, starting to get angry. "Now please, get out of here when I'm working."

Get out of here? I suddenly had a very good idea. The president of the electric company was a friend of mine named Ed Mulligan. I called him at 3 A.M. and said, "Hey, good morning, Ed, how are you feeling? Ed?" He mumbled something and I continued, "This is your favorite mayor speaking. I just want to inform you that by turning off the power without informing anyone, you just murdered two people on the East Side."

You bet they got that power turned on fast.

Nine

fter my conviction in 1984 I'd walked out of the mayor's office into a different universe. For an entire decade just about every single minute of my life had been scheduled; I'd had to make a thousand decisions every day that eventually would affect the lives of countless people, the phones never stopped ringing, and when I finally did get home, my wife and my daughter were waiting there. And then it was all gone, my life as mayor and my family. Gone. Suddenly, the biggest decision I had to make was what time to get up in the morning. Or, sometimes, the afternoon.

I didn't have a job to go to during the day and I didn't have a family waiting for me to come home at night. I didn't have the mayor's limousine waiting out front; I couldn't get the chief of police on the phone immediately; in fact, I didn't even have a desk or a phone. And I certainly didn't have much of a political future. All because I'd found out the woman I was divorcing had been having an affair. I'm not going to claim it didn't hurt. It did. I had given my life to the city for more than a decade and I found out very quickly that it could survive without me. And I terribly missed being with my daughter.

Joe Paolino, the president of the city council, replaced me. We were political enemies; we had fought about everything. I liked to say we were on a second-name basis. When he took over, he replaced almost all of the people who worked for me. In fact, people weren't allowed to say my name in city hall. They had to refer to me as "the former administration," or "prior administration." Freddie Passarelli, who was fired, remembers running into a former colleague at a restaurant who told him how much he had enjoyed working with him in the "former administration." He used that phrase several times until Freddie finally said, "You are talking about Buddy, right?"

I also didn't know what was left of my reputation. I had always been a somewhat-controversial figure in Providence—in addition to the old rape charge against me, while I was in office twenty-one city employees had been indicted for corruption, although not a single charge was ever made against me. But after this episode, I didn't know how people felt about me. I'd done a stupid thing, which I regretted, and I wondered if it had completely destroyed my reputation. When I was invited to be the grand marshal of a Columbus Day Parade on Federal Hill, my first public appearance since my resignation, my question was answered. Two friends went with me and I remember thinking that, just in case things went wrong, they should stay a little bit away from me so they didn't get hit with the first burst. Instead, I got a tremendous reception. For an hour or so it felt as if nothing had changed. The next day even the *Journal* admitted in a headline, CIANCI GETS TUMULTUOUS WELCOME HOME.

The biggest problem I faced was not knowing what to do with myself. I hadn't planned on being unemployed. For a brief time I did consider the possibility of running against Joe Paolino in the special election; some people were urging me to do it, and I believed I would win. But eventually the State Supreme Court ruled that I couldn't run for reelection in an election being held to elect my replacement. Though the law was a little vague on the situation, it was prohibitively expensive for me to appeal, and there was little chance that the decision would be reversed. I finally had to accept the reality that this part of my life was over.

Fortunately, even after settling with my former wife I had sufficient money in the bank to live comfortably. To earn a living I got involved in the real estate business. As mayor I'd been in the real estate business for a decade, building, buying, renovating, and condemning buildings for the city. So I knew the value of property. I also had learned how to make a deal, and my name still meant something to a lot of people. A local NBC reporter once said about me, "He's got 33 1/3 percent of the people of Providence who would vote for him if he shot his mother at high noon in Kennedy Plaza." Even without shooting my mother I could bring people together, I could arrange meetings, and I had access to sources of financing, so real estate was a nice fit for me. I bought a nine-story building in January 1985 for $4.2 million—and nine months later I sold it for a million-dollar profit. I was involved in the construction of another building in South Providence. And I ended up owning a couple of restaurants. So for several years my financial situation was very good. Eventually, I bought the home I had been renting; I had one of three condominiums and was able to rent out the other two to cover much of my mortgage. I also had a beautiful fifty-two-foot boat and a luxury convertible.

But more than anything else, I missed being in the middle of the action. For longer than a decade absolutely nothing had happened in the city without me knowing about it and, usually, having something to say about it. Either I was quoted or criticized in some section of the *Journal* every single day. For weeks after my resignation my name continued to appear regularly in the newspaper, but once it was accepted that I wasn't running again, I officially became old news. Several years later my name appeared on a long list of people with forgotten bank accounts in the smallest type available, causing a friend to remark, "You'd do anything to get your name in the papers, wouldn't you?"

In addition to being written about daily, I had gotten accustomed to having TV and radio reporters sticking microphones in front of me and practically demanding that I comment on the issue of the day. An open microphone to a politician is irresistible. That was usually when I was at my best "Buddy." I knew when to be serious and when to be glib. And I was comfortable on the air. After leaving office, from time to time I was invited to appear on local radio talk shows. One afternoon, for example, I had the opportunity to question a talk-show host who had been extremely critical of me for years and in fact had helped ignite the recall effort after the 1982 election. I thought I was very kind to him as I pressed him to talk about accusations of fraud involving a charitable agency he had founded, then I put him on the spot by asking him if he even knew the difference between accrual and cash methods of accounting. This was the guy who had been relentlessly criticizing me for years. He fumbled for answers. It made for very good radio. A few weeks later I was asked by Bob Fish, the owner of WHJJ, and his program director Ron St. Pierre if I would be interested in actually hosting a radio talk show for a few weeks. I wasn't quite certain exactly what that required. Ron explained, "All you've got to do is talk." Talk? Me? Could there possibly be a better format for me? In March 1985 my third career began. I was given my own show on WHJJ, free to voice my opinions as often and as loudly as I wanted to. It was great. It was like handing matches to a pyromaniac. From the moment I sat down behind a microphone as host of a radio talk show, I loved it. For three hours a day—later four hours a day—my job was to be an entertainer. And at the end of that time I could go home or out to dinner or do whatever I wanted to do without worrying about a city council vote or pushing a program or appearing at an event. My show consisted of interviews, comments, and conversations with callers. Among those callers was "Ray from Lincoln," who I later found out was the son of mob boss Raymond Patriarca. I was also fortunate that many people working in the city government secretly fed me information. I had on a range of guests from the bishop of Providence to radical Rabbi Meir Kahane, from politicians to a woman I'd sung with on Celia Moreau's radio show *Kiddie Review* forty years earlier. I became a pretty good interviewer because I wasn't timid about asking difficult questions. In 1986 there was considerable speculation that I might quit the show and run against Joe Paolino for mayor. I milked it as long as I could, announcing only minutes before the deadline to file to run that I would not be a candidate for mayor in 1986.

I also had an active social life. I was single and successful in a wonderful city. Several years later, in fact, *Rhode Island Monthly* named me not only the state's "Best Politician" but also "the Rhode Islander you'd most like to go on a date with." I dated several women simultaneously and at times it required some deft footwork. One November, for example, I was invited to speak at some sort of conference in Puerto

Rico. I told one of the women I was dating that I would be taking a male assistant with me, although in fact I was taking another woman. Then my assistant spent those four days hiding in Providence, going to a tanning salon twice a day to get a tan. It worked, sort of—he ended up with third-degree burns. He met me at the airport and we drove into the city together.

Eventually, though, I met Wendy Materna, a tall, beautiful woman who had been born in Providence but was then living in Chicago. Wendy was the perfect complement for me; not only was she self-confident enough not to be overwhelmed by my life, but people loved her. She is, in every way, a class act. We went everywhere together and she became quite well known and popular in the city. We had a comfortable life together, and maybe for the first time in my life I understood the appeal of simply settling down. I'd spent so much time running from here to there to over there that I hadn't known what it was like to just stop and relax and be with the one person you really wanted to be with. That was Wendy. Maybe I didn't stop completely, but I definitely slowed down. I knew how lucky I was to have found her, but my divorce had soured me on marriage. We talked about getting married, but I just couldn't do it. I just couldn't do it.

Wendy and I were together for almost nine years. After I won reelection in 1990 she became the First Lady of Providence without all the fuss of a wedding ring. She was so deeply involved in charitable work and assisting me that she even had her own space in city hall. I thought it was a perfect relationship; who needed all the formality and legal connections of a marriage? We were in love.

Wendy needed it. When it became apparent to her that I wasn't going to be able to make that commitment, we separated. I knew she would come back to me, though; I was Buddy, I was the mayor. There was no possible way she would leave me.

Finally, Wendy went to Florida on vacation and met another man. She came back and told me all about it. I was her first choice, she said, but he would marry her. I was such an egomaniac that I just didn't believe it. It couldn't possibly be true. How could she possibly choose to be with someone else after spending all that time with me? I thought she was just pressing me to make a commitment. So I called her bluff. This was right in the middle of the 1994 election campaign and I wanted her to be with me. I was feeling pretty good; I was confident that I had calmed down this problem between us, and I remained confident until she got on an airplane and flew to Barbados to get married.

I called her the morning of her wedding and asked her, "Are you sure you want to go through with this? You don't really love this guy? How can you do this?"

She said, "I'm going to marry him."

I was campaigning that afternoon. People were surprised that Wendy wasn't with me and asked me where she was or when we were going to get married. I had to admit the truth: "She's getting married today in Barbados." I had to smile when I said it, as if my heart wasn't breaking. In response to one question I did admit, "Well, I have had better days."

Public officials are rarely permitted to show their private feelings. It isn't part of the deal. Every time I walked out of the door I had to become "Buddy," the gregarious, energetic, concerned, and personable character the city expected me to be, even if I was dying inside. And it didn't matter that it was my fault we'd split up, I was feeling completely rejected, ripped up inside.

Several weeks later the private line in my office rang. "Remember me?" Wendy said. She was in town to pick up her belongings. Some of her stuff was still in my house, and some of my things were in her apartment. We spent some time together. And then we sat down and together we stuffed her wedding announcements into envelopes, affixed stamps, and mailed them. It was arguably the most confusing thing I've ever done in my life: I was helping my girlfriend mail out the announcement that she had married someone else.

Being involved in that election saved my sanity. I was depressed, and lost a lot of weight. I just got up every morning and did everything on my schedule, trying to hide my wounds.

It was very difficult for me to accept the reality that our relationship had ended. I owed so much to Wendy; in fact, it was primarily Wendy who had convinced me to run for mayor in 1990.

Joe Paolino had announced that he was going to run for governor, leaving city hall vacant, and he had no natural successor. I thought about it, just as I had in 1986, but truthfully I was ambivalent. Though the economy had slumped, putting both of my restaurants in serious financial trouble, I genuinely was enjoying my life. In 1990 my radio show was number one in Rhode Island. Years earlier I'd cautioned a candidate not to run unless he was ready to smell the manure on the streets, and I just wasn't sure I still had that drive. A committee was formed supposedly to make recommendations about the future of Providence, but in fact it was an effort by several of my old supporters to determine if I had any chance at all. Among the members of that committee were Dr. Patrick T. Conley, Paul Campbell, my adman Norm Roussel, and Frank Corrente, who had been the city controller when I resigned. At that time I was a convicted felon with a radio show; there weren't a lot of people willing to stick out their necks in public to support me. A poll conducted by this group found that my only chance to win would be in a three-way race in which support was split. I couldn't even count on getting 40 percent of the vote. While the thought of marching back into city hall as mayor was exhilarating, the reality was sobering. Wendy and I did talk about it. This was my last chance, she said. If I didn't run this time, I would never get another chance to come back—and if I didn't do it, I would be very sad. That was the word she used, "sad."

The possibility that I might run again put me right back on the front page. On my radio show it was the main subject callers wanted to talk about. The station even ran an advertising campaign speculating "Guess Who Wants to Be Mayor? You Could Learn a Lot Today." Most of my listeners urged me to run—of course, if they didn't like me, they probably wouldn't have been listening to my program. Even President George Bush wondered what I was going to do, asking a columnist from *The Providence Journal* at a White House luncheon if I was going to run. But Wendy may have been my strongest supporter. She kept urging me to follow my heart.

I honestly didn't know what I was going to do, but I would get up in the morning and read stories in the newspaper telling me what I was thinking. "Will Buddy run" became a big industry. A few weeks before the filing deadline Wendy got an application for me, but I didn't bother to fill it in. Basically, I had this burning desire to get back into office and prove myself—I didn't like the way I had left, being unceremoniously asked to leave city hall—and of course I wanted to return; I just didn't want to have to go through another rough political campaign.

On the final day for filing Wendy arrived at my house in the morning all dressed up. Several other friends and supporters and a few reporters were already waiting downstairs, assuming I was going to go for it. I'd already had a conversation with Charlie Mansolillo, who at that time was a policy adviser to the Republican governor, and told him I wasn't going to do it. But Wendy didn't know that. "Are you ready?" she asked.

"To do what?" I had to get to the radio station.

"Aren't you going to file?"

"No," I said, and at that moment I meant it.

I went downstairs with Wendy and announced, "I've decided I'm not going to do it." There were some mild protests, but everybody started to leave. Among those people was my longtime aide Freddie Passarelli. As he turned to go I stopped him. "Where you going?"

He said, "I guess you probably want to be with Wendy today."

"Why don't you come with me to the studio," I said. Then I added, "Just in case I change my mind."

As Freddie left my house, a reporter asked him, "What's he doing?" Freddie shrugged. "I don't think he's running."

Charlie also went back to his office in the State House and told people, "He's not going to run. He just told me." His staff asked permission to listen to my radio show. "Go ahead," he told them. "But he's not running."

The deadline for filing the application to run for political office was 4 P.M. It was strictly observed; years earlier a Republican candidate for Congress named John Holmes missed that deadline by five minutes and was not permitted to run against an incumbent who later lost. I drove to the radio station to do my show. I went on the air at 3 P.M., but I kept an eye on the clock. I was wavering. Just in case I changed my mind, I had finally signed the papers and given them to Freddie Passarelli to hold, but I'd told him, "Don't you do anything with them unless I say go."

Almost every caller that day offered an opinion. At about 3:10 a woman named Hope from Somewhere called and said, "I want to tell you that when you were the mayor I didn't like you very much, but I've been listening to you on the radio and you're a different person than I thought. I think you have a lot of compassion and that's why I think you should run again."

Charlie Mansolillo was listening to the show. As he heard Hope from Somewhere talking, he thought, Oh jeez, here we go. He's going to run.

Maybe I was waiting for this call, or maybe I had already made my decision and just hadn't realized it, but I thought, This call means something. Freddie was standing in the hallway outside the studio. I could see him through the window. At about 3:20 I said, "You know what? I'm going to run." I told Freddie, "Go file the papers."

Freddie took off for city hall, racing the clock to get there from East Providence. Freddie remembers being in a slight panic, thinking, I sure hope there's no traffic, because if these papers don't get filed on time, I'm done. As he went flying over a bridge he noticed that a policeman was holding traffic for him, and as he sped past, the cop gave him a thumbs-up.

When he reached city hall, he estimated there were about a thousand people waiting for him, many of them leaning out of open windows. He got there at 3:50. As he parked the car and walked into the building, someone yelled out, "Freddie has the papers," and people started applauding. He walked into the proper room and said with obvious relief, "I'm here to deliver Buddy Cianci's declaration papers."

The clerk said officiously, "Let's not make this a circus. Everybody else out." The moment my papers were officially filed I became a candidate and had to get off the radio. The news director took over. I called Charlie and asked him, "Okay, now what do we do?"

I decided to go to city hall, knowing it would generate tremendous publicity. By the time I got there it seemed as if people were hanging from the rafters; many of them had supported me through several campaigns. As I walked into the building to meet the media I thought, Here we go again.

Mayor Joe Paolino was so upset that I was going to run that to stop me he seriously debated dropping out of the race for governor and running against me. "This was my worst nightmare," Paolino later told a reporter. "I knew exactly what he was going to do if he won. He would go through my administration and try to belittle everything we did, he would find whatever problems we'd had and amplify them, and then he would identify all the problems facing the city that he would have to deal with and blame me for them.

"I knew that he would do that, because that's what I did to him."

Fortunately, Paolino's staff talked him out of making the run against me. He certainly would have been handed the Democratic nomination and would have been extremely difficult to beat. Instead, city councilman Andrew Annaldo was the Democratic nominee, and once again seventy-three-year-old Fred Lippitt was running, although this time as an Independent. They were both good candidates. Andrew Annaldo was young and smart and ambitious, just as I had been almost two decades earlier when he was still a teenager. I'd actually given him a job as a custodian at one point. His campaign strategy was based on capturing the Italian vote, so he was devastated when I announced I was running, knowing my candidacy would split that vote. I liked Fred Lippitt, too; in fact, when I ran in 1974, one of my first fundraising cocktail parties was held at his house. I always told him that if I wasn't mayor I wanted him to have the job. Unfortunately for both of them, I finally admitted that I really wanted to be mayor again. I wanted it desperately.

The Buddy Party was back in business, but there weren't many people willing to join. I had been convicted of assault with a dangerous weapon and had left city hall in disgrace. For anyone who intended to have a long career in Providence government, I was toxic. Unless I pulled off an upset, anyone who aligned publicly with me would be finished in local politics. So it was difficult putting together any kind of organization. Among those people who did join my campaign were

Frank Corrente and state representative Tom Rossi. Neither of them was there because they loved me, but rather because their careers had reached dead ends and they recognized an opportunity. Without me they were going nowhere, so they had nothing to lose by supporting me. And when I did win, Corrente became the director of my administration (although it turned out he thought he was the mayor). I didn't know Corrente that well, but I appreciated his efforts. He was an old-school Democrat and understood the practicalities of politics. During the campaign he was invaluable. It was also during that campaign that I met Dr. Alfred Arcidi. I walked into a restaurant one night and this man I'd never met before invited me to join him. He was a dentist, but he developed nursing homes and rehabilitation hospitals, and made a fortune. We spent the night talking and eventually he volunteered to contribute to my campaign. Eventually though, he became a very close friend and advisor. Several years later, when I had my own financial problems, he loaned me a considerable amount of money. When I went to prison he signed notes that enabled me to refinance my debt. I repaid him, but when a lot of people were disappearing he was right there for me. The only thing he ever got out of it was my friendship. He never got a thing from the city. He remains a true friend who wanted only the best for me.

The 1990 campaign essentially was a referendum about me. It wasn't the future of the city, it wasn't economics, it was me. Did the good people of Providence want "Buddy II," as the media referred to it? As one potential voter told *The New York Times*, "There is an experience quotient that has to be pegged against purity of soul." The reasons not to vote for me were obvious; I had been convicted of a felony, and a number of people in my administration had been convicted of corrupt activities. The reasons to vote for me were in front of people every day—the city had changed dramatically for the better while I had been in office—and I was entertaining. I was perhaps the most effective cheerleader the city ever had, and I had a national platform to boast about Providence. It was impossible to deny the fact that I had a strong support base. As state representative Frank Fiorenzano said wistfully, "I wish I knew what it was. I would like to get it and bottle it and give it to myself."

A Republican state senator was kind enough to suggest a campaign slogan for me, "Let's keep Buddy on the air." But I had my own slogan, which a very good public relations firm created for me: "He never stopped caring about Providence."

Overcoming the scandal of my conviction was the key to winning, so I didn't hesitate to speak about it. "When I left office it was in disgrace," I admitted. "It was a very, very sad time in my life and in the people of Providence's life. I think I've learned from my mistake. Hold me responsible for not knowing [about the corruption]. But don't hold me responsible for being part of a criminal conspiracy, because if I were, I wouldn't be sitting here today." I even quoted from the Bible, suggesting that he who had never sinned should cast the first stone against me—then I waited for my opponents to throw it.

I ran on my record as mayor. My opponents took every opportunity to remind voters about my criminal record. But they had their own problems. When Annaldo challenged me to accept responsibility for the members of my administration who had been convicted for municipal corruption, I pointed out that one of those men, former Democratic city chairman Tony Bucci, was currently an adviser to his campaign. We had one debate at a closed public swimming pool. Annaldo spoke first, talking about those things he was going to do if elected. In my opening statement I pointed at the empty pool and said simply, "When I was mayor, there was water in this pool, and when I'm mayor again, there will be water in this pool again."

And Fred Lippitt vowed, unfortunately, that he would "reopen the pool by January first."

The defining moment of the campaign came during a televised debate. Obviously, corruption was a major issue, and they tried to hammer me on that. It was important that I put gum on my opponents' shoes. Fortunately, my campaign had discovered that both of them had been involved in somewhat-suspect pension deals. Lippitt had been a state representative for twenty-two years; state legislators received a very small salary but did accrue some pension benefits. However, Lippitt had left the legislature and accepted a high-paying job in the governor's administration, and had worked in the State House for slightly more than a year. While working there he had a friend in the legislature submit a special bill that enabled him to receive pension benefits for all the years he'd served based on his highest government salary. That meant his entire pension would be tremendously increased. The one year he'd been employed by the governor raised his pension more than four times the maximum amount that his years of service in the legislature would have entitled him to receive. When reporters asked him about that, he'd replied, "God helps those who help themselves."

As a city councilman, Annaldo had been permitted to join the International Laborers' Union, which entitled him to additional pension benefits. During the debate Annaldo and Lippitt spent considerable time attacking each other, but finally I had an opportunity to speak. Fortunately, I had been positioned between my two opponents. I gestured toward Annaldo and said, "On this side I have the Little Dipper, who's become a member of the Laborers' Union, the union he's going to have to negotiate with. And on this side I have the Big Dipper, who's increased his pension benefits astronomically."

Newspapers picked up that line and quoted it often. The appearance that both of them had done something unethical took away the moral high ground from them, making it more difficult for them to attack me because of my past.

Still, both of my opponents were able to raise considerably more money than me, and the *Journal* attacked me relentlessly. During one of the debates, for example, a *Journal* columnist held up a campaign brochure in which I promised to be strong against crime and asked how voters could possibly take the word of a criminal. And day after day on its editorial page, the *Journal* warned readers not to vote for me.

Fortunately, I received the unanimous support of the Providence Central Labor Council, whose members remembered the substantial gains they had made under my leadership. I had given retired union members paid health insurance a decade before state workers got it. Teachers in Providence had gone from being among the worst paid in the state to among the best. Police officers and firefighters had gotten substantially improved health benefits. "God bless the mayor," said the president of the Teachers' Union as she urged her members to support me.

On election day the polls rated it a toss-up between Lippitt and me. It came down to turnout. We practically dragged our voters out of their houses. This was local politics one house at a time. We reminded anyone who had ever gotten a tree planted or a pothole fixed to make sure they voted. But five minutes before the polls closed, the local ABC affiliate declared Lippitt the winner. At my headquarters that didn't make sense; our internal numbers showed the race was still much too close to call.

The counting went on into the night. Eventually, I won by 2 percent, 36 percent to 34 percent, a total of 317 votes.

Following the election, Lippitt's disappointed supporters sued to prevent me from taking office, claiming that a 1986 amendment to the state constitution disqualified a convicted felon—me—from holding office for three years after completing his sentence and probation. My campaign manager, Tom Rossi, was furious, pointing out, "Buddy's story has been covered from coast to coast. You would have had to have been hermetically sealed in a mayonnaise jar not to have known Buddy Cianci had some problems. This is absurd." The court heard their argument—and then threw out the case. Once again, I had become the mayor of the great city of Providence, Rhode Island.

From my first days in office there had been a taint of corruption around my administration. They investigated. An FBI agent named Dennis Aiken spent nine years and who knows how much money trying to prove his suspicion that I must be doing something wrong. He had managed to convict a few city employees, but spending nine years to convict some minor city employees is not exactly a résumé builder.

I did cut deals; I did reward those people who were loyal to me and punish those people who fought me, and sometimes I was rough about it. It's called politics. But everything I did, I did with the thought in mind of what was best for the city of Providence. For example, I tried very hard to bring my political opponents into my administration. I tried to befriend my political enemies, not simply because it would end their political opposition to me, as has been claimed, but because generally these were bright, knowledgeable people who also loved the city. Fred Lippitt had spent his whole life as a public servant and understood how to work with the legislature to get things accomplished. Why wouldn't I want him working for me? So I made him chairman of an ambitious redevelopment plan, the Providence Plan, which would eventually change the entire city. Andrew Annaldo was smart and ambitious; I made him chairman of the Bureau of Licenses. It wasn't just those two. I was once quoted, completely fictitiously, as saying, "Marry your enemies and screw your friends." Like so many others words put into my mouth by the media, I never said that. I brought my opponents into city hall knowing full well that they would be trying to build their political résumés by succeeding—and that my administration would get the credit for it.

If I had a real political enemy in Providence, it was the man who had succeeded me, Joe Paolino. I had known and liked his father, who was one of the major real estate developers in the city, and I had met Joe during my first campaign when he strongly supported Doorley. That created a wedge between us that lasted decades. Joe liked to tell people that when he ran for city council I had brought in the Army, Navy, and Marines to try to beat him. That's not quite accurate—he forgot the air force and the coast guard. He felt that as mayor I took too many shortcuts and that my administration was corrupt.

When he replaced me as mayor, he blamed me for every problem he encountered, while I spent much of my time on radio criticizing his administration.

I will never forget the night in 1990 when I was reelected mayor. Paolino had lost his election for governor. In his concession speech he made a point of saying that his mission was to keep the crooks out of city hall. It was clear whom he was talking about. When he said that, the crowd cheered, and the TV cameras swept around the room—and who did I see standing in the crowd applauding that statement but one of my own cousins. I'd given him his first job. I invited that cousin to my office and after a few pleasant minutes I told him I had something to show him. Maybe he expected family pictures, but instead I showed him a video of Paolino's concession speech. "Let me ask you," I said, freezing the frame showing him applauding, "what is that? How can you justify that? You're not that polite."

He squinted at the screen, but he had nothing to say. Instead, he started sweating. He kept his job, though, proving blood is thicker than politics.

My relationship with Joe Paolino began thawing when he joined Governor Sundlun and me to help bring the Providence Place Mall into reality. When he had his official portrait as mayor of Providence unveiled, he wanted to do it in the city council chambers—but he wasn't sure whether to invite me. Finally, he decided he had to invite me, but he didn't want me to speak.

Inviting me to a reception and prohibiting me from speaking? That wasn't going to happen. The governor explained the facts of political life to him, and when I spoke at that reception I said only the nicest things about him. Which seemed to make him angry, because afterward he said to me, "I know why you did that. You just wanted to look gracious in front of my friends."

He was wrong. I did it because the two of us love the city and we are members of a very exclusive club. We had governed the city and understood its poetry. And years later, when I went to prison, he was kind enough to write to me. I wrote back a little longer letter. He wrote back, and we became pen pals. Well, literally I was his pen pal. Eventually, he came to visit me there. We spent the day talking politics; he told me how he screwed me on this legislation, I told him how I screwed him on that bill. Typical politicians talking. And over time two bitter enemies have become friends.

That's what I tried to do with all those people who fought me—although with most of them I didn't have to go to prison to accomplish it.

When I took office at the beginning of Buddy II, I was determined not to have the same type of suspicion hanging over my administration. It was during this time that the groundwork Paolino and I had laid for more than a decade finally came to fruition and Providence emerged as America's "Renaissance City."

It had taken two decades, but it had become cool to live in Providence. Different magazines rated the city among the county's "most livable cities"; we were one of the best cities in which to retire, one of the best places for an artist to live, and had some of the best restaurants and best regional theater. At night people would come downtown just to see what was going on. We had trolleys to drive people to the various art galleries and gondolas and water taxis to enjoy the river. It was possible to eat at four-star restaurants, shop at the most elegant stores, see a Broadway production, and shop for critically acclaimed artworks in Providence. Rather than a city that saw a continuous stream of people leaving the city for Boston or New York, Providence had become a destination.

The actions we had taken affected almost every neighborhood and constituency. For homeowners I'd worked with Governor Sundlun to get more than $50 million in state aid, most of it for education, which meant we hadn't raised property taxes. For the liberals we'd hired the first gay liaison to the mayor's office and supported extending health insurance for city employees to same-sex partners, and for the conservatives we'd established America's first gun court. After Providence police officer Steven Shaw was murdered in 1994 by a robber with a long rap sheet, we realized that it was taking too long to try people who had committed crimes with guns and, when they finally were put on trial, they were receiving relatively light sentences. So I established a court to deal only with crimes in which a gun was involved, stipulated that these people had to be scheduled for trial within sixty days of the completion of discovery, and assigned only one judge, "Maximum John" Bourcier, to hear the cases. It had been Judge Bourcier who'd given me the sentence that forced me leave office in 1984. When we asked the legislature to approve the establishment of the first gun court in America, I also agreed that the city would provide three hundred thousand dollars to fund it, so in essence I was paying Bourcier's salary. The National Rifle Association added another ten thousand dollars and actually bought advertising to promote this court. As we had hoped, Maximum John handed down long sentences—and always added a substantial number of years for the gun. After the gun court was in operation several years, statistics showed that it had successfully reduced the time it took to dispose of a case from more than a year to 126 days, and that convicted felons received longer sentences. As a result, the *Livable Cities Almanac* concluded Providence was "the safest city in the Continental United States."

There weren't too many people racing to run against me in 1994. My only opponent was a state legislator who emphasized his support for the elderly, but had missed a substantial number of votes on issues important to those people. But I still ran as though my reelection were in jeopardy.

I almost had another opponent, a slightly deranged man who told city employees, "If I can't run for mayor, I'll have to kill the mayor." But after being arrested, he explained, "I've been on good behavior and I've been taking my medication."

I won that election without much difficulty, and in the following election four years later I was so popular in the city that I didn't even have an opponent. At various times polls put my approval rating at over 80 percent. But at just about the same time I was easily winning the 1994 election, Dennis Aiken, the FBI agent who had invested much of his career in the earlier investigation of my administration, moved back to Providence. Apparently, he encountered a TV reporter who asked him, "Still chasing Buddy?"

"I never give up," he'd replied.

I strongly believe that if a reasonably competent law-enforcement agency wanted to put the time, resources, and money into an investigation of just about any long-term political administration, it could find isolated cases of corruption. It is endemic in the system. When you put a thousand people in positions of authority, some of those people are going to abuse that authority. Unfortunately for me, Aiken had decided to play Javert to my Jean Valjean. I don't think anyone will ever know exactly why the FBI opened another investigation of my administration and spent years and who knows how many hundreds of thousands of dollars pursuing me. But in situations like this there is often a political motive.

In politics, U.S. senators control their state's courthouses—they get to approve judges and are often consulted on other legal matters—while mayors control the city halls. Senators also vote on the budget for the FBI. John Chafee was seventy-two years old when he was re-elected in 1994, and it was apparent he would not run again in 2000. He wanted his son Lincoln to succeed him, although from time to time there were reporters who wondered in print if I intended to run for the Senate when Chafee retired. I never answered that question.

I knew Lincoln Chafee. Earlier in his life Lincoln had worked for several years as a farrier at a harness racing track, taking care of horses' hooves. In fact, at one point he had asked me for a job as a garbage collector. I turned him down, telling him, "I don't think so. It's not good for your image or your family." I actually thought he wasn't qualified for the job. Eventually, he became the mayor of Warwick, Rhode Island, a city substantially smaller than Providence. Now, who else could have been a good candidate for Chafee's seat in 2000? Perhaps the most popular politician in the largest city in the state? When John Chafee died suddenly in 1999, Governor Lincoln Almond, who years earlier had been appointed a U.S. attorney by Chafee, appointed Lincoln Chafee to fill the rest of father's term. Politics is a beautiful thing.

Do I know this happened? Do I have any evidence that this investigation was opened for political reasons? No. Certainly it's possible that it was a coincidence of timing. But if I hadn't run for the Senate, I certainly would have run for reelection as mayor. And there is no doubt I would have won. After running unopposed in 1998, I had only one opponent in 2002, state representative and criminal-defense lawyer David Cicilline. For most potential candidates, running against me at that time was considered pretty much a political suicide mission. In ordinary circumstances I was unbeatable. But as it turned out, Cicilline and the man who was to prosecute me, Richard Rose, were colleagues and close friends, having taught a class together at Roger Williams University School of Law.

Cicilline wanted to be mayor. That could happen only if I died, resigned, or was removed for committing a crime. My plans did not include dying or resigning. Cicilline eventually did become mayor, and several years later appointed Kim Rose, the former wife of his former colleague, my prosecutor Richard Rose, to a $111,395-a-year job as Providence Schools communications director. Before being promoted to that job she had served as chief of staff to the superintendent of schools. As I often claimed on my radio show, her qualification for this position basically was her wedding ring. She was married to the man who made it possible for Cicilline to become mayor.

Do I know that Cicilline and Rose had an arrangement or that anything at all untoward took place? Absolutely not. The fact that one of these men prosecuted me and the other moved into the job I had to give up might well be just another one of those pesky coincidences. But as a political lifer, even I have to admire the symmetry.

The difficulty I have in discussing the investigation that led to my indictment is that I knew nothing about it while it was going on and, though I certainly knew some of the people involved, there were many more involved with whom I had very little or no contact. The FBI gave it the ominous sounding name Operation Plunder Dome, a play on the popular movie *Thunderdome,* supposedly because it all took place under the majestic dome of city hall.

The obvious goal of the entire investigation was to get to me, to prove that my administration was corrupt and that I personally had accepted a bribe, made an agreement for my personal gain, or directly committed any illegal act. In two FBI investigations that lasted more than a decade, the FBI was never able to pin a single criminal action on me. I know they tried to set me up at least once. At one point during the investigation I agreed to have lunch with a man whom I learned later was an FBI undercover agent posing as an air-conditioning and heating contractor. This FBI agent supposedly owned a company that installed air-conditioning and heating systems, and he claimed that he wanted to install his units in all of our schools. I met with him only because a maitre d' at a local restaurant asked me to sit down with him. It took him several months to set up the appointment. This undercover agent told me he would install his units in our schools for free and all we would have to pay him was a percentage of the money we saved on energy costs. "Really?" I said. "Let me understand this. You're going to pay for all the retrofitting and the only thing we're going to pay you is money we save on energy costs?"

"That's right," he said. When I said we would certainly be interested in exploring this, he asked, "Who do I have to see?"

I told him, "The guy who handles that would be our director of public property. His name is Alan Sepe." I volunteered to make an appointment for him with Alan.

And then he asked the million-dollar question, "Will I have to take care of him?"

Meaning, would he have to pay a bribe to get the city's business. This is what I said, and it was recorded by the concealed wire he was wearing: "No one will ask you for a thing. If anybody does, you pick up the phone and call me. I'll cut his balls off and have him arrested." It's on tape, every word of it. But when we did go to trial, the judge refused to allow this conversation to be heard by the jury.

It never occurred to me that this meeting was a setup.

Aiken started his investigation at the bottom of the barrel and tried to work his way up to my office. His chief undercover witness was a local businessman named Antonio Freitas, or Mr. Freon as he was called, who owned a heating and air-conditioning company. Freitas wore a wire for numerous meetings with members of my administration and successfully filmed Frank Corrente accepting a thousand-dollar payment. Freitas's credibility was diminished after several incidents in which he lost his temper and became violent. Given my own domestic problems, this is ironic, but Freitas's first two wives claimed he had abused them—and in the middle of the Plunder Dome investigation he was arrested for climbing over a counter and through a sliding-glass window to confront his third wife, then allegedly punching her in the face. After pleading no contest to the assault charge, Freitas later was arrested for punching his girlfriend in the face. Aiken actually had to arrest his own chief witness. As *The Providence Journal* reported, "The police said they moved quickly after Aiken told them Freitas had threatened to kill his wife, her friend and himself."

Ironically, several years later Freitas surfaced to support Lincoln Chafee's 2006 campaign for the Senate—and when Chafee was asked about Freitas's record for domestic abuse, he replied, "Nobody's perfect. He made some mistakes and he paid the price."

In addition to lowlifes like Freitas, FBI agent Aiken dug up city board members such as seventy-five-year-old Joe Pannone, the chairman of the Board of Tax Assessment Review, who eventually was convicted of selling property-tax reductions. According to Aiken's investigation, Pannone was heard on a wiretap claiming "the mayor knows everything," meaning that I was aware he was accepting bribes. It was absurd, he was talking about $100 bribes. Like so many other people, Pannone apparently used my name often and easily in his own dealings and claimed to be welcome in my office anytime he needed to see me. He didn't even need an appointment, he boasted. My secretary, Linda Verholst, sat directly outside my office for at least eleven years. As she testified in front of the grand jury, "In the eleven years I was there I think I had five sick days. I never changed my office or my desk. You couldn't go out to lunch. If you got to the ladies' room twice a day it was a good day. Even then you were summoned, somebody would bang on the door yelling that the mayor wanted me right away. I was there until seven or eight o'clock at night and so, generally speaking, it would have been hard for me not to know who was coming and going. I never knew Joe Pannone. I didn't know what he looked like, I didn't know his name . . . and yet he testified or said that he and Buddy were such good friends he could go in anytime he wanted. I didn't know the man. The first time I ever saw him was when his picture was in the paper. How could you believe a man who said he was so close to Buddy he brought him money and I never knew the man. It baffles me to this day."

There is no downside for someone like Pannone to make a claim like that without providing any evidence, and there is little I or anyone else can do about it. In fact, during the trial the Feds played the wiretap on which I was mentioned, but refused to put Pannone on the stand where we could cross-examine him. We even tried to put him on the stand as a hostile witness, but we were unable to do that. In law enforcement it's known as Let's Make a Deal. You give me a bigger fish, and I'll make your life easier. It's the theme song sung by prosecutors. I did it when I was a prosecutor, but in this case I was Aiken's white whale.

Charlie Mansolillo used to explain the way it works this way, "As the city solicitor I had to sign any settlement of litigation. For example, say someone had a collision with a Providence police officer and sued the city for a personal injury. The case would have been handled by one of my assistants. That assistant could tell the attorney representing the plaintiff, 'We can get this case settled for fifty thousand dollars, but I got to hand five grand to the solicitor so he'll approve the settlement.' My man takes the money and puts it in his pocket. I never know anything about it. But I get the paperwork, which he has approved, I look it over and it looks clean, an expert had been consulted and agreed this was a fair payment, so I sign the papers and the legal payment is made. Eventually, the negligence attorney goes to the FBI and testifies he had to give five grand to the assistant for the solicitor. To protect himself, the assistant claims he gave the money to me. There is absolutely no way I can protect myself from this. And this type of corruption happens on every level."

For me, the problem that I couldn't overcome in the end was the belief that I knew everything that went on in my administration on every level. I had been the mayor for so long and was quoted in the media so often that people accepted the fact that nothing happened in Providence unless I knew about and approved it. It was a myth, but people accepted it as reality. In fact, I delegated too much authority to members of my administration, and it was that management style that eventually proved to be my demise.

People in my administration would use my name. Almost always they did it legitimately, because they were carrying out my policy. But as I eventually learned, at least some members of my administration also did it for their own benefit. Police Chief Gannon, for example, would often get requests from members of my administration claiming to be speaking for me. He would call me or come down to the office to discuss these requests I knew nothing about. People used my name to get tickets for shows, dinner reservations at booked restaurants and, unfortunately, on occasion they used my name to run their own little private businesses on the side.

Even if I had been aware of Operation Plunder Dome, I probably wouldn't have been terribly concerned. I knew I hadn't done anything illegal. There were many opportunities to steal a fortune if I was corrupt. We'd had construction projects worth hundreds of millions of dollars; we'd built a mall, an ice rink, schools, and athletic facilities; we'd paved streets, and not one accusation was ever made that I had asked anyone for anything. Not once. So it baffled me that I would be accused of making deals for five thousand dollars or less.

In addition to Freitas and Pannone, Aiken successfully recruited Pannone's vice chairman of the Board of Tax Assessment Review, David Ead. Ead was also vice chairman of the city's Democratic Committee and a politically sophisticated person. Ead supposedly told Aiken that I had agreed to sell two abandoned city lots to Freitas for $1,000 each—in return for a ten-thousand-dollar payoff. I could just imagine Aiken's ears perking up at that one. The fact is that Eads showed up in my office with photographs of a dilapidated house and said he had a buyer for it, but that the person would buy it only if he could get the two adjoining lots for parking. We had a program to fight urban blight in which we sold vacant lots to people who would improve them and get them back on our tax rolls. A lot of houses had been knocked down in the city and we had abandoned lots. Nobody was paying taxes on them, and eventually these lots became overgrown with weeds and overrun with rats. I don't remember the particulars of the deal Eads boasted about, but I've read that he claimed it fell apart when we sold one of the lots to another buyer. That's how strong my relationship with Eads was. In fact, when Aiken threatened to throw Eads into prison unless he wore a wire and personally delivered that ten thousand dollars to me, Eads still refused, explaining, "I don't have that kind of relationship with the mayor." Eads knew his bluff had been called; he knew that he couldn't get near me. Aiken arrested him. So much for me accepting a bribe.

The one member of my administration that Aiken did nail for accepting a payment was Frank Corrente, who was caught by a camera hidden in a briefcase accepting a thousand-dollar bribe from Tony Freitas. I first got to know Frank Corrente during the 1990 campaign. He, Joe Almagno, and Tom Rossi supported and worked for me when everyone else was terrified to come near my campaign. After the election

Corrente wanted to be the director of administration; Almagno, who formerly had been the superintendent of schools, became my chief of staff; and Tom Rossi headed Intergovernmental Relations. Rossi, in fact, insisted on being paid one dollar more than anyone else. Eventually we sent him over to the Planning Department to take away his power.

Joe Almagno was completely honest and he and Corrente struggled for power, a fight that Corrente eventually won. At that time Frank Corrente probably had thirty years of experience in city government, much of it in the financial area, and he was well liked, so I certainly believed he had the ability to do the job. My initial mistake was making him director of my administration, but a much bigger mistake was failing to properly supervise him. I left the everyday machinations of city government—the daily headaches—to Frank Corrente. Eventually, he began to believe that he was the mayor; in fact, he told one of my aides, "People in the neighborhoods, they know I'm the real mayor."

Like other members of my administration, Corrente would do a lot of things in my name that I never knew about. But he had a lot more power than anybody else. He would hire and fire people; he would move them into different jobs. Corrente eventually developed his own little fiefdom. He would build personal loyalty by doing favors for people, favors I often knew nothing about. There was a lovely person who had worked in the office for a long time. This person had a relative who desperately needed a job, and Corrente found him a pretty decent job in a city department. And when that person had a problem on that job Corrente protected him. I didn't know any of that. This person was aware of some of the things that Corrente had done without my knowledge, and if there was ever any paperwork that concerned any of it, this person would make sure I never saw it. For example, if Corrente had made an appointment in the school department that I knew nothing about, anything concerning that appointment would always go directly to Corrente. Not me.

From time to time I would find out about something he'd done without my knowledge and we'd have a real fight over it.

The truth is that Corrente's time had passed, and there were several people in the office encouraging him to retire. They would ask him,

"What do you need this aggravation for?" One night, I was told, Corrente came out of my office and he was steaming. "That's it," he said. "I've had it. The mayor is mad at me again. I'm gonna retire." One of my secretaries sympathized with him. "Do yourself a favor, Frank. Retire. Go play golf." Bill Collins, the head of policy, agreed that Corrente should just go enjoy himself. But just when it looked as though he might walk out, our female office photographer literally threw herself on the ground, wrapped her legs around him, and started crying like Mary Magdalene, sobbing hysterically, "Please don't do it. You can't leave us. You know you're the real mayor and the city will fold if you retire."

Corrente was very good at that part of his job that I did know about. He solved problems and made sensible decisions. It was the things I didn't know about that destroyed him. In January 1999 Aiken sent Freitas to Corrente's office with one thousand dollars cash in an envelope and a hidden camera. Corrente was a multitasker; while he was meeting with someone, he would also be juggling phone calls. In this instance Freitas laid the envelope on Frank's desk, supposedly a payoff for arranging a lease. "What the fuck are you doing?" Corrente said. "It's not necessary. Do you hear me?"

Freitas murmured something in response, then Frank Corrente's phone rang. During that phone conversation Corrente took the envelope and put it in a desk drawer. It was there on tape, there was no mistaking what happened, no possible excuses. Corrente accepted the thousand dollars. He didn't solicit it, but he didn't refuse it, either.

Manny Vieira, my director of communications, had lunch almost every day with Frank Corrente. After this video had been shown on television before the trial, clearly proving there was corruption in city hall, Manny asked him, "Frank, why did you take that envelope?"

"He put it on the desk," Manny remembers him answering. "I didn't want that."

Manny said, "Frank, you put the freakin' envelope in your desk drawer. Why would you do that?"

Apparently, Corrente got angry. "I didn't know what it was. And who are you to say that I was wrong?" In fact, based on my experience this was not his typical behavior. I really don't believe he did a lot of things wrong, but this time he got caught. And in fact, I still don't know what he supposedly had done to be paid the money in this envelope.

So that was Aiken's lineup; some low-level people who were taking bribes to reduce taxes who claimed to be better connected and have more knowledge than they actually did, a witness who eventually went to jail for domestic abuse, and Frank Corrente. But no matter how hard he tried, Aiken was never able to link me directly to a single crime.

In Aiken's mind I was the Boss of Bosses, the mastermind running a corrupt organization who was too smart to get caught. In his mind.

I learned about the FBI's investigation early in the morning of April 28, 1999, when the FBI rang my doorbell. Dennis Aiken identified himself. I knew who he was. Aiken was there with another FBI agent. He asked me if I knew Joe Pannone and David Ead. I knew them, I said.

Aiken told me he'd come to my house rather than my office because, he said, "If we came to your office it would have arose suspicion." Suspicion? Meanwhile, fifty FBI agents were tearing through city hall, carrying out thousands of documents. Fifty FBI agents! I never found out where the big push came from, but either the FBI had so few cases to investigate it was able to assign several dozen agents to this one, or someone with political clout had expressed serious interest in "cleaning up city hall."

Aiken asked a few questions and I explained, politely, "I really don't want to talk to you because I think you're asking me questions I don't think I should answer until I talk to a lawyer." They left.

I found out they had been to city hall when I called Corrente. He gave me as much background as he knew, telling me Pannone and Ead had been arrested, but assured me that there was nothing to worry about. "It's about the tax board," he said.

Aiken's investigation continued for another two years. Some people would consider that a meticulous investigation. I prefer to see it as desperation. Aiken already had the tape of Corrente accepting the money; he was cooked. That left me. I can just imagine Aiken's frustration at not being able to find a single piece of hard evidence showing I accepted a bribe. He tried; oh, this guy tried. Eventually, he subpoenaed almost everybody in the office. My secretaries were questioned, my aides, everyone. He tried hard to intimidate them. An assistant told me that Aiken had taken her into a room, put a gun on the desk, put his badge on the desk, and started asking her questions about me. She told him simply, "Go fuck yourself."

Prosecutor Richard Rose had to find some reason to indict me; otherwise, he would be admitting they had sent an aircraft carrier out to catch a couple of minnows. I also knew how easy it was for people facing years in prison to tell a prosecutor anything he wanted to hear in exchange for protecting their own futures.

So I shouldn't have been surprised that on April 2, 2001, I was indicted on racketeering, extortion, bribery, mail-fraud, and witness-tampering charges. It was a ninety-seven-page indictment. Looking at that thing, I was surprised they hadn't thrown in cattle rustling. In response to the indictment, channeling the President Clinton–Monica Lewinsky scandal, I told the media, "There are no stains on this jacket."

When I went to court to be arraigned, I was surrounded by the media mob. This was the biggest story in Providence since . . . since the last time I'd been in court. One reporter shouted at me, "What do you think of this media circus?"

How could I resist that line? "You calling yourself a clown?" After pleading not guilty I was released on fifty thousand dollars personal recognizance. I was fingerprinted and had my mug shot taken. They made me take off my toupee for the mug shot. Then I put on my toupee and went back to work. Naturally, Governor Almond suggested I resign. Apparently being indicted was enough for him to presume I was guilty. I wondered if the governor had any thoughts about who should replace me.

At this time I was a regular guest on Don Imus's national radio show, *Imus in the Morning*. As far as Imus—or E-mus, as I thought it was pronounced—was concerned, I was the wisecracking mobbed-up politician from Providence, the perfect foil for him, and he liked the fact that I wasn't afraid to mix it up with him. I'd been doing Imus's show for almost eight years, and I'd used it extensively to promote events in the city. And, on occasion, myself. During one of our many conversations, for example, Imus thanked me for sending him a jar of my Mayor's Own pasta sauce, but added, "Unfortunately, it had a finger in it."

"Oh, good," I responded. "Apparently you got the right jar."

My nature has always been to use humor as a defense mechanism. This indictment was personally very painful. Almost two decades earlier I'd made a serious mistake and I'd paid for it. Since that time we had transformed the city, but we still had so many things I wanted to do. Providence was on a roll and this was potentially a huge roadblock. A few days after I was indicted, we learned that months earlier the prosecutor, Rose, had violated confidentiality rules by inviting friends into his living room to show them the sealed videotape of Corrente accepting the bribe. As I told Imus, "When I was a prosecutor, I never showed tapes that were sealed and sacrosanct. It's outrageous. It's cuckoo." And then I added, "I guess Blockbuster was closed that night . . . I wonder if he sold popcorn."

Aiken happened to be listening to the show. It turned out the man had no sense of humor.

Ten

never stopped loving my job, even after being in city hall for more than two decades. Every day was an adventure, and as too many people will admit, when it wasn't, I turned it into one. You would think that eventually the job would become predictable, but it didn't, it never did. For example, there was a way to indirectly enter my office from the street, although the door downstairs was supposed to be locked. One day I was working at my desk when a sound attracted my attention. I looked up and a woman was standing in the doorway—dressed from moccasins to headband in Native American garb. She just stood there staring at me. She didn't say a word, didn't make a sound. I wondered how the hell she'd gotten into my office. "How . . . ," I started, then realized what I was saying. I quietly got up and escorted her out—my security detail was really on the ball!

I also pardoned the Big Blue Bug. The Big Blue Bug is a giant bug sculpture on top of the New England Pest Control building along I-95. It obviously was put up there as a sign, but it had become a popular landmark; traffic reporters on the radio would tell listeners, "Traffic is backed up to the Big Blue Bug." When people were giving directions, they would assume everyone knew where it was, "Go two exits past the Big Blue Bug . . ." But one of our city departments ordered the Big Blue Bug exterminated: They wanted the sign taken down because it violated several building codes. They wanted to kill the Big Blue Bug! Absolutely not, I said, and officially pardoned it.

Another afternoon I was walking down a corridor in city hall when an older couple stopped me. They were from New York, they explained, and had heard about Mayor Cianci and wanted to have a photo taken with him. Would that be possible? I said it would certainly be possible. But when they asked me if the mayor was in, I realized they had no idea what I looked like. Fortunately, at that very moment one of my aides, an African American named Wil Fleming, happened to come out of an office. "Mayor," I said to Wil, "these people are from New York and they want to take a picture with you." Wil looked bewildered, but he posed for the picture, allowing this happy couple to return to New York with the only known photograph of the black mayor of Providence.

We also had a priest who was mugged in the old train station, which was a well-known meeting place for homosexuals. This priest had been active in a community group that demanded more police involvement. The police responded that when they tried to crack down this community too often refused to assist the department. During the mugging several diocesan credit cards had been stolen. I called the colonel at that time and suggested, "Let's find out who rolled him." The police picked up a few people, among them the person who committed the crime; apparently, the police caught him with the credit cards. But the priest, who had been complaining loudly about the lack of police protection in his community, was reluctant to identify the mugger. The police organized a lineup and the priest claimed he was unable to pick out anyone. The colonel got so upset that he put the priest in the lineup and ordered the guy who had rolled him to pick out the man he had mugged.

Even I couldn't make this stuff up.

But, looking back, certainly one of the most difficult and unusual situations in which I found myself took place in 1978, when right in the middle of my reelection campaign I was forced to defend Polaroid photographs of students' sex organs as works of art.

In early May 1978 the Rhode Island legislature passed a law defining obscenity. The Supreme Court of the United States couldn't define it, but the Rhode Island General Assembly apparently knew what it was. According to the lobbyist who wrote this law, it was supposed to be used against commercial distributors of pornography, like adult bookstores and X-rated theaters. People whose business was selling pornography. But that is precisely the problem with trying to define pornography. Only days after this law was passed, students at Rhode Island School of Design opened an exhibition called "Private Parts" with the tagline: "Any size. Any medium. Any thing. Any one. Any private. Any part." It was held in a private gallery on the fifth floor of an old building and there was no admission charge. The exhibition included about 110 photographs, paintings, and sculptures, including, according to a description, "an actual rattrap sprung on an unfortunate male," as well as two photo booths, one for men and one for women. Visitors were invited to go into the booths, drop their drawers, and take a Polaroid picture of their private parts, then hang that photograph on a bulletin board as a work of art.

While it did not appeal to me, "Private Parts" obviously attracted public attention. "Vulgarity is a part of life and art," a RISD student told a reporter, and the show drew several hundred people. At least one member of the city council was outraged and threatened to cancel the school's tax-exempt status because of the show, accusing the students of "violating every standard of the community under the guise of art." Me? I didn't want anything to do with it.

Unfortunately, my then chief of police, Angelo Ricci, felt a need to protect the public. Six officers raided the show and confiscated forty-three pieces. In some cases they ripped them right off the walls. Ricci took a look at police photographs of the show and told reporters he shut it down because "it's wrong. If it's obscene, it's obscene. There's no two ways about it."

The situation was completely absurd. One of the more tame photographs in the show was of a house. I don't know why it was in the show, but when a police officer took it off the wall, an artist screamed at him, "What's wrong with that? It's just a picture of a house."

To which the officer responded, "The court will decide that!"

A sculptor whose work was on display said about the raid, "It's awful. It's a disaster. It's like the Middle Ages."

I was furious. There are few worse places for a politician to be caught than between his somewhat-conservative middle-American voters and pictures of penises. While my conservative supporters wanted the show closed, my more liberal supporters believed it was a freedom-of-speech matter. The city solicitor Ronnie Glantz, our lawyer who would have to prosecute the case, actually handled the situation reasonably. "The whole thing is absurd," he said. "The law is unconstitutional. We'd have to put shorts on half the city's statues. Allow this to happen and the next thing, people will be in trouble for selling books with pictures of Michelangelo's *David*."

The judge asked the police department if it had heard about this thing called the First Amendment and ordered all the art returned. But for a time this controversy created a problem for me. About three weeks after the raid I went to the particularly raucous annual congress of representatives of PACE, People Acting for Community Effort. This was a loud, angry group, and among their many complaints was that the police were not providing adequate service to minority communities. When I left that meeting, I was fuming. As I got into my car I saw Colonel Ricci standing on the side. "And you," I told him. "Instead of arresting people for taking pictures of their cocks, why don't you get out there and catch some crooks and drug dealers."

Actually, I had my own methods for dealing with the sex business. For example, there was a strip club across the street from a veterans' hospital and close to a school. I wasn't against strip clubs—we set aside an area for them—I just didn't want this club in this location. The owner was a former cop who was very vocal in his criticism of me. So I decided I would help him advertise his club. I put a police car on the sidewalk in front of the place, its red light flashing. Naturally the ACLU sued the city. By that time the police had found evidence that prostitutes were working inside and raided the place. The police found hidden video cameras recording men getting oral sex. I called the head of the ACLU and told him, "I want you to know we just raided the place and we got all kinds of tapes of men getting oral sex. You still want to represent this guy?" He said no more.

I realized I was stretching my authority by putting a police car in that location. But sometimes that type of unorthodox action was necessary to get things accomplished. I knew that the majority of people did not want a strip club down the block from a school, so I did what was necessary to get rid of it. Sometimes every politician has to do the wrong thing to get the right thing done. I had a similar problem with an X-rated peep show across the street from Trinity Rep. What was once a Packard Motor Car showroom had become a porno emporium. At various times it contained an adult bookstore and peep show, a strip club, and two bars connected to prostitution. To build up that neighborhood so people would feel safe there at night, I knew we had to get rid of the operators of the sex emporium. Unfortunately, those people had signed a long, solid lease and did not intend to move. They knew the neighborhood was getting better and wanted to be there as it happened. That building wasn't in great condition, but it wasn't beyond repair, either—although it was beyond what the owners could afford to pay to repair it. So, when we finally realized they weren't going to move, I decided to use the municipal powers of eminent domain to condemn the entire building—which got rid of the peep show—and then sell it. I figured we might even make a profit. Unfortunately, buying the building and settling the lease cost the city almost $1 million. It certainly wasn't worth that, and it would have required considerably more to do the necessary repairs. For me, that created a serious problem; I knew I was going to take a loss on the building no matter who I sold it to, but if I sold it to someone with whom I had any type of relationship, the newspapers would make it appear to be a sweetheart deal: "Cianci buys building for a million bucks and sells it to a friend for much less." Politically, I would have been crucified. The fact that getting rid of those owners was only a piece in solving a much larger puzzle wouldn't have made any difference at all. Eventually, I sold it to the Chace family—the old and respected Yankee family that had founded Berkshire Hathaway—for $250,000.

I was in my office the afternoon we were going to publicly announce the sale with my friend and supporter Frank DiBiase, a very successful hotel and restaurant owner. I said to him, "I'm going to give you a lesson in urban politics. If I had paid a million bucks for a building, then sold it to you or any other friend of mine, or any Italian or anybody with an ethnic name for two hundred and fifty thousand dollars, the Bureau of Mines, the IRS, the CIA would be banging on my door tomorrow morning to investigate that deal. There's no way anybody would have believed it was a legitimate deal that I made to clean up the neighborhood. But you watch, because I sold it to the Chace family I'm going to be hailed as an urban hero." And that is precisely what happened.

Using Providence's creative community was always an extremely important aspect of my plan to rebuild the city. A city is a completely different place during the day than it is at night. Jobs bring people into a city during the day; the city's culture brings people into the city at night. When I took office, Providence was dead at night. There was no reason for people to come downtown. We had a few struggling theaters, including Trinity Rep, and some restaurants. We desperately needed to create a sense of excitement in the city, a feeling that something was going on that nobody would want to miss. We did anything and everything necessary to transform Providence into a cultural center; we restored buildings, we moved walls, we even moved rivers.

Among the first things I did was provide the funds necessary to keep our theaters in business. The Trinity Square Repertory Theatre, for example, had established a reputation as one of the leading regional theaters in the country, but it was barely able to make its mortgage payments. In fact, it had fallen behind. Trinity's well-respected artistic director, Adrian Hall, came to see me to borrow a million dollars for a week. The Ford Foundation had given the theater a million-dollar grant for a certain purpose, but Adrian had spent it on productions. He needed to show the Foundation that the million dollars was still in the bank. In the creative community you sometimes had to accept creative bookkeeping. In response to that request, I asked, "You play gin rummy?" He looked at me with a puzzled expression on his face. "Why?"

"Because if I do what you want we're gonna end up in a cell playing gin rummy." Fortunately, we were able to solve this problem in another and legal way.

I also used city funds to support the establishment of a black repertory theater and stayed actively involved in the restoration of the Providence Performing Arts Center. The center is only a few blocks from Trinity Repertory Theatre, but they attract very different audiences. Trinity is a smaller, more intimate theater that can afford to stage classic plays and experimental shows, while the Performing Arts Center brings the big Broadway musicals to the city. After preventing B. A. Dario from tearing down the old Loew's Movie Palace—the once-magnificent theater that had opened in 1928—by refusing to issue a demolition permit, I continued to work closely with the Performing Arts Center director, Lynn Singleton, to develop it into the leading regional theater in New England. In fact, when Lynn had someone in town for some business purpose he would usually arrange for me to meet them. He'd call it "The Buddy Show," knowing that I was going to put on my large and effusive personality to persuade them to do whatever it was he needed or wanted. For example, the theater had enough seats to financially support large and expensive touring Broadway shows—at that time, with thirty-one hundred seats it was the second-largest theater in New England—but the backstage area was too small to fit lavish musicals like *The Phantom of the Opera, Wicked,* and *Beauty and the Beast.* That lack of backstage space had kept the theater from becoming a major regional performance center, and instead it was limited to smaller shows running a split week. It didn't attract a large enough audience to that part of the city to support restaurants and shops. For a long time the building next door, which had once been a department store, sat empty and dark.

The *Phantom of the Opera* changed regional theater and revitalized that part of the city. Before *Phantom,* producers of touring shows like *Cats* modified the show to fit into the available theaters. They would take out scenery and restage it so it could be done in the space available, which meant that audiences saw an abridged version of the show. Cameron Mackintosh, *Phantom*'s producer, announced that his touring company would perform the show the way it was done in New York and London; if it didn't fit into the theater, *Phantom* wasn't coming to town.

It didn't fit in our theater as the theater existed. But Lynn was a dreamer; he wanted to tear down the rear wall of the theater and expand it into the middle of Pine Street. Lynn estimated the cost at $7 million, which was almost as much as a new theater would cost. In addition to money that could be raised through normal fund-raising, the theater needed substantial bank loans. Though the banks were willing to make those loans, they wanted a guarantee that the theater would be able to attract major Broadway productions. Governor Sundlun and I both got involved, and the theater was able to get an agreement from Mackintosh that if the show fit, he would commit to a six-week run for *Phantom* and a five-week run for *Miss Saigon*.

Phantom established the Providence Performing Arts Center as a significant, legitimate theater. It became the anchor for the renovation of that part of the city. Alan Chille, the general manager of the theater, said, "If we didn't have this theater, you could have turned the lights off in this part of the city." Once Lynn had the money, he needed twelve feet of Pine Street owned by the city. We did a little of this, a little of that and gave it to him—and then I sent him a bill for $158,000. I knew he wasn't going to pay it, I just wanted to hear how loud he could yell. He did offer a good suggestion, though, while we argued about it: "I know how we can solve the city's deficit problem. All you got to do is sell pieces of streets." Obviously he got his twelve feet and it didn't cost him a penny.

About two weeks before *Phantom* reopened the theater, I went down there to look at the job. Inside, the theater looked beautiful, but outside it was dull. It didn't light up the street with excitement, which is what I wanted it to do. I said to Lynn, "This show is going to bring thousands of people into the city. We need to make the theater look special." Then it came to me. "We need twinkle lights in all the trees." Lynn looked at me as if I was just a little crazier than normal. But two days later we had people stringing twinkle lights in the trees, and when that show opened the entire street seemed to be celebrating.

Lynn really knew how to use me for the benefit of the theater. At one point he was trying to convince the Walt Disney Company to open a national tour of *The Lion King* in Providence. What I did not know at that time was that to get a big show like that, it sometimes requires making a substantial guarantee, just like bringing a convention or the Super Bowl to a city. Lynn asked me to go with him to New York and have dinner with Disney's director of touring. He made reservations at La Cirque. But before we went to dinner he gave me a pep talk, telling me about all the publicity we would get if the show opened at the Performing Arts Center. "That sounds good," I said. "What do we need to do to make it happen?"

Here it comes, here's where he put the strong arm on me: "Candidly, Mayor, I know they're looking at other locations. So to get Disney's attention we need to put some money on the table to underwrite their tour. Like a hundred thousand dollars, maybe two hundred thousand."

I thought he was kidding, "Two hundred thousand bucks? What the hell does Disney need my money for?"

Lynn pointed out, "Actually, Mayor, it's not your money. It's not that much, more of a symbolic gesture." Lynn explained that shows like *The Lion King* generate millions of dollars in economic activity for a city. The big Broadway touring productions create excitement in a city. People come to see the show, they eat in restaurants, they shop and they stay in the hotels, all of it producing sales-tax revenue.

Nice try. I showed him a symbolic gesture. I wasn't going to allow a multibillion-dollar company like Disney to extort money from me to bring one of their shows to town so they could make even more money. I was adamant about it. Then we went to dinner, although by that point I knew this was a waste of time.

At Le Cirque Lynn told Disney's representative, "One of the things the mayor and I would like to discuss with you is the possibility of opening *Lion King* in Providence."

Disney's man immediately began shaking his head. "No, no, that isn't going to work. It looks like we're going to open in Denver."

Denver? Was he kidding me? I couldn't control myself. I blurted out, "Denver! With those cowboys! Are you kidding me? Why in the world would you go to Denver to do this? Listen, if you'll open the tour in Providence I'll give you five hundred thousand dollars." And then I started selling Providence.

Never mind the Disney rep's response, Lynn just sat there with his mouth open. An hour earlier I'd been screaming at him that we were being extorted, and suddenly I was offering Disney half a million bucks to open at the Performing Arts Center. As it turned out, Disney couldn't make the deal, but Lynn knew from that moment on that I would put Providence's money where my mouth was.

For my efforts, The League of American Theatres honored me with the first Star of Broadway Touring Award, given for support of regional theatres.

In addition to supporting legitimate theaters, I also established the Providence Film Commission to bring television and movie production to Providence. We established the program that eventually evolved into the Rhode Island state tax credit to encourage production. Providence happens to be a wonderful place to shoot a TV show or movie. In 1997, for example, we had eight feature films shot in the city or nearby. The first of these was *Code of Ethics,* a thriller starring Melissa Leo about a serial killer who goes after perpetrators of Medicare fraud. A couple of scenes in that film were shot in my office. As the *Journal* wrote, "If the state were looking for a promotional film, it couldn't have asked for anything better."

The range of films shot in Providence includes the Farrelly Brothers' *There's Something About Mary* to *Die You Zombie Bastards,* billed as "The First Serial Killer Superhero Rock 'n' Roll Zombie Road Movie Romance."

The most successful production to film in the city was the appropriately titled TV show *Providence,* which ran for five seasons on NBC. Talk about the best possible tourist promotion for a city. We actually didn't have that much to do with bringing it to town. They were looking at several different cities, although personally I never thought the title *Pawtucket* would have the same emotional impact as *Providence.* We offered NBC every possible inducement to pick our city. They actually could have used any city, except Beverly Hills. It was a drama about a young female plastic surgeon, played by Melina Kanakaredes, who leaves Beverly Hills to return to her home and family in Providence. It was a nice show. One afternoon at a Conference of Mayors meeting I was discussing production tax credits with Baltimore mayor Kurt Schmoke when he complimented me on getting that show: "It's a beautiful show," he said, "the way the city comes across." Then he frowned and added, "We got a show, too."

"Really? What's it called?"

"*Homicide: Life on the Street.*"

Actually, only some of the exteriors were filmed in Providence. Most of the show was done in Los Angeles. The only thing I insisted on was that they make the city look as appealing as possible, and I agreed to do anything possible to ensure they did that. At one point, for example, they were in town shooting exteriors for the next season and I got an emergency call from one of my aides. "We got a problem, Mayor," he said. "The river is too low."

"What are you talking about?" I asked. "It's a river. It gets high and then it gets low."

"They want to film it for the opening sequence and it's down. It looks like crap."

They wanted me to raise the river. I thought about it. The city has a system of five hurricane pumps, built to pump water out of the Providence River into Narragansett Bay to prevent it from overflowing and flooding downtown during an unusually big storm or hurricane. This system was capable of pumping millions of gallons of water out of the river system in a few minutes. "How about if we reverse the pumps?" I asked. "Can't we reverse the pumps and raise the river?"

We found out it was possible and we raised the river for the shoot. I commanded that the waters be raised and it happened. It made me feel like Jesus.

I appeared in one episode, playing Mayor Buddy Cianci in "Taste of Providence." In this episode Melina Kanakaredes's character, Sydney Hansen, volunteers to perform breast reduction surgery for free on a stripper with serious back problems who wants to leave that business, while the city has a cooking contest with a five-thousand-dollar first prize. In the previous episode one of the characters had made an amazing clam chowder by accidently using breast milk, which turned it into an aphrodisiac. But when she made it for the contest, she used real milk, which ruined the taste. The winner of the contest, who supposedly received a scholarship to Johnson & Wales University in

Providence, one of the leading culinary schools in America, was me. I won for my special marinara sauce. But in a grand gesture, instead of accepting the award money, I donated it the school to use for a scholarship and asked the character who made the clam chowder to be the first recipient. I had two lines, I think. But the producers put my name on a production trailer and gave me my own makeup person.

Unfortunately, the original script did not use the name Johnson & Wales, which was extremely irritating for that college. The administration wanted the recognition so badly that they offered to pay my airfare to Los Angeles just so its name could be dubbed in. Fortunately, I was flying to California for a Conference of Mayors meeting anyway. But only in the world of television would I find myself flying from Providence to Los Angeles to do a voice-over for a show called *Providence*.

There were some productions that we didn't particularly want coming to the city. HBO wanted to promote the new season of *The Sopranos* in various cities around the country, including Providence. It was no secret that historically there was a strong Mafia presence in Providence. When I was a kid, I always felt that that was a stain on Italian Americans. As a prosecutor I'd fought organized crime. But frankly, I got sick and tired of seeing the Italian stereotypes; we've said it, we've done it, we've bought the T-shirt. As a politician I'd had some minor confrontations with the mob, but for the most part organized crime stayed far away from my administration, and I had nothing to do with them. I felt *The Sopranos* glorified the Mafia. Though I couldn't stop them from promoting the show in the city, or even filming in Providence—that was their right—I didn't do anything to help them, either. They asked for my cooperation and I refused to give it to them. I certainly wasn't going to participate in any celebrations of this crew coming to town. Then they wanted to buy several cartons of my marinara sauce to use on the show. Filming in Providence was one thing; using my marinara sauce was something very different. Now that was personal.

I created the Mayor's Own Marinara Sauce in the early 1990s as something to sell at a fund-raiser. It was supposed to be a one-time thing. I made it with the owners of the West Valley Inn. We put in a little of this, some of that, added a pinch of whatever; we just kept experimenting. I wanted it to taste just like the sauce my aunts would make on Sunday afternoons so many years earlier. Their sauce would simmer on the stove for hours as they occasionally added their own ingredients until it was slightly better than perfect. But whatever I added, we couldn't get it exactly right—until the Old Canteen's Joe Marzilli suggested we had to add carrots to take away the acidity. Once we did that, hmmm, it was perfect. We bought mason jars, had a label made up, and gave the sauce away. People loved it, so we made some more. Eventually, I formed a company and began selling it, using the profits to give out more than 250 grants and scholarships to inner-city high schools students.

The Mayor's Own became very popular. For several days it was even displayed in the secure windows of Cartier, surrounded by diamonds, on Fifth Avenue in New York City. During a Providence teachers' strike, a union president Paul MacDonald had a press conference that he concluded by telling reporters, "Oh, by the way, the mayor's sauce sucks."

I didn't respond, but I didn't forget it, either. A year later the orchestra at the Performing Arts Center was on strike and Paul and I negotiated a settlement. We had a press conference to announce the end of the strike. The room was jammed with reporters. As soon as the lights were turned on and the cameras started rolling, I reached under the podium and took hold of the jar of my sauce I'd put there. I placed it on the podium so every camera would have to focus on it and said, "I understand, Paul, that you don't like my sauce? Would you like to tell me why that is?"

Paul responded, "Well, Mayor, at that time I didn't like it. But I certainly like it now."

That sauce was close to my heart, the scholarship fund, and my stomach. So I refused to give the producers of *The Sopranos* permission to use it on the show. To add to the scholarship revenue, we eventually also offered for a limited time the Mayor's Own Pizza, which added one dollar per pie to the fund; the Mayor's Choice Coffee; the Mayor's Own Biscotti; and the Mayor's Own Extra Virgin Olive Oil.

We also had a request for a variance to stage a takeoff of *Tony n' Tina's Wedding,* a so-called environmental comedy in which audience members supposedly are guests at an Italian wedding. The bride and groom come from completely dysfunctional families, described as "embarrassing, bumbling, and colorful," which allows the authors to throw in every negative cliché about Italians. Two really overweight women wanted to produce it in Providence but they needed certain support from the city, for example permission to serve alcohol on unlicensed premises. These women actually thought I would support their efforts. I asked the head of the licensing board, Ray Dettore, a high-ranking official in the national Order Sons of Italy to join us at the meeting. They had some shot getting his approval. I said to him, "Raymond, these women would like to put on this play every night. As far as I'm concerned, this isn't an artistic celebration, this is a money-making insult to the Italian American experience.

"But of course you can give them the variance if you think it's appropriate."

One of these very large women said, "Mayor, it looks like we've offended you."

I know on occasion I go a bit too far, and this was one of them. This time I went way overboard. "Let's say, for example, I came to see you and I told you I wanted to put on a show about fat women." Way, way overboard. "Let's say this play is about women who are so fat they can't have sexual intercourse, women who are so fat they can't sleep at night and they have to be rolled out of bed. Then on opening night we could have you come up on stage and I would hand you a key to the city for this celebration of fat people . . . would you be offended?" Way, way, way . . .

The following Christmas these two lovely women proved they had a lot more class than I did. They actually sent me a present. A box of chocolates.

I used artists as the shock troops of neighborhood rehabilitation. It was the artists who gave the city its spice. We had more artists per capita in Providence than any American city. Many of them had originally come to town to study at the Rhode Island School of Design and

Brown and stayed. Artists value space above comfort, and that's what we could offer them. They needed large, inexpensive lofts in which to live and work, and we had an abundance of boarded-up brick manufacturing buildings and old department stores with large empty spaces located in gritty neighborhoods, so we just put those two resources together. I wasn't the first mayor to appreciate the value of artists to a city: They would move happily into the least expensive areas, taking over large abandoned spaces where nobody else wanted to live, and resettle what was basically an abandoned neighborhood. They would create a buzz, and an avant-garde neighborhood would begin to grow. Eventually, a few art galleries would open and the adventurous collectors would find them. A few performance spaces would open in converted spaces, followed by atmospheric cafés and some cutting-edge restaurants. Then the clubs would come, and finally the real estate industry would arrive, rents would rise, and the artists eventually would be pushed to find the next inexpensive neighborhood.

But I was the first mayor in America to create a tax-free Arts and Entertainment District. Though a former Providence mayor once said, "I don't want a bunch of freaks with green hair roaming my city," I saw the possibilities. In 1985 an artist named Umberto Crenca had founded an art space he named AS220, which was essentially a communal endeavor for artists. Any artist was permitted to show any art there. Crenca didn't have green hair, but he did have a completely shaved head, a long white beard, and, dangling from his right ear, a glass fist holding a glass eyeball. AS220 had been commercially successful and Crenca needed a larger space. I needed the artists, the painters and sculptors, actors, song writers, dancers, writers, poets; I needed those people with green hair and dangling eyeballs to inject creativity into the city's spine. It was a perfect match.

I remembered how excited I had been to walk the streets of our partnership city, Florence, Italy, and see the work of artisans being sold on every corner. That's what I wanted to create in Providence. So in 1996 I proposed turning a square mile of mostly decrepit downtown space into a tax-free arts district. In addition to giving 25 percent tax credits to the developers who would rehabilitate these buildings, any artist or performer living in this district would not have to pay state income tax, and their customers would not have to pay sales tax on their purchases. Eventually we expanded that sales-tax break to include all artwork sold inside the district, including those created by artists living elsewhere.

The definition of an artist was intentionally very broad. We established a committee to rule on that, but basically if you claimed you were an artist and wanted to live there, you were an artist.

Governor Lincoln Almond was against the creation of an arts district, claiming that the potential losses of tax revenue "could be substantial." That was ridiculous. As I said then, when was the last time an artist earned enough money to pay taxes? We hadn't even bothered to determine what the potential losses might be because these were mostly kids whose work sold for very little. And providing tax incentives for developers to rehabilitate buildings would breathe life into decaying neighborhoods. When Governor Almond vetoed the bill, I knew I had the votes in the legislature to overturn it. But it became a little more interesting than that.

This governor and I did not get along. When he was a U.S. attorney, he had spent years trying unsuccessfully to find a reason to prosecute me. And in return I took every opportunity to slam him. He was noted for being a particularly uninspiring public speaker, and every time I followed him to the podium I would begin by thanking him for warming up the crowd for me. I used to say that was about all anyone could expect from a man who still used a phone with a rotary dial. So naturally I saw a wonderful opportunity the day I drove through the Public Works garage and spotted a city vehicle with the Providence license plate "1" on it. Traditionally, the governor of Rhode Island had plate number 1, the mayor of Providence was given the license plate 10,000, while the mayor of the state's second-largest city, Warwick, got 20,000. Number 1, I liked that. It must have been assigned to Public Works about the time Henry Ford first mass-produced cars. I told my driver to stop the car, get that plate, and put it on my car. To make it look even more official, my communications director attached two city shields to it.

The governor was not amused. He contacted the state police, who requested officially that I remove that plate from my car. I said, "Absolutely not. That has been a city plate for seven decades." I could have said eight if I had wanted to; there was no possible way of checking it. "It's not coming off."

"Well, you can't have those shields on it, then."

We checked the regulation and discovered I was permitted to have one shield on the plate. Then I contacted the state senate majority leader, Paul Kelly. I'd done favors for him, and we were friends. I told him I needed legislation passed allowing the mayor of the great city of Providence to have a city plate number 1. He agreed. "I think you're a man of distinction and certainly should have that."

The legislature passed that bill just before the session ended. And Almond vetoed it.

Coincidently, Governor Almond and I had cooperated with the Smithsonian Institution to bring an exhibit to Providence, and we were both invited to cut the ribbon. He was furious with me. "You shouldn't have that license plate, you're always speeding," he said so softly only I could hear him. "It's a bad image."

"There you go again, Governor, jumping to conclusions. I don't speed. I don't drive my car. I'm driven by a police officer, and if he speeds then you should have a state policeman arrest him." I understand that the fact that I enjoy needling people so much is not the most appealing part of my personality. But sometimes I just can't help it.

He said proudly, "It doesn't matter, because I vetoed that bill."

I nodded. "I know. That's why the legislature is coming back this afternoon to override your veto."

"We'll see if that happens," he said softly, smiling for the cameras.

"Don't hold your breath, Governor," I responded, also smiling for the cameras.

Believe me, the legislature wasn't coming back into session just to give me my license plate. The only two bills the governor had vetoed at the end of the legislative session were the bills about my license plate and the creation of a tax-exempt arts district. While the only person who cared about my license plate was me, the arts district had substantial support in Providence, including from the presidents of both Brown University and the Rhode Island School of Design and several politically powerful developers.

By this time the legislators had packed up and gone home for the summer. We happened to be in the middle of a heat spell in the city and they were not at all happy to be back in session. The statehouse is not air conditioned, and the temperature inside that chamber had to be more than a hundred degrees. Many of the legislators showed up wearing shorts. The most important thing to them was getting out of there. There was no question that both of Almond's vetoes were going to be overturned, so they curtailed debate and voted. The most supportive arts and entertainment district in the nation came into being, and I got license plate number 1.

Sports were also always an important part of the city's culture, but the only draw we had during the winter was the Providence College basketball team, which played at the civic center. While the Friars had once been a national power, they had become more of a middle-of-the-league Big East team. We also had hockey in the city. I was honored to be selected as an honorary coach of the Rhode Island School of Design's hockey squad, the Nads, and when I had time I led the cheers, "Go-nads!" Years earlier we had had the Providence Reds of the American Hockey League (AHL), a minor league that fed players to the National Hockey League (NHL), but poor attendance and rising costs forced that team to move to Binghamton, New York. In the early 1990s I wanted to get another team into the civic center, especially on Sunday nights when the theaters were dark.

I began discussions with the company that had the concession rights to the arena. They had absolutely no interest in putting minor-league hockey into the civic center. I made it about as clear as ice: I wanted a hockey team and if they couldn't make a deal, their contract would not be renewed when it expired.

They weren't interested. Maybe they didn't believe me, who knows. Fortunately, the owner of the NHL's Boston Bruins was Jeremy Jacobs, who was also the CEO of Delaware North Companies, a multibillion-dollar concession company. I spoke with Harry Sinden, then the general manager of the Bruins, and told him that if he could bring a hockey team to Providence, I would use my best effort to ensure that Delaware North got the concessions in the arena. I don't know how legal that was—but it was effective. It made sense for the Bruins, too, they would have their minor-league team playing an hour from Boston Garden. Ed Anderson, the owner of the Bruins AHL team in Portland, Maine, actively supported the move to Providence. In return we gave the Bruins a great deal: We rented the arena to them for about $2,500 a game and 40 percent of gross revenues. Unfortunately, that's why inside the arena popcorn is six dollars—but it's very good popcorn.

People wondered how we managed to steal a good minor-league hockey team. But my former opponent, Fred Lippitt, apparently was not surprised, telling a reporter, "Buddy could talk a hungry dog off a meat wagon."

The deal was made. Thanks to Sinden and Anderson the hockey team was coming to Providence. We had scheduled a press conference to make the official announcement, but we still didn't have a name for the team. I'd asked Sinden about the name several times, but had never gotten an answer. Finally he told me he wanted to call the team the Providence Jewelers. The Jewelers? Was he kidding me! I could just imagine the headlines: Jews Beaten!

There was no way that team was going to be the Jewelers. I was adamant it would be the Providence Bruins. It made perfect sense to me; this was the Bruins' minor-league team, and we would all profit from acknowledging that relationship. Sinden disagreed, wanting to keep that name only for the parent club, and we spent a lot of time arguing. Finally, I told him, "I've given in on a lot of points. If it's not going to be the Providence Bruins, I'm canceling the press conference."

Sinden reluctantly agreed. The team was an immediate success, averaging ten thousand spectators a game that first season, and eventually setting AHL attendance records. But as important as the revenue, the fact that the team moved *to* Providence added to the growing impression that the city was changing, that something exciting was going on.

Without question, though, the thing we did that attracted the most attention was WaterFire, in which we set the river on fire. In its early history Providence's location at the head of Narragansett Bay had made it an important port city, which brought the railroads into the city, but as other, deeper-water ports developed along the eastern seaboard, our waterfront lost its importance and was replaced by manufacturing. During the Industrial Revolution the three rivers of Providence—the Woonasquatucket, the Moshassuck, and the Providence, which is formed when the first two come together downtown—had provided access to the city for ships traveling to or from Europe. But as the city became "the Beehive of Industry," as it was known, the center of the nation's textile, jewelry, and silverware industries, the railroads and eventually a road system replaced the commercial need for those rivers. Goods manufactured in more than twelve hundred factories were transported over land, and eventually the rivers were mostly closed to navigation; parts of them were filled in, other sections were polluted by factory runoff. Residents said you could tell what color dyes the tanneries were using each day from the color of the rivers, and apparently they often emitted a foul stench. Rather than being cleaned, the rivers were covered with roads and bridges. In fact, in 1988 the *Guinness Book of Word Records* recognized the 1,150-foot wide Crawford Street Bridge over the Providence River as the "world's widest bridge."

Downtown Providence had been separated into two very distinct areas by the railroad tracks, sidings, rail yards, and service facilities that had been built decades earlier to serve a city that no longer existed. Long before my election, numerous city administrations had talked about relocating the railroad tracks to restore the central downtown area. Some of those plans called for covering the rivers to create highways, while others advocated uncovering the rivers to create parks and walks, but until 1978 nothing had ever happened. On June 4, that year we allocated $4.3 million to finally begin planning a massive project to move the railroad tracks—and five years later I presided over the groundbreaking ceremony.

And while I also helped initiate the $40 million plan to uncover and actually reroute the rivers that ran through the city, certainly some of the credit for actually getting it done belongs to my successor, Mayor Joe Paolino. In response to a proposal that would have uncovered the rivers, in 1982 architect and urban planner William Warner proposed replacing the Crawford Street Bridge which would uncover the Woonasquatucket and Moshassuck rivers, and create parks. Warner's original sketches were drawn on napkins over two martini lunches at the Left Bank restaurant. Governor Garrahy and I obtained a twenty-seven-thousand-dollar grant from the National Endowment for the Arts to see if it really could be done. In addition, I put in another twenty-five thousand dollars in community development funds, announcing, "There is no reason we should have to give up our birthright, which is access to the water." The governor and several prominent Providence businessmen also contributed additional funding.

I have always admitted that as mayor my strength was in the big things—developing the mall, relocating the railroads, rehabilitating neighborhoods, building hotels, and providing services—rather than counting the number of paper clips the city bought. I hated that part of the job. The fact that I did not know so many of the details eventually proved catastrophic for me, but that's the way I managed the city.

Uncovering the rivers was one of those big concepts I embraced and supported. There were many people who ridiculed the idea, pointing out that we were Providence, Rhode Island, not Venice. To those people, the possibility that gondolas would one day float gracefully along the Providence River was about as likely as Providence one day being named one of America's Most Livable Cities. To them, we had to know our place and accept it. But the rough sketches that were shown to me were incredibly exciting. We held a series of public workshops to solicit ideas for our new waterfront, and among those things proposed were rerouting I-95, putting in dams and locks, adding marinas, and building a new waterfront campus for RISD.

By the time I returned to office in 1990, much of the foundation had been laid for the new Providence. And while the complexion of the city was beginning to change, there was still much construction to be done. Unfortunately, people would come downtown, enjoy the view, and then they would go home. And at night, beyond a nice walk along the river, there still was nothing for them to do.

The concept for WaterFire, in which fragrant cedar and pine logs are piled into as many as one hundred metal braziers stretching for a half mile along the river and lit to create an extraordinarily pleasing and relaxing experience, came from a Providence multimedia artist named Barnaby Evans. He was well known in the city for his provocative works. In 1990, for example, when people were screaming about burning the American flag, for a piece titled "Protecting the Flag" he froze a flag in a block of ice and then chained it to the front steps of the RISD Museum. I'd been fascinated by a minor installation he'd done in which he first lighted a river.

In 1994 we were celebrating the tenth anniversary of Providence First Night, an alcohol-free New Year's Eve celebration. Barnaby Evans came to see me and told me about his wild idea. He'd been intrigued by the new river system we had created but disappointed in the response to it. He described it as "a concert with no one coming." When he told me about his idea—put eleven blazing pots of wood in the basin at WaterPlace Park—I thought it sounded kind of interesting. I wish I could say I realized instantly that this concept would become so popular it would become a major tourist attraction known throughout the world, but to me it just seemed like a good idea. I lit the first fire New Year's Eve, 1994, the night before my fifth inauguration. It turned out that the natural beauty of fire, smoke, and water at night entranced spectators beyond anyone's anticipation. People just kept talking about it. It was antitechnology art, a performance that could have been staged exactly the same way hundreds of years earlier—people in row boats gliding along a river at night lighting beacon fires. The *New York Times* art critic called it "intoxicating and nearly medieval." We repeated it the following summer, this time with forty pots of fire. WaterFire, as it was named, grew from there to become the focal point of our summers and a major tourist attraction. By the time I left office we were staging as many as twenty-five WaterFires a summer, in which we had four boats lighting and servicing one hundred braziers while classical music played softly in the background. The city made a substantial investment in what was basically a wood-burning project, and the cost was augmented by local industry and private contributions. As gondolas and water taxis moved along the river, hundreds of thousands of spectators a year strolled or sat alongside the rivers to participate in what is truly a magical experience.

And still, there is nothing at all like it anywhere in the world, even in Florence or Venice.

In 1998, the state under Governor Lincoln Almond's leadership attempted to curtail WaterFire, claiming the smoke was polluting the air. This was an election year, and while I had no opponent, Almond was facing a strong challenge. I called him after being informed of this attempt and said, "Tell me, Governor, I was just informed the state wants to stop WaterFire. Where do you want to announce this, your office or mine?"

That ended that problem.

I always felt the best measure of our success in rebuilding the city was the number of new restaurants that opened. Restaurants are a great barometer of economic progress. Just as important, I'm Italian, I love good food. And there were too few places in Providence where it was possible to get a terrific dinner. Those few restaurants that did exist didn't have the slightest idea of how to market themselves. This is how bad it was: I got a call one day from an editor at *Saveur* asking me to recommend a Providence restaurant. At that time there wasn't a great range from which to choose. "The Old Canteen," I said, figuring it would give my friend Joe Marzilli a plug. The Old Canteen was a terrific restaurant, definitely worthy of being featured in the magazine— but it also was one of the few restaurants that was usually busy. The editor called me back the next day asking for another recommendation. "I can't review the Old Canteen," he explained. "The owner won't give me a reservation."

"What? That's crazy. You're *Saveur* magazine." I put the editor on hold and called Joe. "You don't understand, Joe," I said. "These people are *Saveur* magazine, the best in the whole business. They want to put you on the cover."

Joe was tough. "Who needs 'em."

"Why? What did they do to you?"

"They wanna come Saturday night. I got my regular customers on

Saturday night. These people, they come once, then you never see them again."

I explained patiently, "Joe, you're going to do me this favor. You're going to give these people the best table you got and you're gonna cooperate with them." I could almost hear him thinking about it. Finally, he agreed, and the magazine did a wonderful story on the restaurant. This was the type of thinking I was fighting when we began, but by the time I left for my five-year federally sponsored vacation, Providence supposedly had the highest number of restaurants per capita in the country—although apparently we also had the most coffee and doughnut shops per capita in America.

Very high on the list of those things I missed most while in prison were the great restaurants of the city. Believe me, if there was one person who appreciated those restaurants, it was me. And I tried to appreciate a different one every night. In prison, the best meal we had was chicken. We were given one piece of chicken and there were no second portions. But after the meal one night an inmate who worked in the kitchen approached me and whispered, "Mayor, wanna buy an extra piece of chicken?"

You kidding me? "What's it going to cost?"

"Two macks," he said. The medium of exchange in prison was the mack, a can of mackerel, which was sold in the prison commissary for a dollar. You want a candy bar? It'll cost you a mack. Clean my cell? Two macks. This inmate was offering me an extra piece of chicken for two macks. It wasn't exactly a steak on Federal Hill, but it was the best offer I was going to get. "Okay," I said. "It's a deal."

We agreed he would bring it to me at eight o'clock that night. I was lying in my bunk thinking about that extra piece of chicken when I saw him walking down the hallway, looking carefully for the guards. When he reached my cell I got out of my bunk and went to my locker to get the macks. "You got 'em?" he asked me.

I nodded—and he reached down into the front of his pants and pulled out a piece of chicken stored in a mess hall transparent kitchen glove. I grimaced. "You know what?" I said. "I don't think I want it."

He looked disappointed. "What are you talkin'? This is good chicken."

"I understand that," I said, then added, "it's not the chicken. It's the presentation that bothers me."

While I was in office, we did everything possible to cooperate with restaurant owners. The fact that one of America's leading culinary institutes, Johnson & Wales, was located in Providence and we weren't taking advantage of that frustrated me, and I decided to try to do something about it. That attitude began only weeks after I took office when we lifted a decades-old ban prohibiting restaurants from putting tables outside on nice days. In May 1975 we held a nine-day long city celebration of the arts, and a few places put picnic tables outside. There were people sitting at those tables all day; they just wanted to be outside. I never quite understood why sidewalk service had been prohibited, so we encouraged restaurants to apply for permits to create outdoor cafés. One WaterFire many years later I remember walking along the river on a summer night looking at the thousands of people dining outside and realizing how far we had come from one picnic table.

There were a lot of issues that held people back from opening restaurants. It's almost impossible to successfully run a restaurant without a liquor license, so we had to change some laws to make it easier to get that license. City regulations prohibited anyone from serving alcohol within two hundred feet of a church or school—and we have almost as many churches as doughnut shops. Even if someone wanted to open a restaurant, it was difficult to find a suitable location. So we extended the area in which exemptions to that law were permitted, leaving the final decision to the licensing board. Obviously we weren't going to put a nightclub next to a church, but there was nothing wrong with putting a good Italian restaurant in that location. As far as I know, the good Lord has no objection to quality pasta.

When we began the revitalization process, we knew we needed a restaurant development program. Once we brought people downtown we wanted to keep them there, and for that we needed a large selection of restaurants. The problem was that the very last person a bank loan officer wants to see is a restaurateur, because opening a restaurant is a very risky investment. When it became apparent that people who wanted to open restaurants couldn't get financing, we established a restaurant loan program. We used Housing and Community Development funds to set up our own investment bank to support qualified people. It was like a small bank that issued loans at a very low interest rate. We also established what we called a "60, 30, 10" program available to anyone who wanted to open a business. That meant people could borrow 60 percent of what they needed to open that business, we gave them a 30 percent grant, and they put in 10 percent of their own money. When a bank was willing to make a loan, we would take the second position, meaning if that business failed the bank would get paid back before we did. This was all part of our development program.

We put up substantial financing for more than fifty restaurants in the city. These restaurants provided a great number of jobs, and they returned sales tax to the state, some of which eventually came to us. Eventually, legislation was passed giving the city 1 percent of a meals tax, which has been worth millions of dollars to the city over the years. Equally important, these restaurants created another destination. Providence became nationally known for its restaurants.

In addition to that, we took steps to encourage restaurants to open in those areas we were trying to redevelop. In certain areas, for example, we would issue a liquor license to an address rather than an individual. That way, no matter what happened with the restaurant, the liquor license would stay with that property. Those licenses increased the value of the building, which increased the city's property tax base, but also encouraged property owners to put in a restaurant and kept down the costs.

The restaurants were absolutely necessary for the revitalization of the downtown area. We needed the restaurants if we were going to have a viable tourist industry, and to survive the restaurants needed the Trinity Repertory Theater and the Performing Arts Center, the games at the civic center, the galleries, and finally WaterFire. It all came together, and as more restaurants opened they became a destination. People started coming to Providence to dine at the restaurants they'd read about in the food magazines. We began to compete with Boston. In the early 1990s I even issued a mange-a-mange challenge to Boston's mayor Tom Menino: thirteen of our best restaurants against an equal number of their restaurants. The confrontation began when the National Football League selected Providence rather than Boston as the host for a conference championship game. People in Boston responded by criticizing Providence, and naturally someone in the city, not to mention any names, defended our city. It got so rough that the Boston media even attacked my toupee, referring to it as "extraordinarily formidable." Representative Patrick Kennedy took offense to that, writing Mayor Menino, "Your comments gave me more indigestion than the last time I ate Boston baked beans," and pointing out the superiority of my marinara sauce. We had busloads of people going to Boston to judge restaurants, and contrary to accusations, Lloyd Griffin had absolutely nothing to do with the voting. Admittedly, though, we did distribute the ballots in Providence. We won easily.

By the end of the twentieth century our efforts had been recognized nationally. According to *The New York Times,* "Providence has become more like those vibrant European cities with rivers running through them and picturesque bridges joining the two banks." *Money* magazine declared us "a cultural mecca," and *USA Today* wrote, "A spectacular rebirth has made Providence a model for other industrial cities . . . the downtown area is a bustling arts and entertainment district with some of New England's best restaurants, nightclubs and theaters."

What we'd done is successfully combine sensible urban planning with an artistic vision to rebuild an aging city. And I was our greatest salesman. I used to tell people, without pausing for a single breath, "What more can we do for you. You can go to the civic center and see a hockey game or a basketball game. You can see Shakespeare at the Tony Award–winning Trinity Rep, *Miss Saigon* at the Performing Arts Center, or the Rhode Island Philharmonic at the ornate Veterans Memorial Auditorium. You can explore a beautiful museum; you can go to our world-class zoo and explore the heavens at our planetarium. You can drift on the Providence River on a gondola or enjoy WaterFire and then enjoy a world-class dinner at a four-star restaurant. You can stay at a classic hotel and see an eclectic mixture of artists whose work is on display. We're close to the ocean, and midway between the great cities of New York and Boston. So when you've finally done it all here and need some time to relax, you can go to those places."

Eleven

will never forget standing outside in the freezing cold on December 16, 2002, handcuffed and shackled, waiting for the caged bus to arrive to transfer me to the other side of the Fort Dix Correctional Institution. As I climbed onto the bus I wondered, What has my life come to? The great days of rebuilding a city were done. I was in prison. And I just couldn't figure out why I was there.

There was never one day when I believed I would be convicted. After the end of their undercover investigation, the federal government spent two more years investigating the case and presenting it to a grand jury. The government issued more than three hundred subpoenas, went through more than ten thousand documents, and brought more than 150 witnesses in front of the grand jury. As a former prosecutor I understood the grand jury did not determine guilt or innocence, but rather whether there was enough evidence to proceed to a trial. Any prosecutor can direct a grand jury as if it were an orchestra responding to his commands. Most grand jurors don't even realize that they hold the real power, and prosecutors don't want them to know it. Grand jurors are usually laypersons overwhelmed by the majesty of the environment, and they will easily believe almost anything the prosecutor tells them.

As part of the investigation the government scoured my financial records, and they failed to find a penny that I couldn't account for; the last time they had done that the IRS ended up refunding over $200,000 to me. I can't even begin to estimate the amount of your tax dollars and the government's man hours consumed by this investigation. I was indicted on as many as thirty counts. Indicted with me was my chief of staff, Artin Coloian, who was indicted on two counts. Frank Corrente was charged with twenty-four counts; a businessman named Richard Autiello and an auto-body shop owner named Eddie Voccola, who was a convicted felon, were charged with racketeering and money laundering. The charges against me basically involved extorting $250,000 in campaign contributions from tow-truck operators to allow them to continue doing business with the city, accepting a bribe to get a job for a man named Christopher Ise, accepting payment for selling two vacant lots at a reduced price, taking a $10,000 bribe to ignore a $450,000 tax liability, and extorting a free lifetime membership from the University Club by holding up building permits. But the most substantial charge against me was a violation of the RICO (Racketeer Influenced and Corrupt Organizations) Act. The federal government was accusing me of running the city government of Providence as a criminal enterprise whose objective was "enriching, promoting and protecting" our political power and our bank accounts. According to prosecutor Richard Rose, I was Tony Soprano Cianci, the head of a criminal conspiracy. Some gang; we didn't even have a name. But according to this indictment every department in the city government, from the mayor's office to the school department, was part of this criminal enterprise.

A RICO violation is an overarching charge created by the federal government to allow them to prosecute organized crime bosses who successfully insulated themselves from the everyday activities of their crime families, their criminal enterprise. Under this statute, a prosecutor doesn't have to prove that the head of this criminal enterprise even knew that crimes were being committed, just that people under his leadership committed two or more predicate acts. The city government employed more than four thousand people. Under this theory I was responsible for the actions of every one of them, even people I had not appointed or had never met. Under this same theory, the head of any organization is responsible for the actions of every employee. The whole indictment was fiction. There was not a single conversation or video or even a statement that directly connected me to a single crime. There was no evidence that I had ever committed any crime. All they had were a few low-level employees trying to make deals for themselves. But they threw the RICO charge against the wall with all the others and hoped at least some of them would stick.

I was found not guilty of every charge—except the conspiracy. I had no knowledge of anyone accepting a bribe. One of the defendants on trial with me was someone I barely knew, and another I hadn't seen in twenty years. The whole thing was a political joke—but I certainly wasn't laughing. I spent the next few months preparing for the trial with my attorney and continuing to serve as mayor. Obviously I was distracted, but I was certainly cheered by the support of the city. Day after day people offered me encouragement and told me they didn't believe the charges. There was not a single event I attended at which I wasn't welcome. And I went to them all, to Little League games and transsexual shows at gay bars, to christenings, bar mitzvahs, weddings and funerals, to family barbecues and Liza Minelli's wedding in New York. I went to religious festivals, union meetings, and bodega ribbon cuttings. I wasn't going to allow allegations to keep me from doing what I wanted to do.

Personally, I also sold my house and my boat, which the media later speculated I did because I was trying to turn assets into cash in case I lost the case and had to forfeit property. That was ridiculous. The house wasn't even for sale until a family whose children were attending Brown offered me more than a million dollars for it. I was living there alone and it was expensive to maintain. So I sold it and moved into the presidential suite at the Biltmore Hotel. I sold the boat because after Wendy left I didn't use it very much, and anyone who has ever owned a boat agrees with the description that a boat is simply a hole in the water that you pour money into. I sold it for about what I'd paid for it more than a decade earlier.

As for those claims that I was disposing of assets? Cash is an asset and in lawsuits is treated no differently than property such as a house or a boat. It made absolutely no difference.

And finally, I continued going to my office every day and running the city. I drew up the annual budget, settled a strike, negotiated new contracts. I pushed forward with the major development projects, entertained dignitaries, and established objectives. And I began making plans to run for reelection in 2002.

Let me tell you, when something like this is hanging over your head, it never goes away. It's always there. I don't know what it feels like to be guilty of a crime and have to prepare for a trial, but I do know that when you're accused of crimes that you didn't commit, there's a great sense of anger, injustice, and frustration.

While I was awaiting trial the media did everything possible to try to convict me. For example, in what seemed to be an obvious attempt to influence the potential jury pool, the tape of Corrente accepting a payment was leaked to a local news station and broadcast. Looking at that tape, there is no doubt what's taking place, and though I wasn't implicated in any way, the fact that Corrente was indicted with me certainly cast a shadow over me. There was no question there was corruption inside city hall. The person who leaked that tape eventually went to jail.

The first two judges who were assigned to the trial recused themselves, withdrawing from the trial, leaving Judge Ernest Torres to preside. The only thing I knew about Judge Torres was that he had twice been recommended for the bench by Senator John Chafee—and my feud with Chafee was well known. Torres did fine Richard Rose five hundred dollars for showing the Corrente tape to his friends at a gathering in his house and suspended him from the investigation for thirty days. That seemed to me like a minor penalty for the misuse of very serious evidence.

The federal courthouse is more political than city hall and anyone who doesn't believe that is living in a fantasy world. Among the many things that surprised me when the trial finally began was how few residents of Providence were even in the jury pool. And if they weren't in the pool, they certainly couldn't be on the jury. We ended up with an all-white jury and only one person who lived in Providence, a woman who had moved there from Texas to attend Brown a couple of years earlier. A jury is supposed to be selected randomly. Providence is the biggest city in the state and we have a large African American population. What must the odds be that we would end up with a jury consisting solely of white people who did not live in Providence? I'm sure no one on the prosecution team paid any attention to the fact that several months earlier I had spoken at the National Association for the Advancement of Colored People dinner in Providence—well, maybe Richard Rose did, as he had been there. So this was not exactly a jury of my peers.

Though there certainly was the illusion of fairness in the courtroom, Judge Torres made several rulings that were devastating to my defense. The judge refused to allow us to play the audiotape for the jury of me telling Aiken's undercover agent that if anyone tried to solicit a bribe I would cut off their cojones. "Irrelevant heresy," he ruled, explaining that this conversation "does not relate to any predicate act or to any specific matter with respect to which the government has presented evidence." In other words, it didn't relate directly to any specific charge. In fact, the judge concluded that this conversation was a self-serving attempt to cover my tracks from previous acts. The fact that this was the only time I was taped being offered a bribe and I aggressively turned it down didn't seem particularly important to the judge. My attorney, Richard Egbert, one of the best defense lawyers in America, was dumbfounded by that decision.

The first witness against me was David Ead, who testified that I had accepted several bribes from him—although he had to admit that he had never directly handed me any money. Interestingly, before testifying against me Ead already had pleaded guilty to six counts of extortion-related felony charges and was facing as much as 120 years in prison. I was his get-out-of-jail free card, and he tried to cash it in. He claimed that I had accepted a five-thousand-dollar bribe to get a job for a man named Christopher Ise. The truth is that Ead called me and told me that the son of his wife's hairdresser had a master's degree in historic preservation, and asked if I could find a job for him. I had forgotten all about it, but when Ead asked again months later I asked him to come to my office with the kid for a meeting. This was simply a courtesy because Ead was the vice-chairman of the City's Democratic Party. Of course, what I didn't know was that Ead had told Ise that I wanted a five-thousand-dollar bribe. He warned him not to mention one word about the money during this meeting, explaining that he would deliver it to me personally.

I met Ise, I checked his references, and it was obvious he was well qualified to work in historic preservation. I called a contact in the private-sector Providence Preservation Society but I was so powerful they told me they didn't have any openings. I called a couple of private construction companies that did historic preservation work for the city, but they turned me down, too. Then I called the city planning department and spoke with the deputy director, and again was told there was no full-time job available. He volunteered to give Ise a part-time job that paid about nine bucks an hour with no benefits, no vacation time. We were paying a guy with a master's degree in historic preservation nine bucks an hour with no benefits. That seemed to me like a good deal for the city. During the next mayor's administration Ise did such a good job that when a permanent slot opened up, he was hired. More than a decade later he was still working there and had become one of the leaders of the city Planning Department.

But Ead claimed that this kid actually had paid a five-thousand-dollar bribe to get a nine-dollar-an-hour part-time job. He testified that I told him to give the money to my chief of staff, Artin Coloian, who had been indicted for supposedly accepting the bribe on my behalf. As Artin remembers, "Ead testified that he came to my office and said, 'I got the money right here. Make sure this kid doesn't get fucked.' And then he claimed that he handed me the money and I put it in my drawer. When he was asked during cross-examination what denomination the bills were, he testified they were 'fives, tens and fifteens.' It never happened. It was a lie."

Ead even messed up the time of day the bribe supposedly was paid. He also testified that I had accepted two other bribes from him for reducing a tax bill and agreeing to sell those two vacant lots. His testimony seemed compelling, at least until Egbert stood up to question him. While Ead was testifying, we'd gotten a phone call from a former detective who told us "that guy's got the biggest gambling problem in the world." Ead was a totally degenerate gambler. Within a day we were able to get copies of records from Foxwoods casino. It turned out that Ead had been at Foxwoods every single day; in a year and a half he'd been to Foxwoods and Mohegan Sun casinos 450 times. He'd even been gambling on Christmas Day. Egbert asked him, "Would you be surprised to learn that you gambled eight hundred seventy thousand dollars in the past three years?"

And yet Rose expected the jury to believe that his chief witness had willingly handed over thousands of dollars to me. In return for Ead's testimony, rather than serving any of the 120 years he was facing, Ead never went to prison; and I was found not guilty of those charges.

As the trial proceeded it was obvious Rose was having a tough time. As described by author Philip Gourevitch in *The New Yorker,* "Rose, the prosecutor, did have a habit, when the defense took the stand, of making bizarre, writhing faces, clutching at his head as if in torment and emitting phlegmy gurgles from his nose and throat." After Egbert complained several times, Judge Torres warned Rose, "Some of your facial expressions need to be restrained."

As mentioned earlier, I was charged with extorting $250,000 in campaign contributions from tow-truck operators, who were forced to donate several thousand dollars a year to stay on the city's approved list. One driver testified that being on that list was worth at least one hundred thousand dollars a year in towing and storage fees. In fact, the police had a list consisting of about fifteen towing companies, but my administration didn't start it. It probably started when the first Ford broke down. I knew it existed. I also knew it was completely legal. My attorney destroyed Rose's attempt to turn this into the crime of the century when he showed that these towing companies had contributed two thousand dollars a year to Joe Paolino's campaign fund when he was mayor, and nobody was accusing him of corruption or extortion. It was simply a long-accepted way of doing business. No one was required to make the donation, they just did it. Rightly or wrongly, that was the accepted practice in Providence both before and after I served as mayor.

The prosecution's main witness was a tow-truck operator named

Kenneth Rocha, who testified that Corrente had raised the suggested campaign "donation" from two thousand dollars a year to five thousand dollars, which was eventually negotiated to three thousand dollars. Rocha's credibility was destroyed when Egbert revealed that his company had been briefly suspended from the list by the State Public Utilities Commission for over-charging motorists. Ead's claim that I'd accepted a bribe to sell Antonio Freitas two vacant lots, presumably at a great price or else why offer a bribe, took a big hit when we showed that one of those lots had been sold to someone else—without any bribe being offered—for less than Freitas had offered. I was found not guilty of this charge, too.

During the trial I spent a lot of time with Artin Coloian, who was being tried separately. While I was in the courtroom, he was at city hall. We'd meet just about every morning and night to review what had happened in court and what needed to be done to keep the city running. It was tough for me to sit there day after day listening to people trying to save themselves by lying about me. Yes, I was angry; actually, I was furious. I kept thinking, Does anybody believe this crap? Where's their case? Not one witness claimed they ever saw me accept a bribe. Even Frank Corrente, who was also facing serious time, could have improved his own situation by claiming he'd handed me cash. If he had done that, the prosecutors would have been lighting candles for him. But it never happened and he wouldn't lie about it.

It seemed impossible for me to believe that anyone would think I'd take a fifty-dollar bribe. The numbers they were talking about were ridiculous. Would I throw away my career, my integrity, my reputation for five hundred dollars? I wouldn't do it for fifty thousand dollars, but for five hundred bucks? It was preposterous. I did politics. I encouraged people to make campaign donations and buy tickets to fund-raisers. Politics as usual.

The most absurd charge against me was that I extorted a membership I never used to the University Club by refusing to give them needed variances for work being done. Please. Okay, I gave them a hard time, but this was a club that until recently had made women use the back door, a club whose membership believed they were entitled to whatever they wanted, and I reminded them how the real world worked. Was I petulant? Of course. Immature? Okay; it's a stretch, but okay. But did I do anything for which I deserved to go to jail? Well, perhaps those entitled members of the club thought it was proper punishment for standing up to them, but the people of Providence didn't. I was found not guilty of that charge, too.

I didn't testify. There were several reasons for that. My attorney advised me strongly against it. He said he could get everything into the record that we needed without my exposing myself to questions. Admittedly, I wasn't the holiest guy in the world, and there were questions I would rather not have to answer. For example, the prosecutor could have brought up the entire DeLeo assault case, and there was no way that would have made me look good. They could have asked all types of political questions. And if I didn't answer truthfully, the judge could have added years to my sentence.

In addition, if I testified that I had never taken a bribe, Rose would have been permitted to call Ronnie Glantz to respond. Egbert had represented Glantz at an earlier trial. The government had already tried to disqualify Egbert and failed, but if Glantz testified, Egbert would not have been able to cross-examine him. I wanted to keep my attorney.

Finally, I was confident the jury would see the truth.

The trial lasted seven weeks. We presented our defense in three days, consisting mostly of destroying the credibility of the prosecutor's witnesses. As Egbert said in his summation, "If you appreciate sitting here and being lied to . . . while they're trying to bring down a mayor, okay, then fine."

When Judge Torres gave the jury its instructions, he told them, "It is not necessary in proving the existence of an enterprise to show that each member of the enterprise participated in or even knew all of its activities." In other words, he confirmed the fact that I could be convicted of conspiracy because people I barely knew had committed crimes I knew nothing about.

The jury deliberated for almost ten days. Usually that's good for the defendant. I continued working, but at times it got hard. There were rumors being spread, but nobody really knew anything. I waited for the phone call to return to the courtroom. And I waited. Finally, it came. There is no way to adequately describe the feeling of standing there waiting to hear a verdict. I was optimistic but wary. And the verdict was bizarre.

The first verdict read was on the charge of conspiring to violate the RICO act. Guilty. Guilty? I felt completely helpless. I couldn't believe it. I turned to Egbert but he warned me, "Shhhh." Then the court clerk began reading all the rest of verdicts. I assumed if they found me guilty of the overriding charge, they had to find me guilty of at least some of the underlying charges. They didn't. Not guilty. Not guilty. Not guilty. Not even guilty of the actual RICO charge. The jury had not reached a verdict on the charge that I had extorted a membership in the University Club, so Judge Torres sent them back to deliberate. About three hours later they returned to the courtroom. Once again, not guilty. Twenty-six times, not guilty. The jury did not believe I was guilty of a single specific criminal act. But somehow I was responsible for everything. When the verdicts had all been announced, Egbert shook his head and said, "It doesn't make any sense. If I had known that this was going to be the case I would have tried a different case."

Frank Corrente was found guilty of six counts, and the tow-truck operator, Autiello, was convicted of three charges. The charges against Voccola were tossed out. In a separate trial Artin Coloian was found not guilty of collecting bribes. But as I walked out of the courthouse that day I said to a reporter, mostly in astonishment, "I was found guilty of being mayor."

Actually, it was slightly more complex than that. I will always believe that I was found guilty of considering running for the United States Senate.

When you're in public life, you try hard to moderate your words and your behavior. I knew I couldn't say what I was really feeling, so I put on my facade. I was facing ten years in prison for a crime I didn't commit. How do you respond to that? We were going to appeal, so I still had hope this thing was going to be reversed. I've always had hope. But the first decision I had to make, and I had to make it within a few days, was whether or not I was going to run for another term.

Even after being convicted I was still very optimistic I could be re-elected. The night I was convicted I spoke at a high school graduation, and two thousand people gave me a standing ovation, cheering, "Bud-dee! Bud-dee!"

I wanted to run, I wanted that victory, but the reality was that I was going to be spending too much time working on my appeal to campaign and govern. Judge Torres could still reverse the verdict and, failing that, he would determine my sentence. The last thing I wanted to do was alienate him with an act of bravado. Making that announcement was among the most difficult days I've ever had in politics. "This city is my life," I said. "Providence is my passion.... My greatest satisfaction as mayor comes from the realization that the dreams we dared to dream a generation ago have become the magnificent reality of today." After announcing that I had made the decision not to seek reelection as mayor—"It's time for me to move on, personally and for the good of the city"—I got nostalgic. "Twenty-one years is a long time to bear the responsibilities of office, but I have loved being mayor. Together we have achieved something very special. We have restored the hope and pride of every citizen in our city. I remember the one thing that people kept asking me all the time: What is the greatest contribution you think the city has achieved in the last twenty years? I always tell them, you know, people say the mall, the zoo, people say the restoration of the neighborhoods. It's not that at all. It's the fact that people years ago never had self-esteem.... Ask people today and the one thing they have is a sense of this city moving in the right direction, and number two, that they have a great deal of self-esteem and they are very proud of this city. That's what we have achieved. We have restored the hope and pride of every citizen. As I go forward in the months ahead and years ahead, I know that this was our finest accomplishment."

I received a tremendous amount of support. Even my one-time political enemy Joe Paolino Jr. has said, "I think Buddy knows how to pick his friends, but didn't know how to pick the people who worked for him.... The people who worked for him cared about themselves and cared about what they could get away with. I don't know if Buddy knew about it, if he turned his back to it or if it happened under the radar or not. But when I went to visit him in prison I remember thinking, He doesn't belong here."

Three weeks later I left the presidential suite at the Biltmore Hotel and climbed into my limousine, still bearing the license plate number 1, to go to court to be sentenced. The day before, in my final act as mayor, I distributed money in a discretionary fund that I had set up to give away money I won from the U.S. Conference of Mayors. I didn't want to leave it for the next administration, and I didn't want to keep it myself as I could have done, so I divided it up among six or seven soup kitchens.

As I got into the limo to go to court the next morning, a group of people standing on the balcony of city hall, across the street, gave me an ovation. The prosecution had asked for a ten-year sentence. Judge Torres sentenced me to serve five years and four months in prison, to pay a $107,000 fine, and to perform 150 hours of community service. This was beyond the sentencing guidelines. Torres compared this case to the story of Dr. Jekyll and Mr. Hyde, concluding, "My job is to sentence the second Buddy Cianci because the first Buddy Cianci wouldn't be here." He suspended the sentence for three months to allow me to appeal.

If that judge was right about that Jekyll and Hyde comparison, I thought, how come I was only getting one paycheck?

University of Rhode Island political scientist Maureen Moakley told a reporter that even the judge seemed uneasy at this application of the RICO statute, which certainly was never intended to be used for this type of crime, adding, "Then there is the question of the best use of taxpayers' money. I'd like to know how much this trial cost. How much did it cost to carry out what was to a large degree a vendetta?"

The moment I was sentenced, the city council president John Lombardi became mayor. When I walked out of the courtroom my limo was gone, taking with it that license plate. I was driven home in a Nissan Maxima. With an election only a few months away, Lombardi was a caretaker, but he marched into city hall like General Patton on steroids. He immediately engraved his name on the door. He fired my staff and had them escorted out the door by the police, and then began hiring new people—this was for a term of about four months. After leaving office he wanted to be introduced as "the former mayor of Providence."

It was very difficult for me to accept the fact that this was real, that I was going to prison. Me, Buddy, going to jail for five years. For a long time I continued to believe my sentence would be overturned or reduced. But as I prepared to go to prison, I had no choice but to deal with reality. I spent my last few weeks of freedom visiting with the people I cared about. I had dinner one night with Paul MacDonald, a tough union guy whom I'd known and worked with for decades. Paul kept trying to tell me that whatever I needed done, he would be there for me, anywhere, anytime; but every time Paul started talking, somebody interrupted us to wish me well. It actually was funny. But there were tears in his eyes. So I reached across the table and I grabbed his wrist—I do that sometimes when I want to make sure I have a person's absolute attention—and I said to him, "Paul, I want to tell you something. I never took a fucking dime, but I always wanted to learn how to play the piano and now I'm going to have the time!"

I didn't really know what to anticipate about prison. I wasn't going to a country club prison, I was going to a prison with hard cases, although while trying to keep my spirits up I described it as "a very very inexpensive spa." I told people I had a vision of sitting around with several people as we explained what we were doing there. The first guy said he was a serial killer. The second guy had committed a series of armed robberies. The third guy was a mob enforcer. And when my turn came I said as firmly as I could manage, "I'm in here because I got a membership to the University Club."

I did feel awful for all the other people hurt by this, people who had supported me and been loyal to the city for years. In the election that fall David Cicilline was elected mayor. He appointed Dean Esserman the chief of police. Among the few employees remaining from my administration was Manny Vieira, who had been working in the city communications department for twenty-nine years and eight months, eventually becoming the director of the department. Manny remembered being called into Colonel Esserman's office. Esserman said to him, "If you want to come clean, I can help you."

Manny was surprised. In twenty-nine years and eight months he'd done his job honestly and to the best of his ability. He asked, "What do you mean, come clean? What is it that I'm dirty about?"

Esserman said coolly, "Well, I got information that you may know some things about Buddy that could be helpful. We want you to be a team player."

Manny nodded. "Okay, I want to be a team player." But he remembered wondering at that moment, What the hell is this guy talking about? "I'll tell you anything you want to know."

"Good. We have information that you helped hire people."

Manny agreed, "I interviewed people for jobs, is that what you mean?"

Finally, Esserman admitted that he really wanted to know about bribes. He asked, "Were you ever in Buddy's presence when someone gave him money to hire someone?"

"You know something," Manny said, suddenly completely aware that he was being set up. He believed they were offering him a deal: Tell them about crimes he knew I'd committed and he would keep his job. That wasn't Manny. "You're asking me crazy questions. I never seen that happen. That never took place."

The new administration pressed him. Manny met with at least one other director, and as he explained it to me, "They tried to get me to say things that weren't true. They were total crazy off-the-wall things and after a while I told them, 'You people are asking me about things that never took place and it's like you want me to lie.' They said they didn't want me to lie, they just wanted me to be a team player. The next day they fired me."

I have no idea how many other people were offered the same deal. The fact is that there were people who had a lot to gain by claiming I'd committed crimes. But with the exceptions of Pannone and Ead, not one person claimed to have seen me doing anything illegal. Frank Corrente could have made his life easier by claiming he handed me cash in private. The only thing he had to lose was his integrity by doing that, but he refused.

I left Providence on a Thursday in December, in the middle of a snowstorm. It was surreal. About thirty or forty people, members of my staff as well as the media, had gathered to see me off. As I walked out of the Biltmore for the final time, I heard a Christmas carol coming from the skating rink we'd built. A Christmas snowstorm, a magnificent day to be alive and free—and I was going to prison for five years and four months. Several people were crying. "Don't let anybody disparage what we did," I told them. "We accomplished a lot of things together, we're a part of history. We're part of the revitalization and the renaissance of the city of Providence, so keep your head up high."

I got into a van with my driver, a former police officer named Bobby Lovell, and we drove out of the city. My city. As we drove toward Fort Dix, New Jersey, my new home, I had a sandwich and a glass of scotch. Actually, I was glad it was snowing because it took a long time to get there.

I had to report at noon the next day. In the morning I called several people, including my lawyer, and then went to prison. As I walked inside the gates of Ft. Dix a soldier recognized me and asked for my autograph.

I was anxious. I didn't know what to expect. I had to give up my toupee, or as I referred to it, the squirrel. I did that, I told people, "because you can't take pets with you." That bothered me, not because I cared particularly what it looked like—I didn't think it was going to affect my social life—but rather because it was symbolic of the loss of control. For someone who has been in total control for most of his adult life, giving up all control was difficult for me. I'd been living on a schedule for decades—I'd known what I was going to be doing at six o'clock in the evening three months in the future—and suddenly I didn't know what was going to happen in the next five minutes.

I stayed in the administrative orientation section for about a week and a half. Mostly it was terribly boring. Then early one morning they shackled me, handcuffed me, and left me standing outside in the cold for hours to wait for the bus that would take me to the other side of the prison. I was so cold I thought I was going to die. I learned very quickly not to think about my old life, not to think about my life as it had been. This was my life now, shackled and freezing, wearing paper shoes on my feet. I was being transferred.

In my life I'd been called a lot of names, but now I was prisoner 05000-070. A few days after I went inside, *60 Minutes* ran a profile of me. I watched it with my fellow inmates in the common area. Mostly it was good. When it was mentioned that I had once been a prosecutor, I just kept looking straight ahead, hoping no one would pay too much attention to that. In fact, as a result of the piece I earned some early respect.

When I finally got to my new home, my cell block, there were several people from Providence waiting for me. I have no idea how they knew I was coming, but they did and escorted me to my twelve-man cell. A few of them even had photographs taken of me with their kids on the opening day of Little League season taped inside their lockers. Among them was a man named Earl Person, who was in for decades for selling marijuana. Half a lifetime for selling marijuana. He deserved to be incarcerated even less than I did. But Earl apparently had spent all his time in prison building muscle, because he had muscles the size of the Providence Place Mall. Earl knew all about me and welcomed me to prison.

I was in a cell with six African Americans, three Hispanics, and two other Caucasians. The rule in prison is that if you're over sixty you get a bottom bunk. The bottom bunks are coveted. There was one kid named Whoop who had decided he was going to take my bunk and made all kinds of comments about it, but when I showed up with Earl, Whoop never said another word. Nobody messed with Earl, and Earl and I became friends. Being older was actually to my benefit, because the younger inmates respected me. Contrary to the warnings I'd received, I was surprised how considerate so many inmates were toward me.

The most important thing about being in prison is learning how to do the time, not let the time do you. You have to force yourself to ask why you ended up there, and if you can do that, you can become a better person. There are a lot of tough moments, and you have to learn how to direct your thoughts. If you focus on the fact that you're going to be locked in a cage for five years, it can get really difficult. There are times that you have to dig deep into your soul. I told myself so many times that there was a light at the end of this particular tunnel, that other people have gone through it and survived and I could do it, too. It was just a matter of time.

There are two sets of rules in prison, the rules of the system and the rules of the inmates. There were times when these rules would conflict, and that's when I had to decide who I was and how I was going to do my time. When I first got there, I was called down to the office by the security staff. We know who you are, they explained, and we just want to make sure you're going to be safe here. "In fact," one of them said, "you know, you don't really have to stay here."

Oh?

"All you have to do is give us some information about the government in Rhode Island."

"I wouldn't know anything about that," I said. "I was the mayor of Providence." They wanted me to give up anybody and everybody. Make it easy on yourself, they said. "You don't belong here. You don't have to be here. You help us, we'll help you."

I was assigned to work in the kitchen. Me and a kitchen, there's a natural match. But they put me there because I was considered a high-profile inmate and they wanted the other inmates to see that I was not receiving any special favors. They wanted people to see the big-shot mayor serving food and cleaning the floors. I had to mop floors, wash dishes, and scrub pans. Though it was considered the worst job you can get, I actually enjoyed aspects of it because I got to know everyone.

After six months I was able to get a job in the library as a clerk, where I worked for the rest of my sentence. I saw many seasons come and go from that library. I had a good schedule, working afternoons and evenings. One day the warden came in and asked me, "What do you do here?"

"I'm the celebrity host," I told him.

I acclimated. I got used to it. I blended in, replacing the squirrel with a bright orange knit cap. I accepted my situation and I didn't allow bitterness to rip me apart. What happens is, you stop trying to live in the world outside and you live completely by the rules of this world. The things that matter inside are completely different from what I'd spent my life worrying about. You don't own very much, so you protect those few things you do own with your life. For example, I was lying on my bunk when a new inmate from New York was accused of stealing somebody's toothpaste. In prison it doesn't take much to set off a fight, and I could see where this one was going. I tried to stop them, telling them, "Look, if you guys get into it we're all going to end up in the hole." In prison, as in the military and apparently in the city of Providence, there is group punishment. If you're in a room and there is a problem, a fight, or a theft, everybody goes into the hole. The hole is solitary confinement and it is not a nice place to be. You're confined in a space only slightly bigger than a coffin, you're not allowed any outside contact like phone calls, and you're permitted to shower only twice a week.

So I wanted to stop this fight. I called in an inmate who spoke Spanish and tried to resolve it peacefully. The consensus was that most of the men wanted this new inmate out of the room. They were afraid he was going to steal their belongings. Truthfully, I wanted him out, too. Something had been taken out of my locker a week earlier and it was probable he was the thief. But what I didn't want was a fight that was going to end up with all of us going into solitary. Everybody in the room had his say—I think the vote was 10-0—and it came down to me. What do you think, Mayor, they asked.

I said, "I think you're all fucking nuts. Listen, if you send him downstairs to the correctional office, there's going to be an investigation as to who stole the fucking toothpaste. We're all going to go to the fucking hole. And you don't know who they're going to get next." I looked around the room. "Look at you, you're a fucking drug dealer. And you robbed a fucking bank. You, you're a fucking computer hack." I went around the room pointing out each inmate. There wasn't one Scout leader in there. These were hard cases. Finally, I got to the new inmate. "Him? He stole fucking toothpaste. The problem is, he's got nothing, that's why he stole it. Here's what I'm going to do, I'm gonna give him a tube of toothpaste. And if the rest of you are smart, you'll help him out, too. Then maybe he won't need to steal anything." I passed a laundry bag around and it got filled up pretty quick.

There were fights, though; there were a lot of fights. Put several hundred violent men together and the result is going to be violence. It was pretty obvious that I'd gone the distance from Chardonnays to lock-in-the-sock—a combination lock in a sock, a weapon of expediency. Whenever I saw a fight beginning I turned around and walked away as fast and as far as possible. For instance, there were twelve bunk beds in each room, and the rule of the room was that the person on the top bunk cleaned one day and the person on the bottom bunk cleaned the next day. Then the person on the next to top bunk cleaned, which meant each person cleaned once every twelve days. Well, at one point a man with a top bunk finally got the bottom bunk. The way it turned out, he was going to have to clean the room two days in a row—which he didn't think was fair. He started an argument about who was going to be responsible for cleaning. In prison, when people are going to fight they take off their shoes and put on sneakers, so they'll have better footing and make less noise. It was almost ten o'clock, count time. I was thinking, This shit is going to happen and the guards are going to put us in shackles and take us out in the middle of the night. When there is a fight, the witnesses go in the hole as well as the fighters. So I figured I'd better do what I could to stop it. One of these men spoke only Spanish; the other one, a Caucasian, just spoke English. "Just hold it," I said, motioning to the Hispanic. "This is a language problem." I brought in a bilingual Hispanic to translate. This is going to work, I thought. This is terrific, I'm going to get this settled. The translator listened to both sides and then took the white guy's side. With that the Hispanic nodded his head and punched the translator right in the face. Pow! Blood all over the place. A few minutes later the guard came through—and just ignored it. No bodies on the floor, no harm. I guess he didn't want to do the paperwork.

I was lucky, I didn't have any confrontations at Dix. In four and a half years I didn't have a single incident report. I was considerably older than almost everyone else, so when something was going down they made sure I wasn't going to be involved. The word had gotten around that Providence was a progressive city that protected minorities. Providence hadn't always been that way. It was known that I had pushed the city departments to offer opportunities to every qualified person. My good reputation with minorities preceded me. And it didn't hurt that I knew some very important Dominican politicians. So I had my age going for me, some people from Providence protecting me, and no racial problems. And as I wrote to a reporter from the *East Side Monthly*, "There are some nice people here. And then again, there are those who do not have too many branches on the family tree." But I at least never faced any threats.

Eventually I was moved into a two-man cell and I had several cellees, as they're known. Among them was one of the most accomplished computer hackers in the world. He claimed that he had screwed Rupert Murdoch out of millions of dollars by diverting income from his Direct-TV in Canada, but he was arrested for being in this country illegally. I kept thinking that when he got out I wouldn't want to be the FBI agent who caught him; one day that agent is going to wake up and owe $40 million and discover he has a credit rating score of 0.

For three years I was in prison with Charles Carneglia, a Gambino family hit man who was in prison on a RICO violation, but after I was released he was tried and convicted of racketeering charges, including four murders, as well as dissolving some victims in a vat of acid. As a courtesy. Like just about everybody else inside, Charlie never discussed his past. Those people who did talk about their organized-crime connections were either very low level or making it up; the people who really were connected never admitted it. I got to know Charlie well. When I was in the library, I had access to books so I knew who he was and what he was accused of doing, although just like me, at that time he only had been convicted of a RICO charge rather than any violent crimes. He was sentenced to sixty months; I got sixty-four months. The only crime I know for certain that he committed was stealing roast beef from the kitchen; we never talked about anything else. Charlie was a collector: Whatever he found around the prison he kept in his locker. He spoke with his mom every day, that was important to him. He actually went home before me—and then he was indicted and eventually convicted of still another racketeering charge for multiple murders and sentenced to life in prison.

In prison almost no one discussed the reason they were there, at least not with me. I learned very quickly that you couldn't really trust any-one. I mean, it was prison. It was explained to me that just because you were already in prison didn't mean they weren't going to come after you again. There are so many rats in prison, and some of them will pass along any information they learn to make their own life even slightly better. So Charlie never said a word to me about what he'd done, and I never asked.

Without question, the most difficult adjustment I had to make was dealing with the boredom. I used to say that I was one of the few people who had been inside the White House, Windsor Castle, and Fort Dix Correctional Institution. I'd led a life in which every day was different and filled with numerous challenges and decisions. Inside, the biggest decision I had to make was what time to go to sleep. I read hundreds of books; I never stopped reading, mostly historical biographies. I also subscribed to *The Providence Journal,* which allowed me to keep in-formed about the city. What was tough about that was reading about the deaths of long time friends, as well as the unpleasant and often un-true things people said about me without being able to respond. In fact, in 2006 the Providence Preservation Society celebrated its fiftieth anniversary by naming me one of the fifty most important people in historic preservation and inducting me into its hall of fame. It was an honor I felt I deserved. The reason the city had so many renovated his-toric buildings was because I'd refused to tear them down. But it took a lot of guts for the society to include me. When I received my invitation, I responded politely, "I'm sorry I cannot join with you because I am figuratively and literally 'tied up.'"

What was really surprising was the furor my selection caused in Providence. Mayor David Cicilline was outraged, and there were sto-ries that he threatened the society's funding, although he firmly denied the rumors. I had done considerable damage to the city, Mayor Cicil-line said, speaking from the city hall that I had preserved. But though I certainly didn't like all the nasty comments, I was surprised that af-ter being locked away for almost four years I could ignite such passion. I realized then that some people were afraid of me, worried about what might happen when I returned to Providence. As "Buff" Chace, the developer with whom I clashed several times, said, "The timing is wrong, with the prospect of Buddy's returning from prison next year. He could use this [recognition] to help restore himself to a position that maybe he isn't worthy of yet." Some people were worried about that, he admitted, wondering, "How's the big guy gonna act when he comes back? Will he be a positive influence in the city or a divisive one?"

Of course I enjoyed it all, and finished my own statement in which I thanked the board for this honor by promising, "Thanks so much for remembering me—see you all next year."

While I had been kidding about prison being an inexpensive spa, in fact I lost about fifty pounds very quickly. It's not the kind of diet I would recommend, though. I did a lot of walking around the yard, I lifted some weights, I even did some landscaping. And instead of being forced to eat every night at some of the best restaurants in America, I had the option of choosing from several plentifully stocked vending machines. I was probably in the best shape of my life.

One thing I did worry about was the medical care. If you get sick in prison, forget about it, because it's like Dr. Mengele is in charge of the clinic assisted by Dr. Kevorkian. If you're sick, you have to get up very early and report to the clinic. They lock you in a room and they may or may not get to you. There are a lot of people on medication. At four or five o'clock they handed out the pills; I used to call that happy hour. Guys would get their pills and come back to their cells in la la land.

About a year and a half into my sentence I shut myself off from my friends. For more than another year and a half I made it clear to everyone I didn't want any visitors. It wasn't so much that I didn't want people coming to visit me, it was the pain of me having to watch them leave. Oh, that was tough, knowing they were going back to life and I was going back to my room. But eventually I began to accept that reality and I began having visitors again. My sister and my brother-in-law would come, my nephews, certainly my daughter visited. Charlie Mansolillo would come, Artie Coloian visited twice, as did Bob Lovell. A lovely woman named Kitty Cushing also would visit me. Kitty was a Newport socialite, so this might have been the first time she'd ever been inside a prison. Kitty was so loyal, and we forged a close friendship. She would visit quite often. But also there were people I didn't expect. When I was studying for my master's at Villanova, my housemate was a man named Norm Gauss, who had become an engineer at GE and lived not far from the prison. I hadn't seen him at all in years, but he would visit me every two weeks. He rarely missed a visit, and I came to really look forward to seeing him; he became a lifeline, making me forget for at least a brief time where I was. And to my surprise, Joe Paolino came to see me. I remember we joked that with all the Mafioso in there maybe I could convince them to give us our own territory. We decided to start with North Stonington, Connecticut.

The letters I received in prison made a substantial difference in my life. I used to tell people that the service in prison was so good my mail would be delivered by hand; they even opened it for me. In fact, it would be impossible to estimate how many letters I received. One of the guards used to tell me I should have my own zip code. But it would be difficult for me to adequately express how important those letters became to me. I would get as many as twenty letters a day, every day. Some inmates rarely got a letter. These letters kept me sane, and answering them kept me busy. I really formed a friendship with Paolino through the mail. Basically, people would write to me about what was going on in Providence, or simply send me letters of support. The mail was overwhelmingly positive, but most important to me was the knowledge that I hadn't been forgotten, that I'd made a difference in people's lives and they appreciated it. I'd lie on my bunk reading those letters and then answering them, and for those few hours my mind wasn't imprisoned.

Somehow, time went by. Day after day after day, it passed. I kept my mouth shut, stayed out of trouble, did my job, minded my own business, got along with the guards and inmates, and stayed far away from problems. And the years went by. People warned me not to start looking forward to getting out, that the system has a way of screwing up any plans you make. But truthfully, you never forget the day you're supposed to get out. That date, even if it's not a real date, just gets frozen in your mind. And when the months get down to single digits you begin to taste it. For the first time in four years I began to make plans for the future. That was dangerous.

It was always difficult to watch inmates being released and trying not to put yourself in their position. People would leave early in the morning, five thirty, six o'clock. I would watch them from my window, carrying their whole life in a laundry bag, knowing that the chances were I would never see them again. I guess that was one reason I didn't really get close to anyone; we all were there for different periods of time and it was hard watching a friend get transferred or leave. It made being inside even tougher. I'll tell you one thing, I never saw anybody look back.

The way the system normally works is that when you have six months left in your sentence you can get released to a halfway house. The theory is that living back in society, having a job, would allow you to begin the process of returning to real life. As much as I tried not to anticipate moving into a halfway house, it was impossible not to.

My counselor told me that because my record was spotless I was being recommended for the full six-month release schedule. I began to anticipate it, probably more than I should have. Then, one day after count—when the guards made sure everybody was accounted for—my counselor asked me to come to her office. "I've got bad news," she said. "The most they're going to give you is thirty to sixty days in a halfway house."

That news just devastated me. I'd managed to keep up my spirits for years, but losing another four months for no logical reason was incredibly painful. She couldn't explain the decision to me, just that she had recommended six months and it had been cut by someone for some reason. She added, "If I were you, I'd appeal."

I knew I had no shot at that. This was an absolute dictatorship. They do what they want to and don't have to answer to anyone. "Get me the sixty days," I said to her.

Once you're released to a half-way, you have fifteen days to get a job. Through Joe Paolino, I was to be hired by Boston's very upscale XV Beacon Hotel, a place where rooms rent for as much as a thousand dollars a night and include a Lexus with a driver, as a marketing manager. The hotel management felt the positive publicity I would bring to the hotel would more than compensate for the criticism. In fact, the PR director of the hotel announced they were going to have a big party for me when I arrived. Oh shit, I thought, I knew he meant well, but the last thing I wanted—or needed—was media attention. I was sure I was going to get screwed. All kinds of questions went through my mind. I wondered if they would take away my sixty days and make me finish my sentence in prison.

I was right. As soon as it was announced that I was going to work at a luxury hotel the media just descended on the place. Supposedly, the hotel received a barrage of e-mails and letters from clients threatening never to stay at that hotel again if I was hired. The fact that I had gotten a job at this lovely hotel became a major story.

As I got closer to my release date I still didn't know if they were going to let me go. They kept me hanging until the very end. My counselor called me down and asked me about the job. "I don't know anything about all that," I said. "You said get a job so I called a friend and he got me a job." Then I waited, and waited.

In fact, that hotel probably got more publicity simply by hiring me than it had paid for in several years. And for every person who threatened to boycott the hotel, many more people who supported me stated they would stay there. The whole thing was silly. The last thing I wanted to do was cause any problems; I just wanted out. The owner of the hotel, a Providence native I had never met named Paul Roiff, just ignored those complaints, pointing out, "The city [of Providence] was nonexistent. He just got the city cleaned up, started building things, changed the whole attitude about the city. Everybody I knew in Rhode Island thought the guy was terrific." Roiff added that he was stunned at the complaints, adding, "To my knowledge, this man never harmed anybody." Paul proved to be a stand-up guy—who I still have not met—and I remain forever grateful to him.

I was scheduled to be released to the halfway house Memorial Day weekend. But I was worried, I mean very worried, about the reality of that date. They owned my life and never hesitated to remind me of that fact. Finally, on May 29, 2007, I was called into the office and told,

"Call your relatives and tell them they can pick you up at three A.M. tomorrow morning."

I was going to be out in twelve hours! Three o'clock in the morning? What's that all about? I asked. It was being done to avoid the media, I was told. A prison official explained that several reporters had called, claiming to be my relatives and asking at what gate and time they could pick me up.

If I was released through the normal system I would be inundated. Okay. I was told not to tell anyone I was being released, so I didn't have the opportunity to tell anyone good-bye. They told me to be ready to leave after the 2 A.M. count. Years had passed faster than those last few hours. I told one person I was leaving, another inmate who helped me pack up my locker. I gave him just about everything in it, sneakers, hats, food, everything I didn't need. At five minutes after two the guard came and got me. I had two laundry bags and I followed him to the back door of the building. They unlocked that door and I walked with two guards. It was a dark night and for the first time I walked through the prison yard to the discharge center. They handed me clothes that had been sent to me. It was the first time I'd put on gray slacks or a sports jacket in four and a half years. I put on a Providence Polo Club baseball cap that a friend had sent. They gave me the few hundred dollars that was left in my prison account, I told them my social security number, and the gate opened for me.

My nephew and daughter were waiting for me at an arranged spot. The Providence media was still staked out in front of the prison, waiting for me to be released later that morning. I took a deep, deep breath of fresh, free morning air, hugged my daughter, and got into a waiting Lexus SUV. By 9 A.M., as we were driving over the George Washington Bridge, I was on the telephone with a friend, who was watching as a Providence TV reporter explained that the mayor was expected to be released any minute and they were waiting at the gates for him.

After the barrage of criticism I had decided, with the urging of the Bureau of Prisons, that maybe taking that job in Boston wasn't such a great idea. Instead, Joe Paolino offered me a position as assistant to the project manager at a lovely new condominium complex in Providence, the 903 Residences. It was perfect; my daughter was already living there. My job consisted basically of being there, helping generate publicity. While working there I lived at my nephew's house, although for several weeks I had to wear an ankle bracelet that reported my movements. My life was still regimented.

There is no adequate way to describe how I felt. Almost four and a half years had been carved out of my life for a crime I had not committed. I knew I hadn't been forgotten. In 2005 the popular animated show *Family Guy* broadcast an episode entitled "Fast Times at Buddy Cianci Jr. High." A year later Warner Bros. Television had created a show for CBS titled *Waterfront,* which starred Joe Pantoliano as a "fictitious" Italian-American mayor of Providence. The pilot was described as "a charismatic and ethically challenged mayor of Providence, R.I., tries to fire his city's chief of police while dealing with his own scandals and allegations of corruption." Wonder where that idea came from? I'd read about it in *The Providence Journal.* When Lynn Singleton came to visit, I told him how I upset I was that they were using my story, obviously, and I wasn't going to get anything out of it. Lynn responded that rather than being upset I should be thrilled, that by the time I was released from prison the show would be a big hit and I would be known as "the Wild Bill Hickok of mayors."

After one episode CBS pulled the show. On my drive home from prison I left a message for Lynn, telling him, "This is Wild Bill Hickok and I'm out!"

Also, a biography about my life, *The Prince of Providence,* written by a *Journal* reporter and published in 2003, had become a bestseller. It took me a long time to read it, and I think it accurately reflected the negative views of my career pushed by the *Journal.* It cast a dark shadow over all of my accomplishments while emphasizing all my problems. For example, when one of the main witnesses in the Plunder Dome investigation was arrested on several charges including punching his wife in the face, the author of this book wrote that his actions supposedly were "exacerbated by the stress of his year undercover," and as he was booked "some cops fed up with City Hall corruption and meddling in police promotions shook his hand and embraced him."

The night before my ankle bracelet came off, Channel 10 broadcast a show titled "How Should Buddy Be Welcomed Back," and showed a full-length documentary produced by Cherry Arnold, *Buddy, The Rise and Fall of America's Most Notorious Mayor,* narrated by the actor James Woods. The documentary was a very fair presentation of my life and eventually won an Emmy. A poll cited in the film reported that even after I served my sentence, 38 percent of Providence residents would vote for me if I ran for mayor.

Clearly, I hadn't been forgotten. Even before I was released, I agreed to cooperate with a reporter for the upscale magazine, *The Rhode Island Monthly* on an as-told-to story—on the condition that they would put me on the cover. Normally, the magazine has food or fashion on the cover, and I believe only twice have they featured a person—I was on the cover both times. This story was titled "Buddy Cianci Lets His Hair Down." "Prison is like living at the DMV," read the caption of a very nice photograph of me at Joe Marzilli's Old Canteen. "You have to wait in line for everything; getting a sock or a T-shirt may be an all-day proposition."

On July 27, my nephew drove me to the Barnstable Sheriff's Department, where I cut off the electronic bracelet. I was free. It was one of the greatest moments of my life. While I still had two years of supervised release, I could go where I wanted to go and do what I wanted to do. That night, Barnaby Evans scheduled a WaterFire. I attended it with a large group of friends and family; and the media mobbed me.

Now I had to figure out how to earn a living. And I had one very important skill to sell: I could talk. Oh, could I talk. At various times in my life I have been accused of almost everything, except being shy. So I was the perfect person for talk radio; I had experience as the host of a talk radio show, I was well know and considered controversial, I understood the politics of the city and state, I had tremendous sources who would feed me information, I had very strong opinions, and I liked the spotlight. Okay, I loved the spotlight. Even before I was released I had offers from several competing stations. The head of Citadel Broadcasting's Rhode Island stations, Barbara Haynes and program manager Paul Giamarco offered me a multiyear contract. To close the deal Citadel's CEO Farid Suleman came up from New York, and in September 2007, I signed with WPRO to do a daily show. One reason I picked this station is that my show would be produced by my close friend Ron St. Pierre. Two months later I agreed to do regular political commentary on the local ABC affiliate, which boasted in its promotion, "You either love him or hate him . . . he's back!"

I think it's fair to say that there were several people in the state of Rhode Island who were not truly happy when my new jobs were announced. And the truth is, they had every reason to be worried. People like Mayor Cicilline and his police chief, Esserman, had been taking shots at me for several years while I was incarcerated and I didn't have the forum to respond. At times I felt as if I was an animal in a cage being poked with a stick, but there was nothing I could do but wait. Cicilline had been in office two terms and was still running against me. For five years he had attacked me relentlessly. Those people should have known that it's not a great idea to spit into the wind. I waited patiently.

And when I came home, WPRO and ABC 6 gave me a microphone and the opportunity to say anything I wanted to say. And believe me, I had a lot to say.

Before I went on the air David Cicilline had a 62 percent popularity rating and was considering a run for governor in 2010. By the end of 2009, with my help, he had abandoned the gubernatorial race, and his popularity rating was at 41 percent and dropping. And less than a third of poll respondents believed that he had fulfilled his campaign promise to "clean up" city hall.

I admit it, I'm not a good enemy to have. But what could Cicilline do to me? Put me in prison? Been there, done that, and I brought home the T-shirt. Cicilline's biggest problem was that I knew what I was talking about. The truth hurt him.

In December 2007, for example, Providence got hit by a snowstorm. It wasn't exactly a blizzard—the *Journal* reported a total of only six inches of snow—but the city was paralyzed. The streets weren't plowed, highways were completely blocked. It was Cicilline's worst nightmare—a problem he couldn't blame on me! Almost the entire city was gridlocked, and elementary school kids were trapped on school buses for as long as eight hours. Naturally, I happened to mention it on my radio show. In fact, I probably mentioned it more than once, and went through the steps a mayor should take in preparation for a snowstorm, all the steps that this mayor failed to take. Pretreat the streets with sand and salt before it snows. Have a supply of sand and salt in position. Get parked cars off the main streets by towing if necessary so the plows can get through. I knew the answer to that problem from my own experience. This was Mayor 101 and he failed the course.

I have to say in Cicilline's defense that he took complete responsibility for the disaster. He admitted it was a complete breakdown in communications—and then he fired the director of the city's Emergency Management Agency and suspended the school system's chief of operations for a month. How could it have been his fault? He'd only been mayor for five years.

My relationship with Esserman was no better. This guy has traveled around the country claiming he cleaned up the Providence Police Department, that during my administration the police department was corrupt and officers had to pay for promotions. That was not true, absolutely not true, and that charge infuriated me. He claimed that he initiated community policing in Providence, although we had it in the city in 1992. So I decided to use my platform, talk radio, to straighten out the record. His police officers became my best source. I had more birdies talking to me than the aviary at Roger Williams Park Zoo. I found out, for example, that during that snowstorm, rather than getting those kids off the buses he was at Gold's Gym working out. Apparently, earlier that day he'd called a press conference to boast about falling crime rates, and apparently he got very upset when reporters failed to show up because they were covering the snowstorm. And Esserman had eliminated the Traffic Division, which had at least some experience in dealing with a snowstorm. I found out that on Halloween he had used a police car to take his kids trick-or-treating. It was great stuff for radio. One Halloween someone stole a pumpkin from his front porch so, as I informed my listeners, two detectives were assigned to guard the other pumpkin.

Did I ever have police officers guarding my house? Of course I did, I had death threats. But I never had my pumpkin threatened! Eventually, my show became one of the most popular talk shows in Rhode Island. It's a different spotlight, but I'm still in the middle of it.

Slightly more than a year after my release from prison I decided to march once again in the Bristol Independence Day Parade, still the oldest continuously held Fourth of July parade in the country. I'd never really been welcome at that parade by its organizers; I'd marched in it one year as the musical director of a drum and bugle corps, playing the whistle, and another year I'd marched as a veteran; during one political campaign I arrived in a helicopter and basically dared them to stop me from marching. Several years I rode in the parade on a horse. In 2008 I was invited to march as a member of the WPRO contingent. Okay, not invited specifically by name, though obviously I had never let that stop me. But this year was going to be a different, since in 2008 I was a convicted felon. I was curious and for the first time admittedly a little nervous. Two days before the parade *The Providence Journal* wondered—on its front page—what type of reception I would receive? Some people objected strongly to my participation in the parade. One woman wrote to the Bristol newspaper, "It is enormously embarrassing and defies logic and ethics in every conceivable way. . . . Unless we want our Fourth of July parade to become another parade of horribles, we better think twice about who takes part in our celebration."

Of course, the writer of that letter was Mayor Cicilline's sister.

A little after noon I took a deep breath, told a reporter, "Here we go," and started walking the two-and-a-half-mile route. It didn't take me long to discover how the more than hundred thousand spectators viewing the parade felt about me. As the *Journal* reported, "In a parade with hundreds of participants that stretched over four hours, it was hard for anyone to steal the show. But former Providence Mayor Vincent A. 'Buddy' Cianci Jr. came close. . . .

"More than 200 people approached the 67-year old Cianci with outstretched arms, for a handshake, a hug, a kiss. They grabbed his face in their hands, calling him 'so cute.' They thrust their babies into his arms. They handed him American flags. They snapped photo after photo. Everyone at the parade, it seemed, knew Cianci, or at least felt like they did."

One woman gave me a big hug and told the reporter, "I love his marinara sauce. I'd vote for him if he ran."

I was home.

That woman's remarks in the newspaper might well have struck fear in the hearts of a lot of politicians. "I'd vote for him if he ran." That was not the first time I'd heard that said, nor was it the only time someone had suggested I put on the squirrel and run for a political office. I was prohibited from running for local or state political office for three years after the completion of my sentence—so I will be eligible to run for mayor in the next election. Will I? I do think about it, and when I do, I smile at the thought, knowing how delighted it would make many people, and how uncomfortable that thought makes many others. And at those times, when I'm weighing that decision, there is one thing that has become apparent to me about my entire life:

I've never stopped running.

It has been an amazing ride. Amazing! I've experienced incredible highs and devastating lows. I've had my many moments of glory and I've been publicly embarrassed. I'd become mayor of Providence when the city—a desolate industrial wasteland riddled with crime—was on the verge of collapse . . . and seen it transformed into a vital, progressive, culturally rich city. We created magic, and on those beautiful summer evenings, walking along the river as gondolas floated by, surrounded by smiling people enjoying their city, anything seemed possible.

I know what I accomplished as mayor and I know the mistakes that I made. In retrospect, I wouldn't change too much. Certainly I would have made some different decisions, decisions that might have changed the path I took. Maybe I was too aggressive, maybe I was too egotistical, too full of myself. At times, admittedly, I was abrasive. I know that turned off a lot of people. And I do think that had some impact on what happened to me. Or maybe, what I did to myself.

Maybe my mistake was merging the Office of the Mayor with my celebrity status. There are a lot of politicians who don't do that, or who can't do that, but there was something in me that loved the spotlight. I needed to be out all the time, I needed to be in front of an audience, strutting my stuff. That's who I am, or was, for better or worse. But as a result I became a prize, the biggest prize for people with the power to bring me down.

I know I engendered some real animosity. There is a group of people who believe that I have always been corrupt, that I accepted money and secreted it away in some private bank account. There is nothing I can do about that. It isn't true, but I know some people who will never believe that. People believe it happened, they know I went to prison, and they will never accept my claim of innocence. Admittedly, I played the game of politics, for a long time I played it very well. I was successful in maintaining a strong relationship with my base and I was able to use jobs to trade off some of the people who were against me. I wasn't bribing them, I was bringing them into government to use their abilities in the best possible way for the betterment of the city of Providence. Rather than silencing my opposition with bribes, what I did was give them the power to affect lives.

Most of the time I won the game, but when I lost, when I was convicted of the crime of being mayor of a large city, I accepted it. In all honesty, I never got angry. That was the odd thing, I never got angry. I knew in my heart that what I did was not what the jury decided I did. Was I mad? Sure. Was I disappointed? Of course. But I accepted it. I never yelled, I never screamed, I never cried. I wasn't going to give those people who had spent years pursuing me that satisfaction. I had often contemplated leaving office but I knew that the only way I was going to leave was in a coffin or by being indicted. Even on the worst of my days in prison, I knew there would be another day. My victory was coming out of jail and rebuilding my life, putting those people behind me forever. And admittedly, I do get some pleasure believing that the more success I enjoy the harder it must be for them.

So instead of fading from the spotlight and going quietly into the rest of my life, I'm hosting my own very successful drive-time talk radio show and appearing regularly on television and on the lecture circuit. I suspect it just might be the worst of all my opponents' fears come true: Buddy Cianci with a microphone and an audience.

And a happy life!

Index

McLacken, Margaret, 3
McQueeney, Walter, 54–55, 62, 102–3
  homophobia of, 84
Mansolillo, Charlie, 142, 143, 222, 257, 258, 271–72, 328
Marfeo, Rudolph, 18–19
Marrapese, Bobo, 17–18
Marquette University Law School, 12
  Buddy Cianci's rape accusation, 130, 132–37
Marzilli, Joe, 75, 166, 291, 301–2
Matadors drum and bugle corps
  Buddy Cianci marching with, 42–43
Materna, Wendy, 33, 241–42, 254–57, 309
Mauro, Ed, 243
Mayor's Own Marinara Sauce, 290–91, 305, 338
  on display in Cartier's windows, 291
MC5, 28
Melucci, Bruce, 201–2
Menino, Tom, 305
Merman, Ethel, 71
Metcalf, Mike, 201
Millard, Scott
  and the pit bull, 92
Miller, Bill, 66, 70
Millman, Lester, 49
Minnelli, Liza, 174, 309
Miss Saigon (musical show), 285
Miss Teen America pageant, 174
Moakley, Maureen, 318
Mohegan Sun casino, 313
Moise, Mike, 118, 121

Monahon, Eleanor, 11, 64
Money magazine, 6, 305
Moreau, Celia, 9, 253
Moriarty, Father Raymond, 19–20, 21, 22
Moses Brown School, 9–11, 74
Moshassuck River, 298, 299
Muhammad Ali, 110
Mulligan, Ed, 248–49
multiservice community centers, 75
Murphy's Delicatessen, 206
Museum of Natural History
  and the Hawaiian spear rest, 168–70
  Pacific Rim exhibit, 170
"My Buddy" (song), 8

Nads hockey team, 296
Narragansett Bay, 289, 298
  sewage dumped into, 61
National Association for the Advancement of Colored People, 311
National Association of Christians and Jews, 76
National Endowment for the Arts, 299
National Football League, 305
National Rifle Association, 266
New England Magazine, 1
New England Patriots, 179–82
New England Pest Control building
  Big Blue Bug, Buddy Cianci pardoning, 279
New Times magazine, 135–37